To Dmitry —
Friend and incomparable
violinist.

With much affection.

Patricia Tretick
4/22/82

# DAVID OISTRAKH

# Viktor Jusefovich
# DAVID OISTRAKH
## Conversations with
## Igor Oistrakh

Translated by Nicholas de Pfeiffer

Cassell
London

*In memory of*
*Tamara Iwanowna Oistrakh*

CASSELL & COMPANY LIMITED,
*35, Red Lion Square, London WC1R 4SG*
*and at Sydney, Auckland, Toronto, Johannesburg,*
*an affiliate of*
*Macmillan Publishing Co., Inc.,*
*New York*

Translated from the Russian by Juri Elperin
Translated from the German by Nicholas de
Pfeiffer

Cover design: Jurgen Reichert, Stuttgart using
a photograph by Evelyn Richter, Leipzig

ISBN 0 304 302 392

Production in association with Book
Production Consultants, Cambridge

Printed in Great Britain at The Burlington
Press, Foxton, Herts

# Contents

# Introduction

The name of David Feodorovich Oistrakh was for me, even in my youth, an established term. My father, who was not a musician, but who knew Oistrakh when he was young, found that music and Oistrakh were synonymous. This would also prove true for me and remain so. It was through Oistrakh that I discovered the way to music. I will never forget the day I met him, when I was allowed to play to him on my little violin. I remember clearly, how on that occasion Oistrakh spoke to my father about the great difficulties and great joys of the musician. I later tried repeatedly to persuade David Oistrakh to put memories of his development as an artist on paper together with his meetings with other musicians and also to record his views on reproductive art. One day I arrived at the plan for a book based on conversations with him - at the time, he was just reading the recently published *Conversations with Pablo Casals* by Corredor. Oistrakh really needed hardly any persuasion. He was a superb narrator and a master of the word (and as also later appeared, of the pen). He did not find the proposition unattractive. He even began to tell his story and to outline the content of several chapters; however, he persisted in postponing the actual realization of writing the book to some future date: "Oh, sure, one day when I don't have to travel around the world so much ..." I did not know then that Oistrakh was simply unable to cut down on his travelling. Added to this, his kind smile and ability to show no sign of exhaustion or tiredness deceived his conversation partner about the true way he led his life. Of course we all knew he lived a tremendously tense life, without however suspecting that he exhausted himself in the service of music. Oistrakh laboured for music until the very end and sacrificed himself for it.

After David Oistrakh died, I felt it was even more important to publish a book we had planned to, or at least a book which came as close as possible to the one we had planned. I studied Oistrakh's private archives, buried myself in his correspondence, spoke to Tamara Iwanowna, who throughout her life was both wife and comrade to him, and spoke to the musicians who formed part of his permanent circle. Finally, and most important, I asked his son Igor Davidovich Oistrakh to read and comment on part of the information and to answer many of the questions which I had originally intended to ask his father. David Oistrakh's whole life thus passed before me and the unforgettable picture of this great musician appeared even more clearly before my eyes – the picture of the artist, the citizen and the great human being. In this way the shape and form of the report emerged almost automatically as: conversations with Igor Oistrakh with the addition of David Oistrakh's letters and documents.

This volume would never have appeared without Tamara Iwanowna's invaluable help in the selection and arrangement of the material and without the friendly help and important advice of many musicians whose names are mentioned in the text. I would like to take this opportunity to thank them all.

Moscow, March 1977

Viktor Jusefovich

7

# Development

*David Oistrakh as a boy*

'If I think back as far as I can, I never see myself in my youth without a violin,' David Oistrakh wrote in his own autobiographical notes - I was always reminded of this sentence when I recalled his development.

Odessa rises proudly on one of the steepest shores of the Black Sea which surrounds the city in a semicircle. Odessa was already at the beginning of the century one of the largest cities in the south of Russia. Built of yellow shell limestone and washed by warm gentle waves offering the south-westerly winds free access. A radiatingly beautiful city, as the inhabitants insist and visitors confirm. There is an almost unique combination of brackish sea air, the spicy scent of acacias and the slightly bitter aroma of coffee. Straight streets which aim like arrows for the sea, streets which Pushkin and Tchaikovsky, Mickiewicz and Garibaldi had seen. There was the famous Deribassowskaja which was for good reasons compared with the Nevsky-Prospekt. Wonderful buildings: the Woronzow Palace, the old stock exchange and the opera. The latter regarded as one of the most lavish and acoustically superb buildings in the world. And above all: the people of Odessa. A colourful mixture of representatives of many nations, religions and traditions and at the same time an amazing harmony which expressed itself in the temperament of overflowing joy of life as well as unending energy and a fine (in spite of its good nature) sometimes ironically tinged humour. Odessa knew how to live happily and at ease (even in difficult times). Wit and a ready tongue were always admired here, valour and courage respected, art and knowledge adored. People who possessed such characteristics changed even in their lifetime into legend, almost irrespective of which subject they had succeeded in. Among such celebrities were: Max Linder, who appeared in Russia and was known as uncrowned king of silent film far beyond Odessa; Iwan Saikin, the circus wrestler, a hero of the typically Russian style of people's entertainment; Jan Kubelik, the master violinist, who by his exclusive performances in Odessa was only known to a narrow circle of people. Such demigods excited the whole city and their names were on everybody's tongue. Whenever, however, a native of Odessa succeeded and reached the top, he was guaranteed eternal glory. As the years passed the conditions

*Odessa: Opera House on right and Stoliarsky School on left*

changed, but the character and nature of the Odessa people remained.

In the first decade of the twentieth century Odessa was rightly regarded as one of the most outstanding cultural centres of the Russian province. Odessa led a vivid scientific, literary and artistic life. The town had a university, a theatre with rich traditions going back to Michail Stschepkin, the founder of Russian stage realism, many newspapers and periodicals as well as a number of literary circles which vanished as quickly as they appeared. Eduard Bagrizki and Isaak Babel, Valentin Katajew and Juri Olescha, Ilja Ilf and Jewgeni Petrow grew up in Odessa. Their work was published in many languages and has for some time been part of European cultural heritage. However, of all the arts, it was music which enjoyed the greatest prestige. When it came to music only Petersburg or Moscow could possibly challenge the rank of Odessa. Music was being produced everywhere in the town, violinists performed in the tiny cafés and restaurants, the most famous being Saschka Musikant who was mentioned in the novel *Gambrinus* by Alexander Kuprin. Neapolitan bands and brass orchestras played regularly at the Richelieu Square. Quartet and chamber-music evenings were held in the houses of well-known doctors and professors of philology. There were outstanding symphony concerts and opera performances which approached the standard expected in the capitals. All Russian artists of fame and reputation gave guest performances here in Odessa and foreign stars who came to Russia appeared reguarly. Glazunof conducted in the opera house, Chaliapine and Sobinof, Titta Ruffo and Caruso, Anna Pavlova and Isadora Duncan could be seen on the stage. Music was nursed with a passion in Odessa, concerts and performances led to heated debates. The sound of violins could be heard from almost every window, music filled the air. Whoever grew up there absorbed it with his mother's milk and was drawn subconsciously under the spell of this atmosphere so saturated with music. The world owes a debt to Odessa for so many outstanding musicians, among them: Emil Giles and Sviatoslav Richter and a host of outstanding violinists with David Oistrakh at the head.

He was born on September 30, 1908 and spent his first twenty

*Feodor Davidovich Oistrakh, David's father*

years in Odessa. What do you, Igor Davidovich, remember of the stories your father told you about his childhood? Did he like to talk about those distant times?

"Father loved his childhood reminiscences, although he grew up

*Isabella Stepanowna Oistrakh, David's mother*

off, but this never affected the atmosphere in his parent's home. There was always peace and agreement in the family, everybody understood one another and was cheerful, always ready for a laugh, as people from Odessa were expected to be. I am thoroughly convinced: father's optimism and life style were already created in his childhood by the spirit of the city. This trait obviously also came out in his artistic nature as so many foreign critics have commented."

Which parent had the decisive influence on the musical interests of the child?

"His father, Feodor Davidovich, who was very seriously ill even as a child, had a pronounced influence on his son as a human being with his strong family sense and high moral principles. Father often remembered with great love the many talents my grandfather possessed. Although he was not a professional musician he loved music, didn't play the violin badly and also played several brass instruments. Father also told us about grandfather's strict educational methods. However, the decisive influence came from his mother – Isabella Stepanovna. She often took little Dodik (as people called David)

during a period which could be called anything but easy. He was the son of a modest official and an opera singer. They lived in a small, rather dark room which had no windows except for a skylight. They were therefore far from well

to the opera. He would stand in the orchestra pit and listen fascinated to the sounds of the music."

Joseph Pribik created a whole new period in the cultural life of Odessa. He directed the opera orchestra for forty years as its chief conductor and before that, in 1890, he conducted I. Prjanischnikow's operatic society playing Tchaikovsky's opera *Pique Dame* at its première in Kiev. The fact that Pribik was personally aquainted with Tchaikovsky and that the latter recommended him to his musical friends in Odessa gave the conductor special status. For the young Dodik, Pribik remained for ever the key figure in opera. The boy was interested in the orchestra, the musicians and their instruments. When David Oistrakh later talked about Swjatoslaw Knuschewizki and the impression which the sound of cellos made on his sensitive musically trained ear, he also recalled that even a few bars of the cello in ballet performances meant a major event for him as a child.

"Dodik's mother already noticed his pronounced musical sensitivity early in his childhood. And of course, there was his first 'violin', a present from his father."

You say this with some amusement?

*13*

"Not at all, except that the violin was not a real one. In the autobiographical notes *My Road*, which David Oistrakh wrote in the 1950s, he says:

'I was three-and-a-half years old when my father brought home a toy violin, when I played on this I imagined with much pleasure that I was a street musician, in those days a rather second rate but quite common profession in Odessa. I never felt happier than when wandering around the yard with this violin.'"

Who first suggested the boy's musical training?

"His mother let little Dodik take music lessons. He enjoyed relating this story about his first exam: the flautist of the opera orchestra listened to the boy's playing at the request of his mother. Dodik had only just learnt how to move the bow across the strings. After listening to this the flautist declared quite firmly and with an enviable certainty which defied any contradiction: 'Don't torture this poor child; anyway, it's all a waste of time, particularly as the fate of an orchestral musician is not an enviable one. The boy will anyhow never make a solo violinist.' Fortunately mother did not agree with

this. Even Dodik, the victim, didn't appear to approve of this verdict. He later writes:

'It gave me so much pleasure to act the street musician that when I was five years old and finally got hold of a real one – only a one-eighth violin – I abandoned myself fully to music lessons.'

At this point in time father met Professor Stoliarsky, his future teacher."

The persistence with which David Feodorovich already as child preferred the violin is admirable . . .

"Unfortunately, I will have to disappoint you there. Father's aquaintance with the violin was by no means faultless. Like his contemporaries, he was very lively and ready for a prank. He participated in the noisy fun and games which boys are accustomed to and when his violin lessons prevented him from taking part, he would cut the strings of his violin or the hairs on his bow (in spite of all his love for music). However, after a lot of useless scolding, his parents found an effective remedy. If the boy didn't want to practise and treated

*The little David with his first violin*

*14*

his violin barbarically (in most cases he cut the strings on a Friday evening because the shops were closed on Saturday evenings and Sundays), then his mother wouldn't take him to the opera. His desire to stand next to the conductor in the orchestra pit was so overwhelming that he soon gave up his pranks."
Did your father have to apply the educational experience of his parents several decades later?

"I can guess what you are aiming at. Frankly, I only heard what I just told you after I had established a firm relationship with the violin. My father had never told me these things before for special reasons. I loved my father so much that I was anxious to imitate him in every respect, even as a young child. The times are changing and so are the methods."
What do you mean by that?

"I didn't cut the strings of my violin, I simply jumped out of the window and left the violin intact in my room. My own son Valeri has grown beyond the age at which his grandfather used to carry out the daring experiments with his violin and bow. Even Oistrakh senior soon forgot about his pranks once he began to study under Stoliarsky."

David Oistrakh always referred to Professor Stoliarsky as his first and only music teacher. Pyotr Stoliarsky was not old at the time, but he already had a great reputation as a teacher of many talented violinists. He not only enjoyed this reputation but also honest and sincere love. Adults and children recognized him in the street and greeted him, people made room for him on the tram. He had to walk a thorny path in his artistic life. Whilst the romantic dream of the street musician lingered on in the heart of little Dodik, his teacher had really got to know all the "pleasures" of such an existence when he had to play for rich "patrons" at weddings and feasts. In spite of this Stoliarsky kept his temper, kind heart and philanthropic way, his youthful energy, overflowing imagination and kind expression which invited children right until his death – as we shall later convince ourselves. I have read in some foreign reviews of Oistrakh concerts that Stoliarsky had been a pupil of Leopold Auer. This is a mistake, they met in Odessa, visited by Auer on one of his tours. Auer attended Stoliarsky's classes and praised his extraordinary teaching ability. Stoliarsky was taught in Odessa by the famous Polish violinist Stanislaw Barcewicz and later by Josef Karbulka.

"There has been a lot said about Stoliarsky at home, both by father and by his colleagues, many of whom were his pupils. Father admired his teaching very much and praised his natural talent for teaching.

Stoliarsky was on very friendly terms with my father's parents and visited them often. He combined his teaching activity with playing in the opera orchestra and therefore often noticed how the little Dodik listened enthusiastically in the orchestra pit. Father wrote: 'I met Pyotr Stoliarsky before I could hold a violin. I had the feeling that he was waiting impatiently for me to reach the age of five in order to at last make a violinist of me.'

He also described the atmosphere in Stoliarsky's school in his auto-biographical notes. The school was known in Odessa as the 'Talent Factory' and it was attended by eighty to ninety children, even very small ones: 'Lecterns, piled up violin cases and folders stuffed with scores stood in all corners of the large building in which the school was housed. Joyfully excited youngsters were crowded in all the

*Pyotr Solomonovich Stoliarsky,*
*Oistrakh's teacher*

rooms, the mothers sat around in the corridors waiting for their child prodigies, all the time discussing with great excitement and remarkable knowledge the problems of violin playing.' "

Did Stoliarsky devote much time to his students?

"Father told us that Stoliarsky's working day lasted from early in the morning until late in the evening. He couldn't however devote the same amount of time to each of his pupils. He would work with the most talented children sometimes twice or even three times a day. As far as the other students were concerned . . . he told us, not without a touch of humour, how Stoliarsky would sometimes have to listen to the playing of an ungifted 'child prodigy' of wealthy snobbish parents and without making any comments or attempts at improving the child's playing would then send the child home, reminding him of the deadline for paying the tuition fee. It was this money which enabled him to teach the gifted children free of charge if their parents weren't able to scrape together the tutition fee. Father wrote: 'I also belonged to this group and it is questionable whether I would have ever been a violinist without the sympathy and support of Pyotr Solomonovich.' Michail Markovich Goldstein, Professor at the White Russian State Conservatory and once a fellow student with father at Stoliarsky's school, relates this story: 'Everybody, or almost everybody, worked quite hard in our large class, but even we were amazed how Oistrakh managed to find time to learn and remember everything that we were taught.' "

How did Stoliarsky organize his violin lessons? Which principles did he regard as fundamental?

Stoliarsky used his remarkable knowledge of child psychology by enriching the lessons with playful exercises and managed to arouse the children's interest and their desire to study the piece of music he wanted them to learn. He not only knew the musical ability of each individual student but also his character, inclinations and interests. Father told us that Stoliarsky played the violin rarely during lessons and he never demonstrated how any certain passage should be played; however, in listening he corrected the mistakes of his small violinists cleverly and artfully. On such occasions one could tell by the expression on his face exactly what impression the playing had on him.

The fact that all his students also had to learn the viola, play in ensemble and participate in violin 'unisono' and string orchestra performances, as well as their frequent appearances at school concerts, helped to gradually eliminate any

16

stage fright and got them used to the concert platform. Father regarded all these points as important. It was not just by chance that Stoliarsky's school produced violinists of the calibre of: David Oistrakh, Nathan Milstein, Samuil Furer, Jelisaveta Gilels, Michail Fichtenholz and many others. I think it very important that Stoliarsky trained each student to accept high demands and to respect and love work."

I would like to add a few words to your picture of the professor, especially as I discussed the subject with David Oistrakh and a few of his colleagues of the Odessa school.

Stoliarsky's teaching activity was of great value during the days which prevailed in Tsarist Russia with its class system and suppression of non-Russian population. I don't just mean by that that Pyotr Solomonovich was willing to teach poor students who couldn't pay for their lessons. His students didn't limit their activity just to learning the school curriculum; in addition to that they gave free concerts, both solo and orchestral, which gained an ever increasing audience. Stoliarsky thought in an advanced way and he took a very active part in the development of Soviet

musical education. After the military intervention forces were driven out of Odessa and Soviet power had been established and even earlier in spring 1917, Stoliarsky made his political sympathies quite clear.

"This can be seen from father's notes: 'We, the pupils of the Stoliarsky school, led by Pyotr Solomonovich, walked through the streets of Odessa on 1 May 1917, and played the specially rehearsed Marseillaise on our violins which were decorated with red ribbons. The 'International' (Brothers to Sun and Freedom) and other revolutionary songs were soon added to the repertoire.' "

Professor Stoliarsky's lessons were of great importance for the development of the character which formed the artist and citizen, and David Oistrakh was greatly influenced by these lessons.

The years which David Oistrakh spent as a student were very difficult for our country – You have already mentioned, Igor Davidovich, that your father was not even six when World War I began. He wasn't even nine at the beginning of the October Revolution. His childhood lay in the shadow of civil war; the government's laws and money changed

*David Oistrakh as a music student*

more frequently in Odessa than anywhere else. The government changed fourteen times in the first three months after October 1917. The delicatessen had only just filled their windows with coconuts and tropical fruits when the situation changed and Odessa had to live off

17

pancakes made from pea flour. The whole of Odessa was, of course, not affected to such an extent, but social contrast had increased to an unheard-of degree. Black market and corruption flourished in the city. Robberies were a daily event. The poverty of the Oistrakh family increased even further. It was during these days that Stoliarsky's unselfishness towards his pupils became most apparent. Soviet power was finally established in Odessa in February 1920. It still took a long time for living conditions to stabilize. Economic collapse and the lack of fuel were the consequence of the 'Interventionist's war'. The artists and musicians, including Stoliarsky and his pupils, felt that the new state cared for them: 'I remember the first steps towards improving the welfare of the students at the Stoliarsky school. We were given a special bread ration. It was then that we realized with joy that we were needed and that high and important personalities cared for our well-being – for the well-being of the little violinists. I will never forget the day I came home proud and happy and put a whole loaf of bread on the table. This was a week's bread ration given to me by the state.'

Please tell me about David Oistrakh's first concert appearances.

"Father's performances began in 1914. His first concerts were not intended for the public. He made his début at a student's matinée which he opened as the youngest participant (he was then five-and-a-half years old). The final performer was a graduate of Stoliarsky's school – Nathan Milstein.

Father once played together with Milstein in a quartet in Stoliarsky's class. Father the first violin, Milstein the cello.

People could hear him for the first time with an orchestra in 1923. He chose Bach's Concerto in A Minor on the advice of his teacher. He had already studied at the Institute of Music, as the Odessa Conservatory was called at the time. Father was supposed to have shown exceptional feeling for style and exemplary clarity in his performance.

In the following year, the name of Oistrakh appeared for the first time on concert posters. They announced a solo evening with the violinist and the repertoire included not only Bach's Concerto in A Minor, the 'Devil's Trill' by Tartini-Kreisler, Sarasate's 'Gypsy Melodies' as well as several other small virtuoso pieces. A wall in the Oistrakhs' flat was decorated with these posters to the pride of his family, as father told us with his good natured sense of humour. After a short time father began on his first concert tours. He played in the different towns of the Ukraine with the student orchestra of the conservatory during 1925. This tour took him from Odessa to Elisawetgrad (now Kirowograd) and afterwards to Cherson and Nikolajew. Father recalls many years later: 'Even on the first day that I arrived, I was so curious that I immediately went into the town and looked it over. I didn't know then that I would have to travel a great deal in my life. My train journey from Odessa to Elisawetgrad was a great and extraordinarily exciting adventure.' "

David Oistrakh was then seventeen, an ideal age for getting intoxicated with the romantic feeling of travelling and eagerly absorbing any new impressions. On reading the memoirs of Michail Goldstein, who accompanied David Oistrakh on the piano, one finds that the young soloist was far too serious for his age. His interpretation of the Tchaikovsky Concerto was both individualistic and absolutely organic.

"Father himself writes about this: 'Thinking back to those days and the way I played, I feel that I played fairly loosely, freely and in a fairly clean way from an intonation point of view. However, I had to spend many years working hard and persistently on sound, rhythm, dynamics, and most important of all on the deep understanding of the underlying musical idea.' "
And how did your father work in other musical areas?

"Mother often said that she envied father when she worked with him in a group, he would write musical dictation in the solfeggio lessons with such ease as well as singing straight from the score in the excercises for two voices."
What about the young violinist's musical influences?

"Father said, with regret, how little he had been in touch with the interesting musical life in Odessa before the beginning of the Interventionist World War I. This can hardly be surprising as he was after all still only a child. The most important source of his musical impressions during that period remained the opera house in Odessa and Stoliarsky's school. You could later add to this the concerts of guest musicians of such reputation as: Glazunof and Prokofiev, Horowitz, Szigeti and Poljakin.

The participation in concerts of the composer Reinhold Glier, the famous singer Antonina Neshdanowa, soloists at the Bolshoi theatre, who gave performances with the symphony orchestras under the direction of Pribik, Malko and Pasowski, proved an outstanding influence."
David Oistrakh left the Conservatory with distinction in 1926. The program at his diploma examination comprised: Bach's Chaconne; Tartini-Kreisler's 'Devil's Trill', which had brought him much success in the past and which he played this time accompanied by a string quartet; Prokofiev's 1st Violin Concerto and – on the viola – Rubinstein's Sonata. This program alone gives some indication of the orientation of Stoliarsky's champion student. Particularly characteristic is the choice of Prokofiev's Concerto, a composition which had only just begun its early history. It doubtless needed a great deal of courage to perform a major and almost unknown work in a diploma examination. It was a risk of course, but at the same time the best and noblest method by which he could prove himself. We shall have the opportunity of dealing with Oistrakh's attitude to Prokofiev's ingenious score when we attempt to discuss the friendship between the violinist and the composer. I would now like to ask you to tell us what you know about father's meetings with Glazunof, a composer of the older generation? If I am not mistaken, these meetings also took place at this time?

"His contact with Glazunof's music and later with the composer himself made a great impression on father. In autumn 1927, he had to perform Glazunof's Violin Concerto in Kiev under the direction of the composer:

'When I arrived, I went the same day to meet Alexander Glazunof in his hotel. I was feeling extremely tense and nervous as I walked into his room. I was met by large heavy man whose smile both calmed me down and, by its kindness and cordiality, prejudiced me in his favour. He was so friendly and attentive, discussing with me the forthcoming joint concert with such a simple sense of equality that my nervosity soon disappeared. I began to prepare myself for the concert, bursting with joy and energy. It

*19*

*Alexander Glazunof, with the composer's dedication to the young violinist (17.11.1927)*

was extremely pleasant and easy to play with Glazunof. His whole being radiated mental warmth and peace. He conducted sitting down, his tempi were somewhat slower than I was used to playing and hearing them played. This was, however, compensated for by the exceptionally beautiful sound of the orchestra. All the instruments were singing not only in the cantilenas but also in the fast parts.'

During all this, father never uttered a single syllable about himself, as if his violin hadn't 'sung' with the orchestra! It was as if 'joy and energy' were the only feelings which dominated the violinist between the first meeting with the composer in the hotel and the concert under his direction. But we have Goldstein's eyewitness report of the repetition of the Kiev concert in Odessa which took place a few days later:

'I can remember this concert very well. I was amazed not only by Oistrakh's beautifully mature presentation, but mainly by the fact that he was within a few days able to explore the atmosphere and tempi of the whole work ... He later told me how instructive one single (!) rehearsal with Glazunof on the piano had been.'

Father's success with Glazunof's Concerto was even more honourable as this work had been frequently played by Nathan Milstein in Odessa. The same concerto had been played brilliantly by Miron Poljakin under Glazunof virtually the day before Oistrakh's presentation. The audience on that occasion was fascinated by his sensitivity and the beautiful sound of his violin. There hung in father's study for many years a picture of Alexander Konstantinovich Glazunof. A picture which he had given to father on that occasion in Odessa. The composer had written on it:

'To the highly gifted young virtuoso and artist, the outstanding musician David Oistrakh, in remembrance of our joint concerts in the Ukraine. With sincere admiration for his talent – A. Glazunof, 17 November 1927.' There follows a musical autograph: a theme from his violin concerto."

I would now like to interrupt our discussion of David Oistrakh's last years in Odessa in order to give an impression of the young violinist's personality as it was before he left his home town. He went through a period of exceptionally rapid artistic development in the years 1926-28. His repertoire increased, as well as the number of performances and tours. His virtuosity grew and his musical interpretation gained more character and individuality day by day. His first performance of the Beethoven Concerto turned out to be a great success. This performance (under Grigori Stoliarov, rector of the Odessa Conservatory) deserves a special mention because it took place at his beloved Odessa opera house. How many more times would David Oistrakh play this

*David Oistrakh with his wife
Tamara Iwanowna*

concerto and how many different interpretations would he present?
The critics praised the elegant and crystal clear playing of the artist. They also stressed that the secret of the violinist's success did not just rely on his inborn sense of adjustment to the music but also in his remarkable ability of spiritual exploitation and interpretation of the music. They also emphasized how much they enjoyed their fellow-countryman's success and how proud they were as citizens of Odessa that David Oistrakh's artistic origins and developments were taking place in front of their eyes.
I recently had the opportunity to talk to Regina Samoilowna Horowitz, Professor at the Conservatory in Charkow. She was an old friend of David Feodorovich and is well known as a teacher of great personality. After accompanying Nathan Milstein for a number of years on his tours, she (the sister of the famous pianist Vladimir Horowitz) accompanied an unknown violinist, one David Oistrakh, who was also on tour. She told me:
"David Feodorovich knew that I was Milstein's accompanist, he adored Milstein at the time. I was very interested to see what Oistrakh

had to offer in comparison to Milstein's impulsive temperament, the full sound of his violin and his exemplary technique. My first and lasting impresson of Oistrakh's playing was this: he never tried to imitate anybody nor did he attempt to deliberately contrast his interpretation with that of any other violinist. He was a musical personality with his own method of expression. Everything he played was presented in his own natural way which was totally free of any fixed pattern."

It has been stated in some publications about David Oistrakh that he began his artistic activities as master of 'small form', as a brilliant violinist who proved his virtuosity by playing small pieces, and that he only appeared much later on as an interpretor of the great sonatas and concertos. What do you have to say about this?

"I can only reluctantly agree with this, although with some reservation. One has first of all to consider the tremendous differences between public demand on the repertoires in 1920 and those of an audience in the 1960s or 1970s. It was customary in those days to let the program be dominated by small virtuoso pieces and transcriptions.

This would nowadays be regarded as superficial. Furthermore I must point out that father has never entirely been a master of miniature pieces. This must be due to the fact that Stoliarsky did not train him on Paganini and Sarasate but much more on Haydn quartets and Mozart duos, as well as on Bach, Beethoven and Tchaikovsky concertos."

His acquaintance with the pianist Tamara Iwanowna Rotarewa, which developed into a close student friendship and later led to a lasting happy marriage, also took place during his period in Odessa. I assume that you have a lot to say about this?

"I don't want to talk about myself here, neither do I wish to talk about my relationship with my mother nor her relationship with me. She brought me up and bore all the burdens during the terrible time of war. Whenever I think of father, I see mother at his side, his most faithful companion always ready with help and advice, full of loving and a sacrificial care for her Dodik (as she called him). She gave up hopes of making a career of her own in her youth, of becoming a musician with a degree from the Conservatory, in favour of her family and my own education. As I grew up, she accompanied father on his endless tours. She needed unbelievable physical and psychological energy to listen to father's performances. She'd stand behind the curtains because she could hardly ever be persuaded to sit in the hall amongst the audience. The performances lasted twice, no, ten times as long for her as for father himself and for the exulted audience. Mother was always worried about his health, especially after father's severe heart trouble in 1964. She could see how much superhuman strength the reputation of being one of the most famous violinists of the day demanded of father – the overcrowded concert halls in Europe, Asia, America and Australia, where the audience gave him standing ovations as a famous and much loved artist. She tried in vain to persuade and convince father that he should restrict his concert activity and allow himself some relaxation. When he fell ill, she sat, to the doctor's amazement, eleven to twelve hours a day at his bedside. In the end, they had to let her move to the hospital which she didn't leave until there were clear signs of improvement and recovery."

# *Breakthrough*

1928 was a very important year in David Oistrakh's life as it was a major turning point. It was in this year that he had his début as a violinist in Leningrad and chose Moscow as his permanent residence. Who was responsible for your father's invitation to perform in Leningrad?

"Glazunof the composer and Nikolai Malko the conductor. My father wrote of his joint concerts with Glazunof in Kiev and Odessa:

'The best valuation of my concert was the fact that Alexander Constantinovich invited me immediately after the performance to appear with him in Leningrad.'

Malko met my father in Odessa at one of his concerts with the Odessa orchestra:

'I was often invited as "impresario" to important concerts when famous guest conductors conducted in Odessa. I played the violin solo in Miaskovsky's 5th Symphony and Malko expressed the wish to hear me alone. I played him a few pieces and was most surprised to receive the invitation to take part in the opening season of the Leningrad Philharmonic Orchestra in 1928/29.' In order to appreciate the importance of this début in Leningrad one has to remember that this was the first performance of the 'beginner from the province', as David Feodorovich called himself in those days. It was a début in an important musical centre of the country and on top of that the first concert in a series in which conductors such as: Joseph Szigeti, Bruno Walter, Hans Knappertsbusch and Otto Klemperer took part. Father had been engaged to perform Tchaikovsky's Violin Concerto with the outstanding Leningrad Philharmonic Orchestra conducted by Malko. Father told us how excited he was before the first rehearsal. He already knew from his experience in Odessa how demanding the orchestra was and the exceptionally high expectations the musicians in the orchestra had when new 'genii' performed for the first time. This nervous excitement was even more justified as the first rehearsal in Leningrad did not work out very well for David Feodorovich:

'I walked in after Tchaikovsky's 3rd Symphony had just started,' he told us later. 'I thought that I would lose some dignity if I appeared too soon and as a result I was a few minutes too late. Nikolai Andrejevitch Malko said to me sternly: 'Young man, you will have to wait until the second part starts.' This was the first disgrace. However, the orchestra's distrust of the débutant soon disappeared and made way for a well-disposed sympathy."

The young artist got very good press reviews. His success was even more convincing than even the best newspaper commentary could show. Oistrakh was offered a new engagement in Leningrad only one month later – this time playing the Glazunof Concerto.

"However, to father's dismay, Glazunof had fallen ill and Wjatscheslaw Suk conducted.

'The atmosphere was already much more relaxed,' wrote father comparing this performance with the first, 'I also felt much freer and less inhibited in my relationship with the orchestra.'"

David Oistrakh moved from Odessa to Moscow at the end of 1928. This move was undoubtedly as a result of his success. Did he keep in touch with the home town where he spent his youth and did he remain in contact with the musicians from Odessa?

"The extraordinarily intensive artistic life my father led prevented him from giving any town priority. Father loved Odessa in spite of it all, the unique colour of the port with its streets and squares and famous opera house were all close to his heart. He often visited his home town and was of course a well liked guest in the Stoliarsky school and in his college as well as the Conservatory. He dropped in to see the work going on in the violin classes and was very pleased with the performance of its pupils. Some

of them: Olga Kaworsnewa, Rosa Fain, Valeri Klimow, Semjon Snitkowski later continued to study under his direction at the Moscow Conservatory.

Jakow Sak told me about his meeting with David Oistrakh at the beginning of 1945. David Oistrakh saw the prospect of performing outside the Soviet Union for the first time since the beginning of the war:

'I couldn't help noticing that he was more excited than normal, as could be seen from the expression on his face and also on conversation with him. I was told that Oistrakh would also perform in the opera house in Odessa on his way to Rumania and Bulgaria. The mature master, who already before 1941 had performed in important European musical centres was as excited as a young débutant prior to his appearance in "his" opera house and in "his" town.'

"One more point: my father already liked to go as a child with his father to the port and watch the boats coming in laden with water-melons. He had a weakness for water-melons until his last day and he was very proud of his ability to pick the ripest and juciest better than anyone else."

David Oistrakh's human and artistic virtues came clearly to the surface as early as first years after he moved to Moscow. He was totally unknown in the capital. He found a turbulent and interesting musical life there and the music lovers already had their gods, among them: Lew Zeitlin and Miron Poljakin. Oistrakh had to make a name for himself and in order to do this concentrated all his efforts on participating in concerts. He was nevertheless invited to participate in mixed concerts or as he called it "side-plate to the main dish", the 'main dish' consisting of evening performances of famous singers and ballerinas. What really made 'Oistrakh' as we knew him was his gigantic creative will, the desire and ability to work hard, application and the urge for self-perfection. By self-perfection, he not only meant as a violin virtuoso but above all as a musician with wide horizons. Do you agree with this view Igor?

"I am often asked whether father studied with someone special in Moscow. It is difficult for me to give a clear and definite answer to this question. He wrote in his autobiographical notes that he occasionally attended the classes of the most famous violinists and teachers at the Moscow Conservatory: Lew Zeitlin, Abram Jampolski and Konstantin Mostras. It would however be quite wrong to overestimate the importance of the individual observations my father made on these occasions. Being an obviously extremely sensitive person he must have gained something from the lessons of these students with their professors just as he obviously gained some benefit from attending the concerts of the many local and foreign artists (not just violinists) who performed in those days in the Moscow concert halls. Father knew how to listen and he had a uniquely sensitive ear and an equally unique analytical ability to draw useful conclusions from what he heard. He didn't just say by chance that he had learnt a lot from the concerts at which he played as a 'side-plate'. He learnt something from everything, but remained faithful to Stoliarsky and did not study under anyone in Moscow. Indeed, father owes most of his artistic maturity to himself as he searched in all directions for the pinnacles of artistic maturity. One can gather this from his autobiographical notes.

Leonid Kogan suggested the idea that: 'Such violinists, such artists, such phenomena as Oistrakh couldn't really learn much from anyone for a long period, as the sum total of all the secrets of the violin and of musical genius are programmed in them from birth.'" The cultural climate of the capital with its theatre, museums, exhibitions and concerts contributed in no small way to the development of his artistic personality. Did your father tell you which of the violinists in those years had made a special impression on him and had appealed to him?

"Miron Poljakin and Joseph Szigeti, whose concerts father attended in Odessa and whose great ability he only truly appreciated in Moscow, as well as Fritz Kreisler whom he only knew from records. David Oistrakh gave many concert performances at the end of the 1920s and at the beginning of the 1930s. He appeared in all the capitals of the Soviet Union giving both solo performances and concerts with symphony orchestras. His first performance took place on January 22, 1929 in the Mozartsaal in Moscow. The program announced two concerts: one was given by Oistrakh and two days later a concert was given by Béla Bartók in the small hall of the Conservatory. The young violinist's concert included Brahms' D Minor Sonata, Glazunof's Violin Concerto as well as a number of the most difficult pieces from Tartini to Dobrowen." What was Oistrakh like as a violinist at that time? How did he play? Pawel Pawlowitsch Kogan, who organized the tours of Nathan Milstein, David Oistrakh, Vladimir Horowitz and Emil Gilels and who met David Oistrakh in the winter of 1928, later gave his impressions:

'In those days he looked like a seventeen year old . . . shy and taciturn. He gave the impression of being serious and concentrated.

Only an occasional childish smile gave him away, a smile which sometimes played around the corners of his mouth and sometimes flashed from his eyes. Oistrakh's playing was surprising people not so much by its brilliance, effective contrast or virtuoso speed – his recital bore the stamp of natural grace, excellent taste and of some inner charm which was not always immediately apparent. He played in a simple and effortless way, not a single sound was lost and no flageolet scratched at one's ear. The way in which he dealt with his instrument, by treating it as if it was a close dear friend, was appealing to me.'

Which of his concerts did your father prefer to talk about most frequently at the time?

"In his biography, he regarded his concerts with such outstanding violinists as Constantine Igumnof, Alexander Goldenweiser and Gernrich Neuhaus as particularly important and interesting. He only recently admired their outstanding ability and was in close contact with them. These were the young violinist's first steps in chamber-music, a musical area which would bring him and his partners Lew Oborin and Sviatoslav

*"He looked at the time like a seventeen-year-old"*

Knuschewizki triumph after triumph in future years."

David Oistrakh enjoyed his first triumph in 1930 at a violin competition in Charkow, where he won the first prize. Five years later he won another prize in the Second Union Competition in Leningrad. He wrote about it:

'This competition was a test of strength for me, which I had to take seriously. Strictly speaking, after finishing at the Conservatory in Odessa, I was left to myself. The question of whether the path I took from then on was fruitful was answered by the competition.'

There was no ambiguity about the answer. Oistrakh won the first prize. Dmitri Shostakovich remembers that distant year of 1935:

'The young violinist fascinated the members of the jury, the audience, as well as myself with his masterly playing. He played in a virtuoso manner, with incredible ease . . . and everybody in the room knew that he was attending the birth of a great "master".'

This new victory paved Oistrakh's way to the international arena of violinists, which in those days was dominated by Kreisler, Szigeti, Heifetz and Milstein. He reached this 'Olympus' through two international competitions: the Henri-Wieniawski Competition in Warsaw and the Eugene Ysaye Competition in Brussels. In 1935, 55 competitors from 16 countries travelled to Warsaw to take part in the competition which was named after the outstanding Polish violinist Wieniawski. Among these competitors was the twenty-six-year-old Soviet violinist David

Oistrakh. He later confessed that he had suffered from terrible stage fright before the beginning of the competition:

'I simply couldn't imagine a comparison between myself and the foreign violinists.'

An extremely illustrative chronicle of this competition comes from David Oistrakh's letters to his wife Tamara Iwanowna:

'2 February 1935

We are approaching the border. The carriage is rattling so badly that I can't write.

I am feeling well. How many interesting things like ahead of us. Don't worry about my health. We have today been rehearsing on the train. I will write again this evening.

I kiss you and Garik.*

Dodik.'

'Warsaw, 4 March 1935

Dear Marochka,

Well, here I am in Warsaw, I am at least certain that this is true . . . We arrived in Warsaw at nine-thirty. We were met at the station by Adam Wieniawski (the organizer of the competition and nephew of the

*Igor's family nickname

composer), representatives of the Polish violinists and by our consul. We were then taken to our embassy where we have excellent accommodation. It's moving to see how concerned they all are about us. The formal opening of the competition took place yesterday.

. . . You can imagine the state I was in, as I had to listen to the playing of the first competitor and as I formed a picture of the abilities of my fellow competitors and their relative strengths. The first one to play was a Pole who lived in Paris, average performer, then Biro the Hungarian - very poor, afterwards Christiansen the Dane - not very exciting. The fourth and last competitor yesterday was a Polish lady who lives in Paris, a pupil of Thibaud - her name is Grażyna Bacewicz. She played very well, comparable to Ruth Posselt, perhaps not quite so good. Today, however, she was outclassed by a Pole who lives in Switzerland. His name is Broinslaw Gimpel (I have never heard of him), an outstanding violinist with great international concert experience; they are just announcing his concert here. The seven other violinists who played after Gimpel today were each one worse than the other. We still have

to listen to an Englishman, according to hearsay, an outstanding violinist; also an Italian who won a first prize in Italy and a Pole who won first prize at an international competition in Vienna and finally a group of talented French violinists. In spite of this, I believe that I have also got a chance of getting a good place since everything that I have heard so far is not really top class. Everything will depend on how I play and how I feel. At the moment I am feeling extremely well and I am absolutely fit, fairly calm and my hands are in good condition. Let's wait and see . . . I will play on the third (I have attached the time-table and order of performances). I miss you very much, much more than when I travel around in our country. I can imagine how excited you must be. Write to me and phone me. I am going to bring toys for Garik. Please give my regards to the relations. I kiss you.

Your Dodik.

Don't get excited, take an example from me, I am completely calm. The Soviet delegation are very interested over here.'

'Warsaw, 8 March 1935

Maronka,

*David Oistrakh at the*
*Warschauer Competition 1935*

I am writing only very briefly as I am terribly tired, the result of my playing. I have just phoned you for a minute. I must tell you that I am very pleased with my performance at the competition. This was, in my opinion, the most successful performance of my life. The days of calm reasonable work in Warsaw were not wasted.

I was afraid I would be terribly nervous. During the rehearsal in the morning I was indeed so nervous that I couldn't play. However, all the nervosity disappeared in the evening. I was just a little tense and that was in fact useful. I don't know how things will further develop here, there are still other strong violinists yet to play. But for the time being I am just a "nose-length" ahead of everybody. I had an unheard-of ovation from the competitors, professors, reporters and photographers. They congratulated me and interviewed me and photographers took pictures. I simply couldn't believe the reality of what had happened and it appeared to me as if it was a sweet dream, as I never thought it would end like that. I was terribly afraid of my nerves and the resulting uncertainty. Our embassy which looks after us so well, as if we were close relatives, was also happy. Tomorrow I am going to work on the concerto. The chance of success is considerable if nothing unexpected happens. And it is just this that cannot be ruled out. Anyway, for the time being I have done everything that was in my power and I shall try to continue to do everything. My conscience is clear in this respect and I am calm.

Today is one of the happiest days of my life. I write to you so quickly so that you can share my joy since I know that you get just as excited as I do . . . Tell our friends everything in detail.

Tomorrow Antonio Abussi, the talented Italian, will play. All in all, this is really marvellous. I kiss you and our little Garik. Tell granny that her grandson works under "full steam".'

*The fourth letter after publication of the results:*
1st Prize: Ginette Neveux (France)
2nd Prize: David Oistrakh (USSR)
3rd Prize: Henryk Temianka (Poland)

'Warsaw,
17 March 1935
Dear Tamarochka,
I can't tell you how depressed I am that I can't phone and tell you my impressions and feelings with my own mouth. Everything here seems like a sweet dream. I simply cannot accept that everything has had such a splendid end – this is how I judge the result of the competition. But my greatest interest is: are you satisfied with the result? I, for myself, am satisfied, since I find it wonderful to have got the second place despite competing with a number of truly excellent violinists in a program which is by no means the best in my repertoire – and in addition my health and nervous condition. Do you agree little one? I must tell you that I worked in Warsaw as I have never done before in my life . . .

. . . I have to be fair to myself, I took the matter as seriously as it deserved to be treated and as I was able to treat it.

One must admit that Neveux is devilishly talented. I was convinced of this yesterday when she played the F Sharp Minor Concerto (Wieniawski) with incredible strength and intensity. As she is only 15-17 years old it is by no means unfair to give her the first prize.

I played in Wilno on the 21st, Grodno on the 22nd, Łodź on the 24th and in Warsaw on the 26th. There are probably going to be even more concerts if these prove to be financially rewarding, otherwise I will return immediately to Moscow, as I feel homesick as never before. How I would love to do nothing for a week on my return to Moscow. If only this could be possible. I ask you to read this letter to our friends. I am at the moment unable to write further letters. I received a lot of telegrams today . . . The newspaper interviews are a nuisance. I expected your phone call today and ran to the fourth floor fifteen times, to the central office – calls from Moscow, however each time it turned out to be the newspaper reporters. Are you keeping all the press reports and opinions for me? . . .'

The Warsaw press, which dealt with the competition in detail, pointed unanimously to David Oistrakh's talent. The critics called him a 'worthy successor to Bronislaw Huberman', and that was in Poland the very highest praise. The newspaper reports also indicated some degree of dissatisfac-

*29*

tion with the jury's decision.

"Father, however, who always had a lot of time for young talent (as could be seen from his letters) was quite happy with second place and the victory of the young girl (she was in those days sixteen, father didn't know her age exactly). Ginette Neveux also expressed her sincere sympathy and admiration for father and kept this to her last hour. She wrote to father after she had returned to Paris from Warsaw: 'I tell everybody what an outstanding talent you have'."

David Oistrakh gave his first concert performances outside the Soviet Union shortly after the competition ('doing nothing' was obviously impossible for him). His performances in Turkey are particularly worth mentioning. They had little to do with the usual guest performances. A large group of Soviet artists was sent to Turkey at the invitation of Kemal Ataturk, the Turkish President. They stayed there for one month. The group consisted amongst others of: Valerie Barsowa, the soloist of the Bolshoi Theatre; Maria Maxakowa, Alexander Pirogow, also the composer Dmitri Shostakovich, the pianist Lew Oborin and the conductor Lew Steinberg. Oistrakh joined this group a little later on as he made a 'little detour' from: Moscow to Warsaw – Vienna – Budapest – Sofia – Istanbul. The journey took a week and was (as he wrote) 'surprisingly interesting', although he could not quite find complete inner calm:

'I was worried that I hadn't played for a whole week. How could I perform after this?'

*During a guest tour in Turkey in April 1935: David Oistrakh and Dmitri Shostakovich with teachers of the Istanbul Conservatory*

"Father's concern was not without justification. He arrived in Ankara on the 20th of April. He said in a letter of April 23:

'I have already played in a concert for the army on the day of my arrival and yesterday Shostakovich, Oborin and I played at the Conservatory in a matinée performance. A ball began at ten o'clock that night at the Minister of the Interior's in the presence of the whole government and President Ataturk . . . We all performed at the ball . . . It lasted until seven in the morning.'

Father wrote about Ataturk as if the

30

leader of the Turkish people was generally popular – a president who changed the backward country of the Sultan into an economically and politically independent state:

'He said with a loud voice between two of the pieces I was playing: "Our Revolution is not yet finished by a long way. It hasn't even begun yet in music and art. Listen and learn!"

Excellent conditions were created for the Soviet artists; the staff of the Soviet embassy and also the consulate showed them every possible attention. For example: the football fans among the artists (father and Shostakovich were enthusiastic football supporters) were given the chance to go and watch the interesting match of Turkey playing Vienna. Father described his impressions in a letter to mother: 'You cannot imagine the noise and howling with which the Turkish public accompanied each successful shot by a Turkish player, and the deadly silence in the stadium as soon as the Viennese shot a goal. Vienna won by 2-1. The match ended in a row due to unfair play by the Turks who had pushed some of the Viennese players. It very nearly came to a fight.'

Yes, there was football, also picnics, but above all there was a lot of hard work. Father gave solo concert performances, appeared together with Oborin and an orchestra under the conductor Steinberg, as well as playing in Ankara, Istanbul and Izmir. The concerts, which in most cases were free, took place every day and sometimes even twice a day.

'You cannot imagine,' father complained, 'how worn out I am. The evening concerts and the night receptions use up the last of my strength. One has to stand for hours at many receptions – this is the custom here, only ladies sit. When one is finally allowed to sit down, one has to jump up at once as soon as the President or the Prime Minister stands up. It is also no great pleasure to put on tails everyday . . . I dream of a time when I can sleep as long as I like, 48-100 hours uninterruptedly.' "

Nobody had it easy, least of all David Oistrakh, as the physical and mental demands had had their effect on him during the previous few months: immediately after taking part in the Union Competition in Leningrad, he travelled to Warsaw without knowing the result and without being able to enjoy his victory. He travelled to Turkey without having recovered from the Wieniawski Competition.

"Father wrote from Ankara in a letter to my mother: 'The President chose the joke that since we were thought to be a present to Turkey it would only be fair not to let us return, and he would therefore simply keep us here.'

Of course father returned home, but after that time, as mother frequently said, our Moscow flat only represented a temporary home for him."

We shall still have the opportunity to convince ourselves of the intensity of David Oistrakh's concert tours. Following his triumphant success in Brussels in 1937 at the Eugene Ysaye Competition he set out on an exceptionally large series of tours. Before we go back to the letters of the master violinist (where he discusses in the same detail as he did two years earlier), we need to say a few words about this competition. 125 competitors originally put down their names. However, this number melted down to 68 and then to 58 as the composition of the competitors and the jury became known. Both facts had a sobering effect on the competitors. They represented nineteen countries. The Soviet Union sent five competitors:

Jelisaweta Gilels, Boris Goldstein, Marina Kosolupowa, David Oistrakh and Michail Fichtenholz. The outstanding pianist Abram Djakow undertook the accompaniment for all. Oistrakh, now twenty-eight years old, was the oldest Soviet participant. Exactly how difficult the competition was is shown alone by the number of violinists who were admitted to the second and third rounds: 21 to the second and 9 to the third. Baron Buffin de Chosal, Chairman of the Queen Elisabeth Music Fund stood at the head of the jury. The other members of the jury included: Jacques Thibaud, Joseph Szigeti, Karl Flesch (who only took part in the third round), Abram Jampolski, Georg Kulenkampff, Mathieu Crickboom, Désiré Devoe and Marcel Darrieux.

However, let these letters describe the competition as seen through the eyes of the victor:

'Brussels, 19 March 1937
Our embassy gave us fairy-like accommodation in Brussels. It is six kilometres outside the town in an area of extraordinary poetic beauty. A large park with a pond also belongs to the house. Abrascha Djakow and I have a two-roomed flat with kitchen and bath entirely to ourselves in the house which also contains the office and a few embassy working rooms. Opposite, beyond the front garden, there is a building used for receptions, the ambassador Rubinin and a few employees live there. They have offered us an empty two-floored small house at the back of the park for our rehearsals. The little house has four rooms and a kitchen. They delivered a rented piano there today. Let me add that we have absolute peace and quiet here, our food is excellent, the air superb and the weather perfect. You can now understand how beautiful it is here. The daily program is great: we get up at seven-thirty, have breakfast at eight and then we work. We all work like mad and are on excellent terms with one another. I feel well, much much better than in Moscow and my nerves have undoubtedly improved. For the time being, I haven't noticed the slightest nervosity and as far as my mood is concerned, I am all set for the competition. I am unafraid, everything is firmly established.'

'Brussels, 20 March 1937
I would like to give you some news. First of all, the draw was today: the result, I am the 39th. It is now clear that there will be 68 participants and three elimination tests. In the first, which finishes on the 24th, everybody has to play a Bach fugue and the first part of his concerto. In the second round we have to play: a sonata by Ysaye and the first movement of a concerto which can be chosen by the participant. Only 35 to 40 competitors will be admitted to this, the second elimination test. 12 participants will remain in the third round (there will be 12 prizes), they have to play the whole concerto with orchestra and one of six pieces. Exactly which one will be decided by a draw. Odnoposoff, a very strong competitor from Vienna, will participate; he won the 1st prize at an international competition in Vienna in 1932 or 1933. People predict that he, Makanowizki and I will win the top prizes. I shall give a concert in Brussels on the 7th of April. We will all probably go to London to give a concert at the embassy. If only the competition were over. I don't have to explain to you what a 'nerve mill' this is, since I know that you are just as excited as I am. I must say that I feel relatively well and my mood is also good enough for me to fight like a lion. However,

it doesn't all depend on me, a lot depends on how the others will play . . .'

(A third letter has disappeared and the following fourth letter was written after the first elimination.)

'Brussels, 26 March 1937
Tamarochka, my little sun!
A great deal has happened in the two days from the 23rd to the 26th. There was so much worry, joy and nervous strain that it's impossible to describe it all in one single letter. I shall begin by saying that Lisa played in the afternoon of the day that I had my first rehearsal (23rd) and on which I sent you my last letter. She was exceptionally good and since nobody was expecting anything of her (they didn't know her), her performance hit them like a bomb. All predict that she will win the 1st prize. On the 25th, when the second elimination began,

*The jury in Brussels, March 1937. Amongst others: Jacques Thibaud, Joseph Szigeti, Karl Flesch, Abram Jampolski, Georg Kulenkampff, Matthieu Crickboom, Désiré Devoe, Marcel Darrieux*

I was so excited on account of these circumstances that I felt completely ill and shattered. As you probably already know only 21 out of the 58 competitors will be admitted to the second elimination. There aren't any strong violinists amongst them . . . It's marvellous that all the members of our delegation have been admitted. I want to tell you that the competition is extremely difficult and on an exceptionally high level. As I have already written, I felt so awful yesterday, on the 25th, that I played with the idea of giving up any further participation in the competition. Furthermore, two to three hours before my performance I discovered that the jury had decided that the whole concerto (with piano accompaniment) would have to be played from beginning to end in one go, instead of only playing its first part. I had only rehearsed the first part. My knees virtually gave way, and I went in this condition to the competition. I felt sick on the way there and I suffered from such shortness of breath that I decided to give up on my arrival. Furthermore, I wouldn't have been the first to give up. Many just can't stand the crazy tension. Odnoposoff was playing Tchaikovsky when I arrived. He

*33*

played beautifully. I sat being the stage with hanging shoulders and didn't know what to do. But imagine, as soon as I walked on the stage I noticed that all these stupid thoughts just dropped away and that I could play with full force. What do you think - I played the Ysaye Sonata very well and the Tchaikovsky Concerto in such a way that I would never have dreamt of, with such impulsiveness and technical perfection as never before in my life. The success was colossal. All the members of the jury came and congratulated me and it all seemed like a dream.

Everybody again said: Of course he'll get the 1st prize, etc. I collapsed after this superhuman concentration and lay the whole evening as if dead. I spent all today at the competition as I wanted to listen to a few of the other competitors.

If only you knew what a sea of tears and disappointments and shattered hopes this competition is for most of us. Once I am home I can tell you many sad details. Tomorrow is the final day of the second elimination. You can't expect great changes in the overall mood as all the outstanding players have already played. At the beginning of the third round the situation is as follows: in my opinion all five have a chance to reach the final, that means that all five will receive prizes since there are twelve participants and twelve prizes in the final. There is only some doubt concerning Marina and a lot will depend on how she plays tomorrow. There is great excitement in the corridors. By this I don't mean the competitors. Everybody is amazed by the high standard of the Soviet delegation. We shall know tomorrow evening who will be in the nine and who will be eliminated. More tears! An enormous amount of blood is shed here. That's all for the time being. Let me thank you 'little sun' for your warm letters and telegrams. I grasp them desperately, I now need every bit of support to survive this hellish stress. Abrascha Djakow is wonderful, he is great to me, in him I have a true friend.'

'Brussels, 1 April 1937
Tamaronka,
You can imagine what an exciting day today is. The result of the competition will be announced this evening. I played the Tchaikovsky Concerto with orchestra and also the Passacaglia the day before yesterday in the third elimination. It seems to me that I played very well, just as well as in the second elimination. I am very happy that I played with full force all three times. I can't do any better, the rest doesn't depend on me.

It's almost impossible to say who will get the 1st prize at this stage but I no doubt have a chance. By the way, I could also get the 4th prize. There was a reception at the Minister of Culture's after yesterday's performance by our girls. They paid me a lot of compliments, even people like: Flesch, Thibaud, Kulenkampff and Szigeti. Szigeti has only heard me on Moscow radio: the Viotti Concerto and the Ysaye Sonata. I went to bed very happy. However, this morning I am again full of doubts with heart problems and sickness. I wake up at 5-6 o'clock and can't sleep any longer. As I am used to sleeping in the morning this knocks me out, as you can imagine. It will certainly take some time before I am again in good form. If only the result is satisfactory. The chances are good, all I need is a little luck.

I must tell you that we all live together in complete harmony and that we share any joys and unpleasantness between us.

This gives one strength. All the newspapers note the fantastic achievement of the Soviet 'legendary' five. The press only shows our pictures. There is a great deal of noise and turmoil. You have to know how fantastically the other competitors played to understand how significant our success is. The local papers write as if it is a devilish competition.

My nerves are at breaking point, my hands are trembling, I can hardly write.'

'Brussels, 2 April 1937
Hurray, Tamarochka, our position is splendid, I have obtained the 1st Prize! It all seems like a dream to me and I am afraid of waking up. If only you knew what I had to go through yesterday. The hall, which was filled to the last seat, became completely quiet when we, the twelve finalists, appeared on the stage. Charles Houdret went to the microphone. I awaited the decision with my hands clenched into fists. I thought it might be possible for me to win the 1st Prize. However, when Houdret mentioned my name, a storm of ovation broke out such as I have never before heard. I though I would faint. My jaws cramped and I couldn't even bow.

*Before the announcement of the jury's decision*

*After the 'verdict': David Oistrakh as victor*

When the symphony orchestra began to play the Belgian national anthem in honour of the victors, the whole audience stood up. There was such a solemn atmosphere that I nearly had tears in my eyes. In this moment I thought about all the excitements and doubts which you and I had gone through. I knew what you must have gone through during those minutes awaiting the result of this mad competition. I felt that this was one of the unforgettable star hours in our lives. The achievement of the Soviet delegation is extraordinary and had made an indescribable impression here. I am now certain of getting any engagement in any country. There are unheard-of possibilities. I have moved up into the realm of the élite, of the world's best artists, owing to this success. I had a phone call from Moscow today and was told that *Pravda* had devoted a front page article to us. That is colossal. Cables are arriving here all the time today. I got a telegram from Litwinow. The photographers

and interviewers won't give me a free minute. I feel like a boxing champion – I had to prove my superiority once more and I can now afford some peace and play chess. But don't think that I don't intend to work, etc. On the contrary, I can see how much I am capable of achieving if I work, and I intend to keep my status!'

The results of the competition were a triumph for the Soviet violin school. Of the first six prizes of the competition five went to the Soviet competitors. This was a surprise for many people. Neither the Belgians, the French nor the Germans reached the finals. In spite of different attitudes, the Belgian, as well as the whole West-European press admitted that the Soviet state made a great effort in looking after its young musicians. David Oistrakh and the other Soviet competitors at the Brussels competition had the best conditions in which to prepare themselves. They were thus able to work in peace on the competition's program for several months, whilst many foreign violinists were forced to combine their preparation with daily rehearsals in operas or with symphony orchestras by whom they were employed. The Soviet artists were in addition supported by the best violin teachers (although Oistrakh, as reported earlier, prepared his program on his own). All the Soviet competitors were given first-class Italian violins from the state collection free of charge, during the training period as well as for the actual performance. Furthermore, they came to Brussels with their accompanist Djakow, an outstanding pianist, whilst the foreign violinists had to rehearse in a great hurry with unknown accompanists. And finally, and perhaps above all, every Soviet competitor was aware of the care and attention paid by his country in whose name he came to Brussels. Karl Flesch wrote after the result of the competition had been announced:

'As soon as Russia knew the competition rules a pre-competition was organized a year in advance in Moscow and this was to select the five best violinists who would go to Brussels with the instruction to defend and honour the Soviet flag.'

"That's putting it rather bluntly – of course there couldn't be an 'instruction' and there wasn't. The statement is however correct in principle: it was a matter of honour for David Oistrakh and his colleagues to defend the reputation of the Soviet violin school and the whole musical culture of their fatherland.

In his report Flesch also mentions the points which the victors were awarded: David Oistrakh (USSR) 1st prize, 1620 points; Riccardo Odnoposoff (Austria) 2nd prize, 1564 points; Jelisaweta Gilels (USSR) 3rd prize, 1551 points.

The difference between the number of points father got with those of Odnoposoff was remarkable. Their names were mentioned throughout the competition as contenders for the first prize and people compared their playing. As father said, there were even bets for fairly large sums amongst the audience."

The rivalry between Oistrakh and Odnoposoff was even more exciting as both played the Tchaikovsky Concerto in the final. We shall later see how your father presented this concerto. I would now like to mention an important circumstance which contributed to your father's success. By this I mean the interpretation of the works of the outstanding Belgian violinist Euguene Ysaye, after whom the competition had been named.

"Father always showed the greatest admiration for Ysaye's personality and creations. He described the author of the famous Six Violin Sonatas as the great reformer of violin playing. Father often played his works in different parts of the world and included them in his student's curriculum. He always received the warmest reception in Belgium."

As the master interpretor of Ysaye's works?

"As a violinist who had done a great deal to make Ysaye's work popular with all musicians."

In 1958, on the occasion of Ysaye's 100th birthday, Oistrakh arranged a concert with the students and candidates of his violin classes. It was perhaps on this evening that all six violin sonatas were for the first time played one after the other together with other pieces and musical arrangements by Ysaye. If I am not mistaken, you Igor Davidovich also participated in this concert?

"Yes, I remember that the success of this concert exceeded father's expectations. Moscow's musical public took a lively interest in the Renaissance of Ysaye's music. The room was overcrowded, the atmosphere festive, the whole evening had a special atmosphere. Candidates were followed by first-term students, violinists with no concert experience. These were followed by violinists who had already been hardened at international competitions and had already won prizes. And it seemed to me that father had achieved his ambition. From that day the Ysaye sonatas became a firm part of the repertoire of most students in our class. On that occasion I played the *Elegiac Poem* and the Third Sonata (the *Ballad Sonata*) which I performed for many years on my tours."

Did people in Ysaye's home country know about this concert?

"I am not quite sure – I think so. Anyway nine years later Antoine Ysaye, the son of the composer, said on awarding father (the Honorary President of the Eugene Ysaye Society) with the society's medal and diploma:

'You were not satisfied with winning the Grand Prix of the Eugene Ysaye competition and went on to make great efforts for a deeper understanding of his chamber-music, which you included in your repertoire and teaching program in recognition of its importance. You were the first violinist who made records of the *Elegiac Poem*, *Extase*, *Etude in Waltz Form* (after Saint-Saëns) and of the sonata *At the Grave* (after Locatelli). It is thanks to your example that the sonatas which you regard as an essential basis for the study of violin technique are now ranked with Bach's sonatas and Paganini's caprices as some of the world's top musical achievements. It is thanks to you, David Oistrakh, that Eugene Ysaye's work has stepped out of the shadows of oblivion.' "

Jakow Sak, Professor at the Moscow Conservatory, mentioned to me that one shouldn't overestimate the importance of David Oistrakh's victories at competitions and forget the importance of his individuality as an artist. Amongst other things he told me:

'I remember in detail a meeting with Oistrakh at the railway station in Warsaw. A group of Soviet competitors for the Chopin Competition greeted the violinist who was passing through Warsaw on the way to Brussels. We already had the competition behind us. The violinists still had to fight for the laurels. I was amazed at Oistrakh's nervosity. He simply didn't appreciate his own value. It didn't even dawn on him that he towered above his rivals and was far ahead

*37*

of them in maturity. I never forget that Constantine Nikolaievich Igumnof described him, as early as 1933, after a number of brilliant concerts in Moscow, as one of the best violinists of his time. On that occasion Oistrakh really played like a dream, with sparkling brilliance, without the slightest concession to bad taste and in a very virile and daring way. I repeat, he had no idea of his own value. The level of his playing or the 'artistic standard', as Genrich Gustavowitsch Neuhaus liked to call it, was already outstanding before Brussels and Warsaw.'

"Jakow Sak is right, although what he said doesn't only apply to father in that competitions in general can establish the reputation of an artist rather than leading to the discovery of new talent. Brussels was the cornerstone of his artistic career. It was the moment in which he devoted his whole life to world-wide artistic activity and tours to all parts of the earth.

'Let me give you my timetable,' father wrote in April 1937 to mother after his return from the concert in London to Brussels. 'Luttich on the 16th, I am going to Paris on the 17th, Radio Paris on the 18th, all five of us are supposed to take part in a semi-official concert on the 19th, reception at the embassy on the 20th. Between the 17th and 20th I have to make a recording for Columbia. I return to Belgium on the 22nd. I am playing in Antwerp on the 23rd, in Amsterdam on the 25th and in The Hague on the 27th. There is a sort of mixed concert on the 30th. If you read this letter carefully you will convince yourself that this is a deadly timetable, hardly any free days.'

This already represented the rhythm of my father's life as I knew it in the 1950s and 1960s."
Oistrakh played the first part of the Mendelssohn Concerto and Wienawski's Polonaise in D Major at the Soviet embassy in London on the 12th of April. In spite of the limited audience, the newspaper reporters made Oistrakh's name well know in England (and not only in London newspapers). Amsterdam awaited Oistrakh with impatience. The news from Brussels about the triumphant success of the Soviet violinists sounded like a fairy tale. The *Telegraph* later wrote: ' . . . Sceptics try to catch every imprecise sound to check the credibility of the enthusiastic Brussels reporters.' And the result?

'The sceptics suffered a complete defeat.' Let's read on: 'After the first sounds came from his violin they already classified him as an artist of world rank.' Oistrakh's performance of the Tchaikovsky Concerto for the Amsterdam Radio Orchestra was described by the whole Amsterdam press as 'The coming of a violinist of new format'.

"The following outline of a letter from Brussels gives some idea of the atmosphere at the Oistrakh concerts following the competition:

'The concert yesterday was fantastic. All tickets were sold out five days earlier. The first time this has happened in the five years since the concert hall was built. Many members of the audience sat on the stage and stood in the corridors. A seat on the stage cost 30 francs. The success was amazing. I had to give over a 100 autographs and played six encores. They literally tore the buttons off my coat at the exit.'"
David Oistrakh's letters from 1937 are informative psychological documents. They are addressed to his wife and represent his thoughts and feelings sincerely and concretely. His triumphant passage through the most important European concert halls, the offers

of engagement by the best-known impresarios of the old and new worlds and the best-known record companies were not yet familiar to him and therefore impressed him even more. It was necessary for him to overcome overwhelming exhaustion which struck him again: just try managing a marathon when you are only a sprinter. There moved in front of his eyes for the first time (mostly through a car windscreen) visions of Big Ben and the Eiffel Tower. But it was impossible to find time to look at them more carefully or even to visit the Louvre. Homesickness, longing for his wife and for you, his son, in those days still a little boy, made him return to Moscow over and over again. The knowledge of the task ahead of him also dominated the necessity for further work and self-perfection, only this could turn his dream-like life into lasting reality.

"I think that father would have made a first-class research object for a psychologist at that time. Only when one knows father's character, his modesty and unwillingness to use empty words can one really understand the sentences in his letters to my mother:

'I must tell you that one can easily make a world-wide career if the concerts (in autumn) continue as they do now. Believe me, I am not overstating the possibilities.'

'I feel that I have now benefited from the extraordinary interest people have in me. I now have the chance to take one of the top positions among the world-famous violinists ... We have already achieved this in Belgium. The autumn tour must bring about the decision. In any case one can say that my appearance in Europe has been described as the birth of new, very bright star. Everything will depend on this star not fading away prematurely.' "

On returning to Russia Oistrakh again dived into intensive concert activity. He was travelling again. Everybody wanted to hear him playing and he was available to music lovers and audiences up and down the whole country. They now got to know the man whom they only recognized from the one photo which had been published in *Pravda* after his success in Brussels.

"It was at this time that father got into closer contact with many Soviet composers. They turned to him more and more often with the request to perform a new composition in public. And it wasn't always the well-known composers or the musicians from Moscow. It was of course physically impossible for father to accept all proposals of this kind. But even the amount of Soviet music that he did perform reached a size that would have seemed almost impossible for a violinist to manage in a whole lifetime. He would have need a second life. There were concertos for violin and orchestra by Prokofiev, Miaskovsky, Shostakovich, Kabalevsky, Rakow, the classics of contemporary Lithuanian music, the Concertino of the Georgian composer Taktakishvili, the violin sonatas of Prokofiev, Shostakovich and Weinberg. Many of these compositions were first performed by father."

It wasn't just that Oistrakh played these works for the first time: many of them were only created thanks to your father's artistic standard. They were inspired by him and this allows us with no doubt to call them 'monuments in the honour of David Oistrakh'.

"We shall discuss in greater detail how my father arranged some of these sonatas and concertos of the composers when we come to his friendship and cooperation with contemporary composers."

At the end of the 1930s violin enthusiasts could be divided into two groups: on the one hand, David Oistrakh enthusiasts and on the other supporters of Miron Poljakin, one of Auer's best pupils and Glazunof's darling at the Petersburg Conservatory (Glazunof once gave him the mark 5 + + * after an exam). Poljakin returned to the Soviet Union in 1926 after a triumphant tour lasting eight years through Western Europe and the USA. Poljakin, Professor at the Leningrad Conservatory and since 1936 at the Moscow Conservatory, was loved and known as a pronounced romantic in his interpretation. The critics compared his violin playing with the piano playing of the romantic Vladimir Sofronizki. Poljakin, who rarely visited the concerts of his colleagues was a frequent guest at David Oistrakh performances and compared the latter's artistic potential with his own. As far as Oistrakh was concerned, he had always shown the greatest interest in Poljakin's art even in his youth. He visited almost every concert which the violinist gave and had a particularly high opinion of his in-

*5 is the highest mark and corresponds to a 1 in our marking.

terpretation of Bach's Chaconne. He regarded Poljakin's performance of the Brahms D Minor Sonata, which Poljakin played with Genrich Neuhaus, as the summit of the art of interpretation. The expression of emotion particularly impressed him.

It was by chance that Oistrakh and Poljakin occasionally faced one another more or less as rivals. We have only to remember that David Oistrakh's successful performance of the Glazunof Concerto in 1927 under the direction of the composer which took place in Odessa occurred virtually one day after Poljakin's masterful interpretation of the same concerto in the same city. The artistic parallelism of the two master violinists proved in the end to be of value to both.

"In one of his comments on the rivalry between the Oistrakh followers and the Poljakin followers, Genrich Neuhaus quotes Goethe from his *Conversations with Eckermann*:

'The public has now been arguing for some twenty years as to who is the greater: Schiller or myself, and they should be glad that there are still a few fellows dotted around the place about whom one can argue.' - 'How wise!' Neuhaus states.

'We should indeed be happy that there are still a few chaps dotted aound the place about whom we can argue.' "

The entire accustomed way of life was with one stroke destroyed in a single day: on June 22, 1941 the great patriotic war began. It was for thousands and thousands of artists as well as the whole of the Soviet Union a period of the greatest suffering and trials. This applied to masters and celebrities as well as to beginners and unknown artists. All those who performed at the front or in the large towns disproved the old Latin proverb 'inter arma silent musae' (when the arms sound the muses are silent).

Moscow, 1941. The enemy advanced furiously towards Moscow. Here, in front of Moscow, Hitler's armies were to suffer their first defeat since the beginning of the war. The situation at the Moscow front was extremely dangerous in the autumn of 1941 and the winter of 1941-42. In spite of this, many musicians refused to leave the capital. Musicians such as: the conductors Nikolai Anossow, Sergej Gortschakow, Nikolai Golowanow; the musicians of the famous Beethoven Quartet, Dmitri Zyganow, Wassili Schirinski,

Wadim Borissowski and Sergey Shirinsky, the pianists Maria Judina, Vladimir Sofroniski, Jakow Sak, the young Sviatoslav Richter, the composer and organist Alexander Gedicke, the singers Nadeshda Obuchowa, Natalia Roshdestvenskaya, the mother of the conductor. It was thanks to their efforts that the Moscow music life continued almost uninterruptedly. The musical programs on the radio, which were not only transmitted in the Soviet Union but also to foreign countries, did not stop for one day. This was the voice of the undefeated, the voice which sounded in the heart of the fatherland and bore witness to its fortitude and faith for the future and final victory.

One could hear mostly classical Russian music in war-time Moscow - Glinka, Borodin, Tchaikovsky, Glazunof. People experienced the music as the embodiment of national greatness, as an impassioned plea to protect the native culture. Western classics were played, including those of the German composers - even at the time when the German armies stood outside Moscow and Leningrad. Germany was never associated with National Socialism in the Soviet Union. In this way, Beethoven's music, which was transmitted by Soviet Radio, was of great symbolic importance. Each day produced new compositions by Soviet composers written with their heart's blood as they tried to come to terms with the gory events of the war. There were so many first performances that they became a regular feature of the concert repertoire.

The memories of some musicians can give us an impression of the concert life at the time and recreate the atmosphere. 'The audience sit in the hall clad in fur coats and padded boots,' according to an entry by Wadim Borissowski in the diary of the Beethoven Quartet after a performance in Moscow. 'It's very cold in the hall (about 4 degrees); a great success ... The mood of the audience and musicians is outstanding ... The audience particularly appreciated those artists who had stayed in Moscow and shared the joy and suffering of its inhabitants.' Professor Maria Judina emphasizes the interest of the Moscow inhabitants for symphony and chamber music evenings: 'The concert had to take place under the protection of mounted police as the rush of music lovers was so strong that it threatened to virtually 'burst' the building ...'

In the same year 1941, Leningrad. The defense of the city belongs among the greatest events of the patriotic war. The German troops managed to get to the outskirts of Leningrad. The town was encircled and according to the Wehrmacht the fate of the city was clear. General Field-Marshall von Leeb, commander of the 'North' Army Group had nothing better to do than to have invitations for a banquet at the Hotel Astoria printed to celebrate the expected fall of Leningrad. The Leningrad defenders were of a different opinion. The obstinate defence of the city on the Neva lasted for two and a half years, from September 1941 to January 1944. The surrounded city was attacked without interruption by the Luftwaffe and artillery for 900 days and nights with the objective of levelling Leningrad to the ground. In this way the city became the 'front', as it was cut off from land and was only connected to the fatherland behind by one solitary artery - the so-called 'road of life' - over the frozen lake of Ladoga. The food reserves disappeared in a

41

catastrophic way and the same happened to fuel and other raw materials. You could reach the 'front' with the tram from the centre of Leningrad because the front-line positions were only six kilometres away. The true front, however, went through the heart of the people and their consciousness. Michail Swetlow, the Soviet poet, wrote about the defenders of Leningrad (of which he was one) with the following words of an Arabian legend: 'They poured the Sahara through a sieve and the lions remained behind.'

The faithful allies of Leningrad enjoyed the arts even at this time of severe trials. The poets, musicians and actors who remained in the town helped along with the rest of the population in the building of lines of defence and stood on the roof tops to sound the anti-aircraft alarm during the uninterrupted air attacks. There still exists a photograph of Dmitri Shostakovich during one of these watches on the roof of the Leningrad Conservatory. But the most important thing was that the artists continued to work and perform day after day. Dmitri Shostakovich composed a new symphony. The pianist Vladimir Sofroniziki, the young cellist Daniil Schafran, the Leningrad Radio Symphony Orchestra (under Karl Eliasberg) and the operatic theatre (theatre of musical comedy) all performed uninterruptedly. The posters announcing the first performance of Kalman's *Countess Mariza* were stuck next to the slogans on the walls such as: 'Beware! This side of the road is particularly dangerous under artillery fire!'

Beethoven's 9th Symphony was performed on November 9, 1941 in the overcrowded Great Hall of the Leningrad Philharmonic. During those days this symphony was regarded as a symbol of the faith in the human ideals of mankind, which the genius of the German had proclaimed. Exactly seven months later, on August 9, 1942, the people of Leningrad heard for the first time Shostakovich's 7th Symphony, which was composed in the encircled city and which was dedicated to Leningrad. The performance of the symphony took place shortly after its première in Kuibyschew and after its fantastic success in Moscow and New York. Shostakovich praised the high ideals of world justice and humanity, the heroism of Leningrad and the Soviet people. 'The red army created an enormous symphony of world victory,' wrote the Soviet writer Alexander Tolstoi. 'Shostakovich put his ear to Russia's heart and played the song of triumph.' The performance of the symphony in the encircled Leningrad also turned out to be an act of heroism. The Radio Orchestra had lost half its musicians during the blockade. It seemed impossible for them to manage the score, because of its very difficult parts and because it needed a very large orchestra. However, the orchestra was complete, thanks to the enthusiasm of the conductor Eliasberg: the missing musicians were miraculously found in the city and were called away from front-line positions of the Leningrad front at the request of the conductor. The concert took place on a day when the Germans started an attack to conquer the city. It was only made possible by the Soviet artillery which covered the enemy position with uninterrupted heavy artillery fire. The necessary silence in order for the music to be heard was thus forced out of the enemy. On the evening of the 9th, the whole of Leningrad seemed to be united in the decorated hall. 10,000 people sat in front of the loud speakers awaiting the transmission of the concert. The Leningrad première of Shostakovich's 7th Symphony was more than a musical event, it was the victory of the morale of the Leningrad people and of their steadfastness. This is how Moscow and Leningrad lived in the time of war - tense and fulfilled. David Oistrakh was one of the musicians who had not left Moscow. He also flew into the encircled Leningrad to play for its defenders. You, Igor Davidovich, can surely tell us what your father's life and that of your whole family was like during the war?

"Our family was separated by the war. Mother and I were sent to Swerdlowsk. Our life meant waiting: waiting for father's next letter. Mother spent the whole day in the hospital. Although she was employed as a librarian she did every kind of work - carrying the wounded and night duty caring for the severely wounded. She saw more than enough pain and sorrow in these years and she herself had to suffer and endure a lot."

And your father? We know that he still played during these years, did he also continue to teach?

"Yes, the teaching which was interrupted in October 1941 was again started in March 1942. He also appeared frequently in public. During the first months after our departure father lived along with many other musicians in the Savoy Hotel (now the Berlin Hotel), where he also ate his meals. Heating was irregular and rehearsal difficult. His fingers froze, became stiff and unmanageable, but it was even colder at home. Father felt deserted in the empty flat. In spite of this he returned there and wrote in a letter to mother:

'It's very cold in the flat, it hasn't been heated for two days, but I have to work with the students at the Conservatory and that is a real refrigerator, as cold as on a skating rink.'

Some of our belongings were left outside in the Datscha, it was almost impossible to get there:

'I can't get to Schodnja; the trains take all night to do the 30 kilometres.'

In spite of this he remained in Moscow, for a number of reasons. The main reason was, as I see it now, an inner desire not to abandon Moscow in this difficult hour. His departure would have been regarded as desertion, as fleeing from the battle field.

Father warned us again and again against a premature return to Moscow. At the same time he showed, in one of his letters in 1942, sympathy for those who had remained in Moscow in spite of the danger of new attack. Father became a member of the Communist Party in those times most dangerous for the Soviet Union, and he served its ideals until the end of his life with his art and many social activities."

How intensive was his concert activity during the war?

"Judge for yourself. In spite of all pressures, father not only played in Moscow but also undertook tours to Swerdlowsk, Tscheljabinsk, Magnitogorsk, Wologda and even to Leningrad. He was a member of the Military Commission for Conservatory Sponsorships and participated in concerts which were arranged under the organization of the 'Conservatory for the Front'.

In the first years of the war, the first rehearsals and concerts of a trio began. A trio whose members were: father, Lew Oborin and Sviatoslav Knuschewizki. You could often hear his violin on the radio.

'I have a hell of a lot to do,' father wrote, 'I play every day for the radio, solo, trios and sonatas . . . all need intensive rehearsal and practice . . . I have to work a lot . . .'

Father told us how difficult even the trip to the radio station was, particularly with transmissions to foreign countries which took place after midnight most of the time. He had a pass which allowed him to enter the streets of Moscow at night, but he often had to run through the darkened city during the night as all the traffic stopped during curfew.

Father played in Leningrad in March 1943:

'I am flying to Leningrad . . . The town is bombarded ten times daily by artillery,' father states in a letter to mother. 'Jascha Flier is here at this moment. He started out on the 2nd and only arrived on the 8th. He had to sit in Tichwin for five days. He can't get back for the time being. Planes fly rarely. . .'

He also wrote to me shortly before his departure to Leningrad:

'Moscow, 23 February 1943
Dear Garinka,
I am just driving to the airport. I am flying to Leningrad where I will give concerts. Although I am very busy I would like to write you a few lines. I am flying to Leningrad, a town which has been encircled by Fascists for almost one and a half

*David Oistrakh and Jakow Sak 1943, in front of the Hotel Astoria in Leningrad*

years. Just think, the Fascists are closer to Leningrad than Sokol is to Moscow (at the petrol station where the road branches for Moscow and Chimki). The Fascists have formed a firm ring around the city and want to freeze out its population. They are destroying the city with a daily bombardment from heavy long distance artillery. In spite of it all the city manages to live, work and fight against the enemy and even amuses itself. Art and music are so essential to the people, they love the arts so much that they go to the theatre, attend concerts and listen to music even in these inhuman and difficult times. Just imagine how beautiful it is for me to play in this heroic city for the soldiers and commanders who

defend it and to visit the great battleships which shell the Fascists, to play whilst at the same time knowing that my music gives them pleasure and enjoyment in their free time.' "

David Oistrakh played in the Leningrad Philharmonic with the Radio Orchestra under Karl Eliasberg – the legendary musicians who had performed Shostakovich's 7th Symphony. There was still hunger, cold, suffering and unrest in the city.

'And in spite of this the Great Hall was overcrowded, although the members of the audience had to keep their coats on because of the cold.' David Oistrakh later wrote. 'The alarm sirens began to howl just as I began to play the Canzonetta from Tchaikovsky's Violin Concerto. Nobody got up. I completed the concerto.'

Oistrakh also gave a concert in the

editorial building of the paper *Leningrad Pravda*, which was at the time situated in a wonderful mansion on the Fontanka road. Oistrakh played in a medium-sized room, without a stage, in front of some fifteen listeners.

'Strength and tenderness, a storm of emotion flowed into our hearts and gave us an inner courage with which everyone could strengthen themselves and which brought out the best in us. Even the women had forgotten how to cry during the blockade, but today . . . we were embarrassed to look at each other,' the journalist L. Nikolski later wrote. A few hours later a fragmentation bomb weighing one and a half tons hit the editorial building. One could surely not think of tours to foreign countries in those days?

"Of course not. However, many music lovers in foreign countries were able to hear father's violin playing by listening to the Soviet radio broadcasts. Father was again all over the world as soon as the much longed for peace arrived. Already in spring 1945 he played in Bulgaria, Rumania, Yugoslavia, Austria and Czechoslovakia. I can remember these tours very clearly. Father told us about the enthusiastic reception which the public gave him, the public who longed for nothing more than peace, music and kindness.

'The concerts were received enthusiastically,' he wrote from Sofia. 'The concert halls are full to bursting point and performances in the provinces turned into demonstrations . . . Judging from the critics and the local musicians we can regard our task as fulfilled.' "

Oistrakh met a group of Soviet artists in Vienna, amongst them the ballet dancer Galina Ulanowa, the singer Natalia Spiller, David Oistrakh's trio partners Lew Oborin and Sviatoslav Knuschewizki. In addition to his performances with the trio (Shostakovich's Trio was tremendously successful) Oistrakh played Miaskovsky's and Chatschaturjan's violin concertos as well as Prokofiev's 1st Violin Sonata. This program was of particular importance since the Austrians hadn't had the opportunity to hear Soviet music since the beginning of World War II. They only knew Shostakovich from his 1st Symphony and had no idea who Chatschaturjan was.

"Father played with the same success in Czechoslovakia. He was very popular in Prague. It was not just by chance that he had been a frequent participant of the traditional music festival 'Spring in Prague' (since its formation in 1946). As a rule he played in several concerts – one after the other, which made him very tired. Playing with Czech orchestras and conductors always gave him the greatest pleasure.

'Every day, I am like a dog chasing his own tail, from 7.30 in the morning until late at night. I couldn't dream of greater success than I have had here,' father wrote from Prague in 1947.

He was also invited to the 'Jubilee' – the thirtieth 'Spring in Prague' festival which took place in 1975. Father dreamt of this concert and worked very hard for it. This is understandable, for he had to conduct Beethoven's 9th Symphony. I still have the score with father's comments, which he studied in depth during his last summer in 1974, when he rested in the German Democratic Republic. However, this dream was not to be fulfilled . . ."

Was Oistrakh junior a participant in the Jubilee festival?

"Yes, and I was able to convince myself again with what high respect the people of Prague regarded Oistrakh senior."

45

# *World fame*

The war retarded David Oistrakh's international fame. The decades after the war opened a new chapter in his artist's biography in which he reached even greater maturity and celebrated unsurpassable triumphs throughout the world. Which of his many tours during the first half of the 1950s do you consider as being particularly interesting and laden with responsibility?

"I would first like to stress that father prepared himself for each concert with the same sense of responsibility, quite irrespective of which country and town he was playing in. Over 150 towns in the Soviet Union, large and small, near and far, heard David Oistrakh's violin. He played (and not just once) in almost all of the Soviet Union's republics, in the 'heroic cities' Leningrad, Wolgograd, Odessa, in Middle Asia, in the Urals, in the Donez valley and in Kusbas. Father's tours to foreign countries took him through many places. I am not just referring to father's journeys to numerous international competitions – this is a separate subject.

He went overseas for the first time in 1954. He participated in concerts at the International Film Festival in Mar-del-Plata, the Argentinian coastal resort. He also played in the Colón Theatre in Buenos Aires and then in Montevideo, the capital of Uruguay. The tropical flora, the almost endless golden beaches on the Atlantic, an audience full of temperament which gave father an exceptionally cordial welcome – all these impressions remained in his memory for a long time. Father met the well-known Soviet film actor and director Sergej Bondartschuk over there, who later made a film of Tolstoi's *War and Peace.* He also met Bondartschuk's French colleague Michel Simon, whose performance in the film *Monsieur Taxi* remained an unforgettable experience for many people.

The meetings with important musicians in Argentina and Uruguay were important to father. Such encounters during his travels helped him to obtain a deeper knowledge of the art and culture of other countries and peoples.

Father was very happy that the final of the world chess championship took place in Buenos Aires during his visit. He made many friends among the participating Soviet chess players.

The journey to Latin America was on the whole not his most difficult."

Do you remember your father's concert which was attended by 40,000 listeners?

"Oh, yes, that was in Mar-del-Plata, in addition to the 15,000 visitors to the summer concert hall under the open sky there were another 25,000 in the nearby streets and squares who came to listen. Father amused us with the follow-

*Concert with Nikolai Anossow*

ing story: All participants at the festival (he was also one of the stars this time) were introduced by an announcer and welcomed with a tune from their home country. When the Soviet delegation appeared on the stage they were greeted with the sound of the small country ditty 'Barynja'.

In discussing the 1950s tours which placed particular responsibility on father, we must above all consider the concerts in England, Japan and the USA."

November 1954. England hears Oistrakh. The first concert in the Albert Hall was sold out. Some of London's best known musicians were in the audience. David Oistrakh included Beethoven's and Prokofiev's First Violin Sonatas and Ysaye's Third Sonata in his program as well as several pieces from Kreisler and Tchaikovsky. It was a resounding success. Oistrakh then played two concertos with the orchestra - the Brahms and the Chatschaturjan, the latter under the composer's baton. Oistrakh as well as Chatschaturjan were participat-

*47*

*David Oistrakh at the beginning
of his international career*

ing in the 'Month of Anglo-Soviet Friendship'. After subsequent performances in many English cities, Oistrakh concluded his tour with the Beethoven and Tchaikovsky concertos in London.

"I gave my own début one year earlier in 1953 in the same famous hall in London. At the same time I played a Beethoven Concerto and the same Chatschaturjan Concerto.

I still recall that father always liked to remember his appearance in Manchester. Although the hall was not full, the audience greeted the Soviet artist most cordially. There were many workers among the audience.

A critic wrote: 'A violinist who has always got to look for something his equal, played in Manchester yesterday . . . As soon as people here realise who he was, thousands of music lovers will curse the day they allowed themselves to miss yesterday's musical event. I can predict this with certainty.'

In those days comparisons were for the first time made between David Oistrakh and Jascha Heifetz in England – this happened quite often later on.

The year 1954 gave this another chance to occur. I quote another press report:

'The first round of the world violin championship took place yesterday. The 53-year-old Jascha Heifetz, the leading violinist of the West, performed Brahms' Violin Concerto in the Royal Festival Hall. The second round will take place next Thursday in the Royal Albert Hall where the 44-year-old David Oistrakh, the leading violinist of the Soviet Union, will play the same Concerto.' "

David Oistrakh was expected in Tokyo in February 1955. The plane was delayed by hours. Over a hundred musicians, artists and journalists waited until 2 o'clock at night in the airport. Finally the SAS plane arrived. David Oistrakh and the pianist Wladimir Jampolski appeared on the steps. A cordial welcome: people welcomed a Soviet artist in Japan for the first time since the war.

"Even before the war only a few Soviet musicians had gone to Japan. The composer and pianist Sergey Prokofiev, the violinist Michail Erdenko, the singer Irma Jaunsem – all visited Japan in the 1920s. The anticipation of the visit by the Soviet artists was particularly high.

A direct air link between Moscow and Tokyo didn't exist in 1955 and father had to fly via Helsinki and Stockholm.

'The flight was incredibly interesting,' reported father. 'It was like turning the pages of an atlas: Sweden, Switzerland, Italy, Iran, Pakistan, India, Thailand, the Philippines. The Scandinavian winter made way for the Italian spring and we were nearly dying of heat after a few hours ... '

Father wrote that the enthusiastic welcome in Tokyo made him totally forget how tired he was:

'They overwhelmed us with the greatest care and attention from the first minute of our arrival.'

On his return he said:

'We saw a group of young Japanese dressed in the same grey jackets and dark pullovers already at the airport. They smiled at us from the crowd. It turned out that the Radio and TV centre had designed a special uniform for our group of guides. We did this, they explained to us, so that you can spot your colleagues without difficulty ... Indeed, the young people were always there and made every conceivable effort to help us.'

Father's tour took him to six of Japan's largest cities: Tokyo, Osaka, Kioto, Fukuoka, Nagoya and Yokohama. The success of the twelve concerts and the special concert given for the Red Cross was tremendous and the concert halls were always overcrowded.

"All public concerts were already sold out in advance,' father told us. 'Many photographs, interviews, and press reports, etc. I yesterday

*In Japan 1955 with young violinists of the music school in Tokyo*

played at a matinée at 2 pm (with Konoye conducting), Mozart, Prokofiev and Tchaikovsky. The hall with its 3,500 seats was packed in spite of it being a week-day. Tokyo is a very large, beautiful city with its population of seven million. Unfortunately we had far too little time to see the sights in Japan – the work was so enjoyable.'

Father stressed the exceptional love the Japanese have for music in his letters and on his return home. He was very impressed by a Unisono of 1,000 violinists which he heard in the Tokyo Music

49

School Shai-no Kyoiku (Teaching of Talents) and also by the high standard of the four best Japanese symphony orchestras with which he played. He also liked the works of the modern Japanese composers, particularly the top composer Kosaku Jamada, who had visited the Soviet Union as a conductor before the war. Father brought many scores back to Moscow and actively supported efforts to perform the Japanese compositions. Next to a pile of scores lay a large pile of letters from music enthusiasts who thanked him for the artistic pleasure his concerts gave and which pointed to the necessity of closer political and cultural contact between Japan and the Soviet Union."

David Oistrakh talked with particular warmth about a special concert: on his return to Tokyo after his tour through Japan the organizers announced a concert in the closed sports hall of the stadium. 16,000 people were able to attend this performance. The seats were not numbered and only cost one-tenth of the price of tickets for the Hibia and Kyoritsu halls. All tickets were of course sold in no time. The concert took place at lunch time. As everybody wanted to

have a good seat people were already arriving at the stadium early in the morning, coming from all parts of the city. The hall had a loud-speaker system, and there was a poster with the names of the violinists in Russian and Japanese above the stage. The success surpassed all expectations. After many encores the crowd began to sing the Soviet song 'Far is my Homeland' for the artists.

"It was in this way that father 'discovered' Japan for many Soviet soloists and ensembles. He now had his first performance in the USA ahead of him, probably the most exciting of all."

November 20, 1955 was a great 'day of the violin' for New York. This was a rare event, even in this city which has seen all the world's violin virtuosos. Three master violinists followed each other on the stage of Carnegie Hall: Mischa Elman played in the morning, David Oistrakh at lunch time and Nathan Milstein in the evening. Not bad company for David Oistrakh at his first concert in the USA, don't you think?

"Father received his first invitation for a tour of the USA as early as 1937, immediately after his victory in the Ysaye Competition in Brus-

sels. On his return to Moscow, he did however concentrate all his efforts on strengthening his success with more intensive practice (Jakow Sak was surely right when he said that father didn't know his own value at the time). His début in the USA was constantly delayed: at first because of the outbreak of war, then because of the Cold War. One couldn't overlook the tension between the two countries even in 1955.

These circumstances added considerable weight to David Oistrakh's début. He already had a good reputation in the USA, mainly through his records, although they weren't widely distributed in America. Reports from experts, Szigeti and Menuhin, who had heard him perform in Europe also added to his reputation. Father's arrival was awaited with much impatience."

Was David Oistrakh, as in Japan, the first Soviet artist to give concerts in the USA after the war?

"No, this time he was the second – after Emil Gilels whose successes preceded father's American tour by a short period."

David Oistrakh and Emil Giles – these musicians, both world famous, have much in common:

Both were born in Odessa and grew up in that city. Gilels was eight years younger. Both showed musical talent from their earliest youth and both were educated by leading music teachers, Emil Gilels first by Berta Reingbald, whom he remembers with great gratitude, and then by Genrich Neuhaus in his outstanding famous school, who changed him from being a brilliant pianist into a real musician. When Gilels was still living in Odessa he often came to Stoliarsky's class to accompany his younger sister Liza. Although he was familiar with Pyotr Stoliarsky's teaching methods, he later nevertheless often went to him for advice when he himself was teaching. After their successes in their home town both pianist and violinist only reached full artistic maturity after moving to Moscow. Both musicians had to pass the Szylla and Charybdis of Soviet and international competitions: Gilels achieved the same outstanding success as Oistrakh in Brussells one year later - a further contribution to the world reputation of the Soviet music school.

Gilels, like Oistrakh, had gone through the war, remained in Moscow and flew several times to give concerts in Leningrad. They now met in New York in 1955.

"Father's début in the USA went superbly well and can be called a triumph without exaggeration. It was not without interest that Elman's, Milstein's and father's programs on this day contained the 'Devil's Trill' by Tartini-Kreisler. Friends advised father against changing the program: 'Let the others take tranquilisers,' Walter Legge later said.

The hall, which was designed to take 3,000 people, couldn't take all the people who wanted to hear father. Part of the audience sat on the stage of Carnegie Hall.

Father prepared himself very carefully for his first tour of the USA and spent a long time considering the content of the program. In his archives you can find programs of concerts by Francescatti, Stern, Menuhin, Heifetz, Elman and Ricci in the 1954/55 New York season. These were obviously sent to him by friends at his request. As a result of his consideration father proposed several programs to the Americans, which included, among others, the following pieces: Tchaikovsky's and Brahms' Violin Concertos, Mozart's 5th Concerto, Shostakovich's and Prokofiev's 1st Concertos and also some sonatas for violin and piano as well as a series of small violin pieces."

David Oistrakh told me that he wasn't very happy with the program for his début.

"To be more accurate, he wasn't too happy with the second part of his début concert. On the advice of many friends, father changed the second part to 'loosen up' the first part, which consisted mainly of sonatas (Beethoven's and Prokofiev's 1st Sonatas) with pieces by Tchaikovsky, Tartini, Medtner, Ysaye and Chatschaturjan. He later regretted this change. However, this multitude of violin pieces allowed him to demonstrate the whole range of his violinistic flexibility with impressive strength."

The audience demanded an encore after the concert. Nine out of ten débutants would not have missed the opportunity of ensuring their success by playing an effective virtuoso piece. Oistrakh, however, played Wagner's 'Blatt aus dem Musikalbum' as his first encore, a piece which doesn't demand more, but also not less, than that the artist should allow his violin to sound in its most noble timbre.

The morning papers of November 21 unanimously reported the concert's great success. Howard Taubman, the well-known American critic, wrote in the *New York Times* that David Oistrakh was a true magician on the violin. The *Daily News* headed its discussion with 'Oistrakh's brilliant début in the USA'. Louis Biancolli, critic of the *New York Telegram and Sun* stressed:

'As a stylist and musician, David Oistrakh has hardly got anyone his equal among the violinists of his generation. There is nobody who surpasses him.'

David Oistrakh played three days later at Carnegie Hall for the second time. The excitement surrounding this concert was indescribable - also in the press.

"I can well imagine father's condition, as he stepped onto the stage (already suffering from stage fright) to see: Fritz Kreisler, Nathan Milstein, Mischa Elman, Isaac Stern, Zino Francescatti, Samuil Duschkin, Tossi Spivakowski, William Primrose, Raja Garbusowa, Pierre Monteux, Elisabeth Schwarzkopf and Paul Robeson sitting in the front rows. 'A nice collection?' father asked me jokingly in a letter after the concert.

The critic weighed up each violinist's mastery of the instrument. One of the critics wrote under the title 'A great violinist':

'After attending two Oistrakh concerts at Carnegie Hall in the last week, I reached the conclusion that he is the best contemporary violinist and the best violinist I have ever heard. This opinion is by no means the result of unlimited enthusiasm - violin concerts don't any longer produce that enthusiasm in me. It is the result of careful analysis of his way of playing and

*During a recording in New York of Shostakovich's 1st Violin Concerto*

of a comparison between him and other violinists who have visited us before.'

New York was father's first stop during his tour of the United States, a tour which lasted one and a half months. He described his heavy timetable in one of his letters to me: he hardly had a single day without a concert. Add to this the fact that he gave more than one concert in the three cities - New York, Philadelphia and Chicago, this meant that he had to be continuously on the move, either by train or plane."

David Oistrakh included Dmitri

Shostakovich's Violin Concerto in the repertoire for his USA tour. Prokofiev and Shostakovich are now regarded as classics of the twentieth century. However, David Oistrakh included their violin concertos in his program a long time before these two composers achieved this world-wide acknowledgement. He was one of the first to play Prokofiev's 1st Concerto in the Soviet Union and played it at his final examination at the Odessa Conservatory. The first performance of Shostakovich's 1st Concerto took place in Leningrad thanks to Oistrakh. He brought it with him to New York immediately afterwards and later to a number of West-European countries. He was of course aware of the fact that some of his listeners, also some of the Americans, didn't want to hear such modern pieces, preferring well-proven concert pieces which had been accepted for decades. You didn't have to think when you listened to these concertos, you just enjoyed them as a 'delight to the ear'. He ignored this, and as in his youth he again went his own way and succeeded against the conservative part of the public, against the average taste. He dared, and each time his audacity proved to be artistically justified.

"The American first performance of Shostakovich's Violin Concerto became a musical event. Father already gave press interviews in New York before the concert in which he described the concert as 'From a musical point of view one of Shostakovich's deepest and most interesting creations'. He put the concerto on the same level as the composer's 10th Symphony. Father told us on his return from the USA, that he was literally told only in the last minute before stepping on the stage to play the concerto that the performance would be broadcast over the entire country. It is not difficult to imagine his nervosity. A recording of the concerto was made available shortly afterwards, just as after the first performance with the New York Philharmonic under Dimitri Mitropoulos.

Father gained many strong impressions of American musical life. He was above all impressed by the American orchestras. He got to know the country's best symphony orchestras, the Boston, Philadelphia and the New York Philharmonic. To be more precise, he played with them under their conductors: Charles Münch, Eugene Ormandy and Dimitri Mitropoulos. Each orchestra had its own specific style (which was obviously partly due to the conductors) and its own 'face' and both were in their own way exciting. Father spoke with particular warmth of the outstanding technique of the Philadelphia, the French timbre of the Boston, and the modern style of the New York orchestras." And what did he think of the violinists? America is a country with first-class violinists, as a quick glance at the guest list of Oistrakh's concert at Carnegie Hall showed.

"The timetable did not allow father to listen to all of these violin virtuosos. However, even the short passing impressions from meetings with famous violinists and discussions with many members of the string orchestras allowed him to make clear conclusions, which I would like to summarize as follows:

It could not be hidden from father that the Soviet and American violin schools were superior, but it should be noted that they shared common roots. We reach this conclusion without implying any doubts as to the standard of the other violin schools - the French, German and in the last decades the more and more important Japanese schools. I often heard father com-

*In America: from left to right –
Nathan Milstein, David Oistrakh,
Isaac Stern, Eugene Ormandy,
Salomon Hurok*

*David Oistrakh and Zino
Francescatti*

ment on these common roots. Most of the prominent American violinists are directly and indirectly linked with the school of Leopold Auer who was previously Professor at the Petersburg Conservatory. Or they were alternatively linked with the student of the past Professor, Naum Blinder and his pupil Ivan Galamian in Moscow." Just an additional comment: the contemporary art of piano playing gives the same impression. The overwhelming majority of American pianists who are now currently recognized were students of previous Petersburg or Moscow teachers. I would like to mention as an example Rosina Lewina, who trained such brilliant pianists as: Van Cliburn, Mischa Dichter, Eduard Auer. As is the case with violinists, we also find with the pianists a predominance of the Soviet and American schools. This brings up the question: did David Oistrakh make new friends in

54

America?

"He certainly gained the symphathy of many thousands of listeners and the friendship of several outstanding musicians such as: Eugene Ormandy, Charles Münch, Isaac Stern, Zino Francescatti, Grigori Piatigorski, William Primrose.

'Dear friend,' Piatigorski wrote to my father. 'A whole week has now gone by but the sound of your violin is still with me. Will I ever forget your concert in Philadelphia? No, never. Impossible. An impression of such depth is an impression one keeps for one's whole life. I grew to love you not only as a great artist but immediately and with a full heart as a true human being! How happy I would be if I knew this love were mutual!' "

What was the relationship between your father and Salomon Hurok, his American impresario, like?

"Father's first American tour wasn't organized by Hurok, but by the concert agency Columbia Artists. After father met Hurok he became Hurok's permanent 'client'. The connection between them, which grew stronger with the years,

*With Grigori Piatigorski*

was really a friendship. They often talked about art and life. Salomon Israilevich was a frequent visitor in our home and invited my parents, myself and my wife to his home in New York.

I met him myself in London in 1961 during a tour which father and I did together. I completely shared father's enthusiasm for this untiring impresario.

Hurok was no longer a young man when father met him and was certainly wealthy enough not to have to work, to get rid of all worries and to enjoy the evening of his life. But he never thought, even in his dreams, of giving up his office on 5th Avenue. He was as full of energy as at the beginning of his career, when thanks to his efforts America got to see Anna Pavlova and Feodor Chaliapine. At the beginning of his seventies he gave America the 'present' of the Igor-Moissejew Folk Dance Ensemble and afterwards the Berioska and the famous Bolshoi Ballet."

Surely the reason for the sympathy between the two, David Oistrakh and Salomon Hurok, was the task of uncompromisingly serving art and through art the good cause of cultural exchange between the Soviet Union and the USA?

*55*

"Of course, Hurok's attitude to father was above all guided by his admiration for him as a violinist and musician. His own mentality and nature corresponded with father's. If you want to search for more reasons for their mutual respect you can recall Salomon Hurok's words which outlined his attitude to his activity as an impresario. 'This is no profession,' he said, 'but an incurable disease.' Father could have said the same about his own mission."

Oistrakh's first American tour would not be a bad place for us to start talking about the intensity of his artistic activity.

"I would prefer to talk about father's 'intensity', not only as a violinist but in all other areas of activity, later, when we discuss his character. The way of life which is dictated to us musicians this century has no easy rhythm, and yet I know a number of musicians who know how to take care of themselves and therefore to compensate a little for the over excessive demands on them. Father was different. But I am contradicting myself if I start talking about this now. Let's stay with the USA tour.

Father, together with Emil Gilels, became the real centre of the New York music season. Many critics regarded their stay in America as the most important event in the country's cultural life. The *Boston Post Friday* wrote for example about father's concert in Boston:

'His début was not just the most attractive event of the season. The crystal clear perfection of Mozart and the rainbow like spray of colours of the Brahms Concerto made the evening an historic event, almost as important as the day King Henry won the Battle of Agincourt. All those who were in the hall will tell their children and grandchildren that they were there when Oistrakh played Mozart and Brahms with the symphony orchestra under Charles Münch. It was one of those concerts which rarely occur, concerts which make the listener feel deeply happy, disturbed and proud that human beings are occasionally able to lift themselves to such summits in the most subtle of all arts.' "

A few words about the political aspects of David Oistrakh's successful American tour and beyond that about all the artist's foreign tours in the period after the war. You often hear that music and politics are subjects on different levels which have no point of contact at all. However, they interacted very frequently in Oistrakh's life. The joy of victory after the war was soon clouded by the Cold War and the general political tension. Under such conditions, David Oistrakh's foreign tours were not merely of artistic importance, especially when he was the first Soviet violinist to play in countries such as the German Federal Republic, Latin America, Japan and later in Australia, New Zealand, Spain and Portugal – his violin made 'politics'. His concerts proved to be the most effective method of strengthening cultural contact between the countries which differed in their social and political systems, and they added to the reputation of Soviet music and culture.

Oistrakh had his début in the German Federal Republic in 1954. A newspaper headed its concert discussion with the slogan: 'Bravo, but why not earlier?' The violinist played often in the German Federal Republic, particularly in the 1960s and 1970s. His tours took him to the most important musical centres: Hamburg, Cologne, Stuttgart, Munich, Dusseldorf, Kassel, Nurenberg, Freiburg and Bielefeld.

Oistrakh played sonatas by Beethoven, Brahms, and Prokofiev, compositions by Leclair, Bach, Mozart, Lalo, Debussy. He included Beethoven's Violin Concerto in his symphony program with Karl Bohm conducting, and the Brahms and Tchaikovsky Violin Concertos under Eugen Szenkar, whom Oistrakh knew from his Moscow period in the 1930s. He played with Kurt Sanderling and Eugene Mravinsky conducting on a tour with the Leningrad Symphony Orchestra in 1956. On this tour he played Mozart's 5th Concerto with Sanderling and Shostakovich's 1st Violin Concerto with Mravinsky, which was still new to the music trends in the German Federal Republic. He acquainted them with Shostakovich's Violin Sonata years later.

Oistrakh already had a good reputation in the Federal Republic because of his many records. Each of his visits was expected with great impatience and the press was unanimously enthusiastic: 'Star without sensation', 'The tsar of the violinists', 'The Russian violin phenomenon', 'The fanatic of tone purity'.

Oistrakh's tours of the German Federal Republic in the 1960s and 1970s were organized by Walter Vedder.

" 'Each impresario,' he wrote in his short memoirs about the Soviet violinist, 'dreams of representing an artist who combines all good properties. He should be a master in his field. The public is expected to go in crowds to his concerts and applaud him enthusiastically, the artist should be an example of modesty, human kindness and warmth.

It's in the nature of things that this dream is never realized except on rare occasions.

Among the many artists whom I have had the honour to represent, David Oistrakh was the realization of such a dream – a true exception.'

I am also well acquainted with Walter Vedder and have had the privilege and pleasure of working with this outstanding impresario for many years. Father always brought back a mass of musical impressions from the Federal Republic. The strongest was in 1954. The visit to Beethoven's house in Bonn. The atmosphere of this house in which the greatest composer of all times – that's how much father valued Beethoven – was born. The simple furniture, the musical instruments which once belonged to the master,

all this was for him moving and unforgettable. Father told us many times about the enthusiasm for music in the Federal Republic. The relationship between the USSR and the Federal Republic varied during the decades following the war; however, father always stressed in his press interviews that the citizens, the people of the Federal Republic were full of the same desire for peace as all other people on earth. He was particularly glad that the concerts he gave in the Federal Republic helped to break down the prejudices which still existed against our country in the 1950s.

To round off this picture we must mention the recordings which father made in the Federal Republic – above all the complete album of all the Mozart compositions for violin and orchestra. This was completed in 1974, and I also took part in it.

Father also played with Herbert von Karajan. Karajan had visited Walter Legge in 1954 and had listened to some of Oistrakh's records (they had seventy-eight rotations and were of poor quality): from the Bizet - Sarasate Fantasy to scenes from *Carmen* and the Chatschaturjan Concerto. Both Herbert von

Karajan and Walter Legge (as Legge later said) were fascinated by Oistrakh's playing. I played, five years later with the Berlin Philharmonic under Karajan, Tchaikovsky's Violin Concerto in Kiel, I also drove with him in his car from Kiel to Hanover. 'I would love to play with your father,' he said at the time. This could not be realized until 1961 in Vienna with the Brahms Violin Concerto. My parents had experienced Karajan as the conductor of Verdi's *Othello* in Salzburg and a few years later in Milan with Puccini's *Bohème*. In 1970 Karajan was conducting at the recording of Beethoven's Triple Concerto. Soloists were the three 'stars' Oistrakh, Rostropovich and Richter.

In the second half of the 1950s father undertook a particularly large number of tours and became famous in all the countries he visited. After the successful solo concerts and the performances with Lew Oborin in Paris in 1953, after his participation in the month of Anglo-Soviet friendship in London in 1954, after the triumphs in Japan and the USA in 1955, father again appeared in England – this time in several cities. He took part in concerts and performed on radio and television. He also made records.

Father remembered this English tour in 1956 with particular pleasure: the success of Shostakovich's 1st Violin Concerto (this was the first performance of the work in Western Europe), the final performance in the London Albert Hall (which holds 8,000 people) with Sir Adrian Boult conducting, and finally the meeting with Nikolai Malko, who conducted the Shostakovich Concerto.

I will return to discuss Malko a

*David Oistrakh with Herbert von Karajan in Vienna*

little later on. Father met him two years later in Sydney. I would now like to mention the present which father was given at the end of his English tour. Victor Hochhauser, the impresario of the Soviet artists in England, gave him the original of an unpublished letter of Tchaikovsky's, addressed to the violinist who for the first time performed his violin concerto, Adolf Brodsky, Professor at the Moscow Conservatory. The letter was dated June 3, 1881 and refers to the first performance of the concerto by Brodsky in England. Father looked after this rare letter as he did his

own eyes."

David Oistrakh performed in Austria in the same year.

"1956 was the Mozart year: Austria celebrated the 200th birthday of this ingenious musician. The most important European soloists, orchestras and choirs came to honour Mozart. Father gave violin evenings and played with the symphony orchestra of the Leningrad Philharmonic under its chief conductor Eugene Mravinsky. His attendance at a Bruno Walter concert, the only one which he was ever to attend, with Mozart's 'Requiem', became a deeply felt musical event for him. Father repeated over and over again, he had never felt anything similar as on that evening."

There were reasons for his being so moved. Bruno Walter was not just a great conductor to David Oistrakh, just as Mozart was not just an ingenious composer to him. Although such a statement may sound controversial, the combination Mozart - Walter - Oistrakh appears to me to be natural and logical, since the work of each radiates light, goodness and sun.

In 1957 Oistrakh performed in the German Democratic Republic, Turkey, Italy and Czechoslovakia.

*With the conductor Franz Konwitschny*

He also often played with you, Igor Davidovich?

"In the second half of the 1950s father appeared more and more often with me. We played many compositions in concerts and on record, especially for two violins with piano accompaniment and with orchestra, works from Vivaldi and Bach to Honegger and Prokofiev. The joint tours were an irreplaceable 'school' for me. You could call it my musical university. We appeared in many cities during the tour of the Democratic Republic, which you mentioned before. I particularly remember the final rehearsal of the Concertos for Two Violins by Bach and Vivaldi with the Leipzig Gewandhausorchester under Franz Konwitschny. Father liked playing with this inspired master conductor. He greatly valued his cooperation at the recording of the concertos by Mozart (the 5th), Brahms and Tchaikovsky.

The tour of Italy was planned in such a way that the cities with the most important buildings and art treasures (Rome, Florence, Venice, Milan, Naples, Genoa, Bologna, Perugia, Siena) would be visited. There was, however, once more not enough time to see everything that he would have liked to see. Father's most important impressions were musical, the strongest impressions came from the Italian symphony orchestras and chamber ensembles. Father met Carlo Zecci, who had already played in the Soviet Union before the war but who now spent most of his time conducting. He also met the conductors Pietro Argento and Renato Fasano. The first of these accompanied him with the orchestra of the Accademia Nazionale di Santa Cecilia in

59

Rome, he heard the latter as conductor of the chamber orchestra I Virtuosi di Roma. Whilst father was in Rome he visited the widow of the Italian composer Respighi, a student of Rimsky-Korsakof.

In the beginning father was puzzled by the reserve of the Italian audience which did not seem to comply with the numerous reports of the excited behaviour of the passionate Italians in the opera houses. He soon found out the reason for this: it lay in the class difference. Everybody goes to the opera - philharmonic concerts, however, are only attended by certain layers of society, the Italians themselves regarding this audience as unapproachably cold.

'The audience is extremely reserved and contact is only gradually created,' father wrote. 'On the other hand at the end of the performance the audience gives expression to its feelings in a very stormy way.'

Father conquered another continent in 1958. He played in Australia. The journey to Australia and New Zealand was particularly interesting for him. We knew little about the musical life in these countries in those days, almost nothing in fact. But the thought alone of this exotic area far away fascinated him.

'Can you imagine where I got to?' father asked in a letter to his childhood friend Viktor Goldfeld. 'Take the globe, look at it and don't be shocked. Indeed, far away from home. We have already been travelling for two months and another month of touring is ahead of us. The tour is difficult, I have already had twenty-two concerts and recordings, but everything is very interesting. We have seen many beautiful sights in Australia. A picturesque landscape, beautiful cities, especially Sydney. We flew from London to Melbourne, over New York, San Francisco and Honolulu, and we will be flying back via the same route.' "

You promised to tell us more details about your father's meetings with Nikolai Malko. You will admit that a meeting after almost thirty years, first in London and then in Sydney, with the man who supported Oistrakh's début in Leningrad in 1928 must have meant a great deal to him?

"Malko accepted the directorship of the Sydney Symphony Orchestra one year before father's trip to Australia. The musical life of this town, previously rather provincial,

*In Sydney with conductor Nikolia Malko*

thus began to develop. Malko spent many years outside his home country and did a great deal to spread Russian classical music as well as Soviet music in particular. Nikolai Andreyevich asked father about his musical colleagues, whom he had known as youngsters. He

60

was interested in the Soviet orchestras, their artistic level, and the young generation of conductors from Leningrad and Moscow."

When Malko met Oistrakh in Odessa in 1927 he commented, not without a touch of irony, after the very young violinist had played Debussy's 'Doll Serenade': 'You have already grown out of the age when one plays with dolls, but you haven't yet reached the age when one plays serenades' Did your father ever remind Malko of his witty comment?

"I think so, father had a good memory for such things. But he also remembered very well the helpful role which Malko played in his artistic development. It was for this reason that he looked forward to the possibility of playing the Beethoven and Brahms Violin Concertos under Malko - now at an age which 'corresponded' to the depth of these masterpieces. He was especially looking forward to playing the Tchaikovsky Concerto with Malko, which he had played at his début in Leningrad. Malko conducted in four Soviet cities one year later."

David Oistrakh was fifty years old in September 1958. He refused to have an official celebration.

"I wasn't in Moscow at the time. Father wrote to me modestly in one of his letters: 'The students congratulated me sincerely on my half century and gave me many presents, so did the conservatory - I received some 500 well-wishing telegrams.' "

Oistrakh's second tour of America (1959) was the end of the 1950s for him. In his symphony program he played concertos by Bach, Beethoven, Tchaikovsky and Sibelius. He played sonatas by Tartini, Beethoven (Kreutzer-sonate), Franck, Hindemith and Aram Chatschaturjan with Vladimir Jampolski as well as compositions by Vitali, Brahms, Szymanovsky and Prokofiev.

"Little changed in father's life and working style in the 1960s. The Conservatory class, which already then had produced several first-class violinists, demanded more and more time. It meant a great success when Valeri Klimow won the 1st prize in the 1st International Tchaikovsky Competition."

You, Igor Davidovich, have out of modesty kept quiet about your own success at the International Wieniawski Competition in Poznán in 1952. It was in fact you who began the series of successes of

1st-prize winners among the students of David Oistrakh's class. But we were just talking of Oistrakh's working rhythm . . .

"Mother used to repeat that we never went on a tour in a relaxed way; Dodik and I used to fly off as if we were literally shot out of Moscow by a cannon, because he worked up to the last day and the last hour at the Conservatory before leaving for the airport. His concert activity didn't slow down, and as the years went by it didn't get any easier for him. There were still six heavily loaded American tours: 1960, 1962, 1963, 1965, 1968 and 1970."

David Oistrakh once jokingly remarked that he didn't feel like a musician but more like a travelling businessman. Such a lifestyle could easily have changed an artist into a smoothly functioning machine. Tickets, timetables, suitcases, cars, airports, jets, delayed planes, receptions, hotels, halls, studios, rehearsals, concerts, applause, flowers, departures, railway stations, express trains, in short *perpetuum mobile.*

"Father's tours remained completely successful. He was certain of the warmest reception by the audience. The press comments couldn't have been more favourable and this always made him forget his exhaustion.

'I gave a concert in the Carnegie yesterday,' father told me. 'I found it easy and calming to play and I believe that it was indeed a successful concert. Today's press comments are excellent.' "

Oistrakh was at that time in 1962 invited to take part in a gala concert in the main hall of the United Nations building. After he had played the Kreutzersonate, the security council went over the daily agenda, David Feodorovich was allowed to sit in the conference room and attend the discussions.

"Father realized an old dream in the 1960s: he began to conduct. He had already taken the first steps towards a début in this new role before the war. Father confessed one year after his triumphant victory at Brussels: 'I am really more a musician than a violinist', and talked of conducting as if he had made up his mind. It is easy to explain why he was only much later able to realize his dream: just imagine what a psychological burden such a début must be for a man whom the whole world knew as a master violinist. Father's modesty didn't allow him to chase after

sensations. Furthermore the time-tables for his tours were so packed that he had to postpone his intention of giving a début as a conductor to more convenient times. I still remember how he came from Kiev in the 1950s and how he excitedly talked about the rehearsal for the Brahms Concerto which he was to play with Knuschewizki. He took advantage of the conductor's late arrival and conducted the first movement of the concerto himself ('it was all much simpler than I thought!').

Father's début as a conductor took place on November 14th–17th 1960 in Moscow at the recording of the Brahms Violin Concerto in which I played the solo part.

I played a Beethoven Concerto in Swerdlowsk with father conducting on December 27, 1961. I remember that I confused father, who was already nervous, at the first rehearsal of the Beethoven Concerto, because I didn't pull the bow upwards as father always did, but downwards (I was searching for the most precise bow movement and phrasing).

Father accompanied me in the same year at the recording of the Bruch Violin Concerto in London. 'We made the recording without

any difficulty and it was good in my opinion,' he wrote. 'The Royal Philharmonic Orchestra and the soloist were both happy, I enjoyed this greatly.'

Father's first performance as a conductor took place in the Great Hall of the Moscow Conservatory on January 17, 1962. Accompanied by father, I played Bach's Concerto in E Major and the violin concertos by Beethoven and Brahms. Father suffered from stage fright as he was very conscious of his responsibility at his first performance.

Prior to his career as a conductor, father confessed that even the thought of standing at the conductor's desk almost gave him heart failure, although his violin performances didn't frighten him in the least. However, everything soon changed when he became a conductor. He remained calm on the day of his appearance at the head of the orchestra but he would start feeling nervous on the morning of a violin concerto performance".

The success of his début as a conductor was extraordinary and earned him a large response: the leading world orchestras invited him as a guest conductor. He conducted in London, Vienna, Tokyo, Chicago, Boston and Philadelphia.

He was particularly closely connected with the symphony orchestra of the Moscow Philharmonic under Kyril Kondrashin.

"Father often worked with this orchestra and conducted a wide range of compositions, played concerts, performed with chamber-music soloists from the orchestra and went on overseas tours with the Moscow Philharmonic Orchestra." We must also mention his first appearance in Leningrad in 1963. The unknown musician from the Ukraine had thirty-five years earlier undertaken the task of playing the Tchaikovsky Violin Concerto with the Leningrad Philharmonic Orchestra. It was the orchestra musicians who were the first to enthusiastically applaud him and with this remove the doubts of the young musician.

And now another début, but this time with the conductor's baton in his hand. How it went is best shown by a letter that the musicians of this famous orchestra wrote to Oistrakh. Because these musicians are the most critical judges of soloists and conductors, they are the people who can best judge 'Who's Who' in the arts:

'Dear David Feodorovich,

The musicians of the Symphony Orchestra of the Philharmonic have for many years enjoyed your great ability as a master violinist and were looking forward with great impatience to meeting you as a conductor. We were all convinced that the first meeting would be interesting, but not even the greatest optimist could foresee that this first performance would become such an event for us.'

Oistrakh's repertoire as a conductor grew so quickly that it sometimes threatened to drown him. 'Owing to a misunderstanding, three concerts in Leningrad and Moscow were announced instead of one, and what's more they are very complicated,' he complained in the summer of 1963. 'In Moscow *Harold*, a String Concerto by Bacewicz and the Mozart Concerto with Lew Nikolajewitsch (Oborin - the author); with the second orchestra in Leningrad, Bacewicz, Mendelssohn's Concerto with Gutnikow and Prokofiev's 5th Symphony (!) and with the first orchestra Beethoven's 4th Symphony, Mozart's *Kleine Nacht-musik* and the Brahms Concerto with Klimow! How is this going to turn out? I am lost. I will have to give up the violin. The first orchestra in addition insisted that I should also conduct it, but when am I (poorest of all people) supposed to rehearse all this?'

"Fortunately father managed to avoid giving up the violin and packing it away, not only in the first period of his new career but also later when conducting had a firm place in his artistic activity. Father often performed as violinist and conductor in the same evening. To, for instance, conduct a symphony by Brahms or Mahler and then afterwards to appear on stage with a violin is not easy even when one is young."

Conducting became an additional burden on Oistrakh's health. On the one hand because he in no way reduced the amount of violin playing and on the other (this was the true reason) because his body, arms and muscles couldn't quite cope with the physical load which he had to carry with his increasing repertoire as a conductor. In the case of young conductors, the body with trained arms gradually adjusts to this load.

"Mother knew only too well how unbearable such a life was for father. The usual arguments about the intensity of father's way of working reached a peak in the 1960s. Mother had always said that

father had neglected his health for far too long."

Illness slowly crept onto David Oistrakh and hit him in May 1964 in Leningrad. A serious heart attack forced him to stay in hospital for a long time. This news spread like the wind among the musicians. Telegrams and letters came to Leningrad from all over the world. Friends, admirers and colleagues expressed their sympathy, encouraged him and ensured him that they would soon be able to applaud David Oistrakh's violin again. Many Soviet musicians wrote, so did Pablo Casals, Yehudi Menuhin, Gaspar Cassadó, Marguerite Long, Georges Aurik, Darius Milhaud, Jean Rouart, Salomon Hurok and Bernard Gavoty.

Queen Elisabeth of Belgium, as always, showed moving attention. She had been fascinated by his art since the competition in Brussels. A pilot of the Belgian airline delivered a very cordial telegram and a basket of fresh strawberries to the Europa Hotel, where Tamara Iwanowna was living at the time.

"Father did not pay the necessary attention to his first heart attack. Soon after his recovery (if this word

**64**

is applicable for severe heart disease) he again worked as teacher and artist, as violinist and conductor and all this with a dash and vigour as if he wanted to compensate for the 'uselessly wasted' months in hospital. Father never told anybody how much this stoicism cost him. If one ever touched on the forbidden subject of his recovery he would change the conversation, with a disarming smile, to the great artistic satisfaction that such a life brings."

David Oistrakh appeared in front of the orchestra and audiences with the same charming smile and without allowing any sign of exhaustion to be shown. This exhaustion was invisible to a stranger's eye. This was so after the first heart attack and also after the second, which he had in London in 1966.

"You say: 'This was so' – perhaps it would be better to say: 'This is how it seemed.' A revealing photograph was published in the Democratic Republic's illustrated publication *David Oistrakh,* taken by Evelyn Richter. The camera caught father in the moment when he was leaving the stage: the concert was over, conductor and musicians were still standing at their desks, father had bowed to the audience and now walked past behind the stage. Look more accurately at his face and you can see the whole weight of the last years expressed in his features. But these are only a few seconds. In a moment he enters the artist's dressing room which is always overcrowded: enthusiasm, gratitude, requests for autographs ... And father is once more the David Oistrakh with his usual smiling face, as all these people knew him."

Alexander Plocek, the Czechoslovakian violinist, who knew David Feodorovich for a long time claims in his memoirs: 'When he had the violin in his hands he didn't know the meaning of exhaustion. The violin gave him strength, just as the earth gave it to the hero of the 'Antäus' legend.' This sounds very good; however, it isn't quite true. We can only now get an idea of the superhuman burden which Oistrakh in vain tried to get used to in the last decades of his life if we look at David Oistrakh's letters to his friends and to you, Igor Davidovich. Let the letters speak and let us forget that they were written partly before and partly after the period which we have just described:

1955. Boston. To I. D. Oistrakh
'The concerts follow each other so closely that I don't even have time to change the hairs on the bow, the old ones are practically useless.'

1959. Brussels. To I. D. Oistrakh
'The timetable for the competition is grinding, every day from three to six-thirty and from eight to eleven. There are thirty-three competitors playing. The programs are long and difficult. I am laden with a lot of work. In the time between the 2nd and 3rd rounds I play four concerts in Holland and one in Luxemburg ... Afterwards here with Menuhin.'

1958. No place mentioned. To W. M. Goldfeld
'I don't feel well, I am completely exhausted. The travelling has become unbearable and the longing for a quiet little corner turns each journey into a torture. But to give up travelling would mean giving up artistic activity, which would be just as difficult.'

1962. London. To I. D. Oistrakh
'I am writing to you at two in the night. I am flying to Budapest at eight. I have just returned from a recording session. Mama will tell

you how tiring and difficult this journey was.'

1965. Moscow. To M. M. Goldstein
'I spent two grinding days in Moscow between two exceptionally difficult journeys. I have neither the time nor the strength ... In one word – I feel as if I am in flames! But at least it's burning beautifully ...'

1969. Mannheim. To W. M. Goldfeld
'As always there is a terrible turmoil. We are living at a most unbearably difficult pace. But it just can't be done in any other way. I am in a great hurry as I have to try to get at least a few hours sleep.'

1971. Moscow. To W. M. Goldfeld
'I feel as if I am living on a volcano. I can hardly find time to breath ...'

1971. Moscow. To M. M. Goldstein
'I am sending you the review. Please forgive me for the delay. The reason for this is my martyr's life which I can't endure any longer. At the same time I am too weak to change anything. In one

*Aram Chatschaturjan drinks to David Oistrakh on his 60th birthday. On David Oistrakh's right: Tichon Chrennikow and Leonid Kogan*

word, I am trying to cope with everything, but I am doing it rather late in the day and rather badly.'

And finally a few lines from 1945: a glance back? No, more like a prophecy:

1945. Moscow. To W. M. Goldfeld
'You are right when you write that one should take it easy. But you certainly know that I never succeeded in doing this. My only hope is that I won't even find time to die. Now, enough of this. You write that I am burning the candle at both ends (this is surely how it was?), presumably from more ends than two. I shall probably only find peace when all these ends are completely burned.'

David Oistrakh was sixty in September 1968. He had been active as an artist for half a century. Several generations of violinists had changed on the concert stage during this period and also several generations of listeners in the concert halls.

As we know there have also been comic situations, above all when the second name Oistrakh junior appeared on the posters?

"Exactly. I remember father talking of an amusing event which happened on one of his tours. After a concert he noticed among the audience who had come to greet him a lady who looked at him with a particularly moving expression. You know, there are 'fossils' in every concert hall, listeners whom you are not sure if they don't know the music better than some professional musicians (this does happen), or, and this applies to father's admirer, whether their ability to take in what they hear hasn't already been overtaken by fixed impressions accumulated over many years.

Controlling her shyness she approached father and said: 'You have played beautifully, outstandingly. I am your old and faithful admirer.' And overwhelmed with the feeling of her superiority which lifted her far above the musicians who filled the dressing room, she added: 'After all I even heard your father playing.' "

Just as he had done ten years earlier, David Oistrakh turned down a jubilee celebration. Students, friends, colleagues from the conservatory congratulated him heartily on his sixtieth birthday. There were of course flowers, speeches and presents. The most valuable present was a violin sonata by Dmitri Shostakovich, who had written as a dedication: 'To David Feodorovich Oistrakh on his sixtieth birthday.' The violinist played the sonata with Sviatoslav Richter.

"At the age of sixty one makes philosophical observations. One thinks about life, its purpose and one looks back. In a letter from this period father writes:

'The years fly past and the day approaches when I shall pass the age of sixty. I cannot say that I am happy about this. I don't belong among these 'unique' people, such as Casals or Rubinstein. May God give them many years of the best health! I already notice the burden of my years very much. In spite of this I am not complaining about my past. It was beautiful with its hopes and disappointments.' "

In these words lies the whole of Oistrakh! What a clear understanding of the past road! How much optimism! Yet these were - to use David Oistrakh's words - the years of the triumph with the painful heart.

" 'I don't think that I would now have the courage to perform with the heart pains as I did in the last seven years,' he confessed in 1973 in one of his letters.

1973 was the most difficult year for father. He was again bedridden for several months. The battle with his heart disease lasted almost the whole year with changing success. Dependent on this his mood changed. He said: 'What is happening to me is called "heart attack" behind my back.' He described himself with a sad smile as a 'particularly dangerous relapse criminal'. . . The events of this year are too fresh in my memory and it is difficult for me to talk about them."

The disease which lurked in the background attacked Oistrakh treacherously after each improvement, severing his artistic plans for the future, his tours, and killing the hope of complete recovery. David Oistrakh couldn't travel to Salzburg to appear there with his friend and duo partner Paul Badura-Skoda. He also couldn't realize his intention of conducting *Eugen Onegin*.

"That had been father's dream for a long time, and he was par-

67

*In Vienna: Igor Oistrakh with his wife, the pianist Natalja Serzalowa, Professor Rudolf Gamsjager and David Oistrakh*

*Receiving an honorary doctorate's degree at Cambridge University*

ticularly sad that it couldn't be fulfilled. The love of opera music and for the opera house had lived with him from his childhood days.

The well-known German musician cembalist and musicologist Professor Hans Pischner, Oistrakh's friend and partner at recordings of a cycle of Bach sonatas, had offered, as Intendant of the German State Opera, to Oistrakh that he should conduct *Eugen Onegin* and that he should take charge of the new production of the opera. A few letters addressed to Pischner tell the story of this unrealized opera début:

Parnu, August 2, 1968
'The concerts in West Berlin are supposed to take place around December 10, 1970. We can fit the beginning of the work on *Onegin* to meet this deadline. But do you think that I will be able to manage this task? I have so far never conducted an opera. I hope that you will give me your friendly and sincere advice as to whether I should attack this task.'

Florence, May 24, 1969
'I am studying *Onegin* and hope that nothing will stop me from taking part in the rehearsals of the opera in your theatre in November/December 1971 as agreed.'

Moscow, May 20, 1973
'As long as I am still in hospital it is hardly possible to predict how long I have to stay here. As I am not yet allowed to get up, I of course have the score and the tape recorder here with me and I wish deep longing for the realization of our plans.'

Moscow, February 6 1974
'Surely you know that I was for a long time ill between February and December. My state of health has changed several times during this

period. Sometimes there was improvement, sometimes relapse. I was only allowed to go home two months ago and I have wanted to write to you for some time. The only thing that stopped me was that I didn't want to put a dot over the 'i' in *Onegin* [this is a Russian term of speech which means: making a final decision – the author]. I always hoped that I would recover faster and that I could again work and play the violin, and then I wouldn't have to give up the thought of *Onegin*. Two months have now passed and I already feel much better, but my work is restricted to teaching two students a day and playing one hour at the most myself. It is for the time being uncertain when I will be able to start to really work again, that is giving concerts, going on tours, in other words to live a life that I have been used to . . .

Considering these facts I regard my dream of conducting *Eugen Onegin* as unrealistic as I would hardly be able to meet the physical burden which the rehearsals of the great performance demand, and on top of that in a branch of art which is new to me.

I therefore think that I should give up the dream which I have nursed for years, and that I should apologize to you and at the same time thank you for your most friendly understanding and offer of enabling me to conduct an interesting piece of work at your superb opera house.

I will consider myself happy if *Onegin* succeeds without me and I hope to visit Berling once more, if fate allows this, and have the opportunity of listening to the performance in your opera house. Perhaps tears would then come to my eyes.' "

In January 1974, the news reached David Oistrakh that he had been elected Honorary Member of the Gesellschaft der Musikfreunde in Vienna. He was very happy about this.

"Father had many such titles, he was Honorary Member of the Society of Teachers of String Instruments in Japan, the Accademia di Santa Cecilia in Rome, The Eugene Ysaye Society in Brussels, the German Academy of Arts in Berlin (German Democratic Republic), The Royal Academy of Music in London, the American Academy of Arts and Sciences, Honorary Dr of Music at the University of Cambridge as well as Professor and Honorary Dr of a number of European Conservatories. However, his election as Honorary Member of the Vienna Philharmonic Society gave him particular pleasure. He loved Vienna, the city which was filled with the sound of music and art and he regarded each of his performances in Vienna as a 'feast' on its own.

'After my long illness things are going up-hill again and this gives me the hope that nothing will stop me from taking part in this year's concert at the Vienna Music Festival,' father wrote to Professor A. Moser in Vienna."

David Feodorovich had no more ardent wish than to 'remain himself' and fate appeared to smile on him once more.

" 'I will never forget Oistrakh's first concert after his long illness in 1973,' remembers Frida Bauer, the pianist who took part in the concert. 'That was in March 1974 in the Scientific Club in Tschernogolowka near Moscow. As he stepped on the stage with his violin to test the acoustics of the hall before the concert, all the lights went on, and an expression of such happiness appeared on his face that one only sees on a child who has just been given a long-awaited birthday present. He played in a

remarkable way on this evening and the artistic pleasure which the violinist felt transmitted itself freely to the listeners.' "

David Oistrakh played in Vienna in May 1974 also with great success, his love was returned with equal love.

'The Viennese audience idolize him,' wrote Professor Rudolf Gamsjäger, Director of the Vienna State Opera. 'He was loved by everybody from the simple stage workers to the top people of the Philharmonic Society. His arrival always meant a 'feast' for us.' As a true artist Oistrakh couldn't imagine an existence without an appearance on the stage. He couldn't live or breath without the stage atmosphere. He always loved playing the violin, but now each performance meant a special joy for him and success with an audience moved him more than usual.

"At the beginning of October in 1974, father received a letter from an unknown radio listener from Kuibyschew:

'Comrade David Oistrakh,' she wrote. 'You play the violin so well

*David Oistrakh's rehearsal in October 1974 for his last concert in Moscow*

that one could go mad. You are a terrific chap and how lucky you are! This makes me so jealous that I can't even express it. Oh! Ho! One would just like to call out. Fortune has been more than kind to you. May you, your friends and family remain healthy and cheerful. Play on the radio more often. I will always listen to you. I perhaps don't quite understand music, but I have a very well developed feeling for it. I sometimes wonder why I am the way I am and not like most others. This makes my life difficult. Please accept my deep thanks and sincere gratitude. I hope that your violin will once be exhibited in a museum so that everyone can see and know what a wonderful artist you are on this violin (the queen of music). A thousand times bravo ! ! ! '

The doctors welcomed father's decision to return to the concert stage as they thought that his condition was stabilizing. They naturally insisted on a gradual return to his previous rhythm of life. But father didn't quite succeed in this.

He was already writing in March: 'I have unfortunately again got to teach a great deal, but what can I do? The students have been waiting for me from April until December (1973), and on top of this I have to

prepare four students for the Tchaikovsky Competition.'

In the summer of 1974, immediately after the end of the 5th International Tchaikovsky Competition (which made great physical demands on father), my parents travelled together to the German Democratic Republic where they rested in a sanitorium for heart sufferers, Falkenstein. Father was very happy with this rest period and visited the beautiful surroundings with the car which was made available for him. He played Schubert's Sonatinas and studied the score of Beethoven's 9th Symphony."

The 1974-75 concert season started for David Feodorovich with a series of concerts in the Soviet Union and in other countries. He played and conducted in Stockholm, accompanied by the Moscow Symphony Orchestra with Kyril Kondrashin as conductor. He played at the Kiev Music Festival in the autumn. According to the opinion of many musicians in the orchestra and of listeners, he played the Brahms Concerto with exceptional brilliance and verve. He afterwards conducted in Moscow. I had the chance of attending the morning rehearsal for this concert (the season in the Tchaikovsky Hall was always opened with the Brahms program), I also had the opportunity to talk to him. He was cheerful, witty and felt well. This was furthermore confirmed by a snap taken by the photo reporter of the periodical *Sovetskaya Musyka.* One day after the concert - who would assume it was his last concert in Moscow - he travelled to the Netherlands.

The Soviet pianists Bella Davidovich and Jakow Flier, who played the solos under his baton, also took part in this tour. David Oistrakh's condition was consistently good, which was not only confirmed by Jakow Flier and Bella Davidovich, but also by a photograph taken on October 23. The exceptionally severe heart attack which the artist suffered during the night of October 24 was for this reason even more surprising - heart attack which he was not to survive. Death reached him on the same day. Oistrakh died in his wife's arms. 'It will soon pass,' were his last words. Tamara Iwanowna arrived in Moscow with her husband's coffin on the following day.

The obituary stated: 'Soviet musical culture has suffered an irre-

*Amsterdam 23.10.1974: David Oistrakh's last concert*

placeable loss. David Feodorovich Oistrakh died on October 24, 1974. He was the 'people's artist' of the USSR, winner of the Lenin State Prize, Professor at the Moscow State Conservatory, a violinist whose name is connected with outstanding achievements in our art and its world-wide recognition.'

'D. F. Oistrakh's merits for Soviet art were highly recognized by the party and government . . .

D. F. Oistrakh, the artist and Communist, educated in the Soviet country was a man with a great social sense of responsibility who gave his talent freely to the people and for the development of the Soviet socialist culture.

David Feodorovich Oistrakh's bright picture will always live in our memories.' "

During these difficult days sympathy arrived from all over the country, from the whole world, from friends and unknown people, from statesmen, musicians and listeners. People wrote to Tamara Iwanowna Oistrakh, whom sorrow had made silent and benumbed. People wrote to you, Igor Davidovich. You must have been a great help to your mother in those days, in spite of your loss and sorrow. You and your mother continuously received letters full of sympathy, love and admiration.

" 'I heard the news of David Oistrakh's death with deep sorrow. In the name of UNESCO and in my own, I would like to express our sympathy. The general assembly which was meeting at the time interrupted its session to honour the memory of the great Soviet musician.

René Maheu, UNESCO, Paris'

'May I express my sincere sympathy for you on your husband's death. The news of David Oistrakh's death has also been received with shock and sorrow in the German Federal Republic. David Oistrakh was not only a blessed artist whose interpretations were for us again and again entirely new events of great violin music. He was also a human being, who by his work has contributed to a better understanding between the people of our two countries. May I assure you that the admiration which he enjoyed to such a high degree in his lifetime will also be payed to him in the future?

Walter Scheel, Federal President'

'We heard with deep shock the sad news of the death of the violin virtuoso and conductor David Oistrakh, who as an internationally celebrated artist personified the high school of the Soviet art of interpretation. Like many people from all continents, the citizens of the German Democratic Republic mourn the loss of this great master, whose work served the culture of great achievements in the music of our nation as well. He has given his entire energy and his outstanding ability as Communist and musician to the glory of his fatherland, the USSR. We shall always remember David Oistrakh.

Erich Honecker
First Secretary of the Central Committee of the SED
addressed to the General Secretary of the KPdSU,
Leoid Ilyich Brezhnev'

'Dear Tamara Iwanowna and Igor, We join you in mourning the loss of our dear David Feodorovich!

With love. Your Shostakovich family. Moscow'

'The tragic news reached us the same morning when our beloved David left you, Igor and his many friends and admirers. The world has lost one of the greatest human beings we ever met.

When I gave the news to the orchestra, which loved him so much, and which David loved so much, the orchestra players were shattered. Isaac [Stern - the author] and I talked about him over and over again during this day. We felt as if we had lost a brother and we couldn't understand that this wonderful noble man was no longer with us.

Philadelphia, Eugene Ormandy'

'We are all shattered by the news of the death of the great artist David Oistrakh. He was for me the true heir to Joachim and Ysaye and I shall never forget his art.

Paris, Artur Rubinstein'

'Everybody who like me had the great luck of knowing David Oistrakh personally will treasure the memory of his honesty in everything connected with music and the life of musicians like a jewel.

Dusseldorf, Dietrich Fischer-Dieskau'

'He didn't spare himself, he left us too early, his music, however, and the memory of his work will live as long as art lives.

Moscow, Kyril Kondrashin' "

73

Creative works

# The violinist

There is a considerable collection in David Oistrakh's flat: carefully piled up boxes full of tapes and an enormous number of records with sleeves of every colour. A great many record companies tried to record Oistrakh's playing, in addition to Melodia from the Soviet Union, firms from Poland, Czechoslovakia, England, America, Holland, France, German Democratic and Federal Republics and Japan all tried to record him. The companies Victor, RCA Victor, EMI, Monitor, Angel Records, Columbia, Pathé Marconi, Le Chant Du Monde, Supraphon, Ariola-Eurodisc, Deutsche Grammophon, Eterna and many others approached David Oistrakh. Records which were released in one country would normally later also be released in others. We came across Oistrakh on record as violinist, chamber musician and conductor. There are no composers that you cannot find in his gigantic repertoire, nor are there any music styles and forms of music that cannot be found on his records!

"I must first of all say that you shouldn't think that father only collected his own records. His record collection contains virtually all the outstanding violin interpretations which were recorded in the last decades."

And not just violin interpretations. David Oistrakh tried to make tape recordings of all compositions which interested him, or to get hold of the corresponding record.

"One of his musical friends wrote to him: 'I once came to visit you after your illness. Although you found it difficult to move your legs, you went to the record player and put on a Berlioz record and listened to it totally absorbed. I can't forget this, because I am used to people who put on records just to listen to certain artists and not to the music itself.'

Father called the tape recorder his note book. He always had it with him and there was hardly a day when he didn't listen to two or three recordings (repeatedly as a rule)."

I am not just by chance referring to David Oistrakh's records. They preserve his undying art for the coming generations and I use the word 'undying' quite deliberately. It was only fifty years ago that even those who recognized reproductive art also as a creative achievement were of the opinion that this art dies with the artist. This is now quite different.

"You say, 'even' those who 'also' recognized reproductive art as creative achievement and as art. What do you mean by 'also' and 'even'?"

The question here arises: In what does the mission and the life objective of the reproducing artist lie? This is by no means just a rhetorical question and it leads over and over again to passionate discussions. Some people insist that the artist is obliged to interpret the composition and reproduce it in a creative way. Each generation in reshaping the music of the past discovers domething new in it, something that escaped its predecessors, something that related to the feelings of the times. Nikolai Medtner, the Russian composer and pianist expressed this view in a very picturesque way in a letter to Sergey Rachmaninof: 'I can't force myself to play music on my Steinway á la Mozart just as you can't travel in your car with the snail-like speed of a post coach of the good old days.'

"This is an accepted fact for me, an axiom that one can't even begin to doubt. What could one possibly say against it?"

The opposers of your axiom talk of the duty of the reproducing artist to limit himself entirely to the most precise reproduction of the author's score possible, or as one sometimes says to 'information about the score'.

"They probably start with a fact which they themselves cannot dispute: the composer has put in his score neither more nor less than what he intended to say.

I can't agree with this view, just as my father couldn't agree with it. The notes which he made at the 1966 Tchaikovsky Competition contain a few appropriate words which don't lack a touch of humour. After a very talented violinist had played Chatschaturjan's Concerto, father noted: 'I like everything about his playing except the interpretation. Does he know anything about it?'

Interpretation was always a high art for father, a creative act. I am certain that if he had ever doubted this, he would have immediately changed his profession. However, I can't imagine father in any other profession."

The creative concept of reproductive art has etymological support. The English verb "to conceive" can be translated into German as either *erfassen* or *empfangen*. The conception (*Erfassen*) of the composer's intention and exploration of objective structure of the composition give the work new life each time it is interpreted. To put it another way: when words cannot express certain feelings, one uses song or music. This is a fact. The system of writing down the music (the notation) is, however, still after centuries of development even now imperfect. By chance? Hardly. A person's thoughts and feelings, his inner experience that the music expresses and to which it turns are so manifold, subtle and sometimes impossible to measure that the notes can only approximately record them. Paul Valéry wrote on this subject: A composition only represents the text which is strictly speaking nothing more than a type of recipe. The main part is played by the cook, who cooks according to the recipe.

"Are you trying to say that cooking might have been the other profession for my father that I couldn't think of earlier?"

You are very witty, Igor Davidovich. By the way, Kyril Kondrashin told me that Aram Chatschaturjan invited Arturo Beneditti Michelangeli (who was giving a concert in Moscow at the time) to his house and asked the pianist what his greatest wish was. Michelangeli replied: a tiny taverna with three tables to serve guests in my spare time. Cooking is also the hobby of the English violinist Arthur Grumiaux. So much for your witty remark. But joking aside, once we have recreated David Oistrakh's attitude to the task of the reproducing artist we should recall what he himself was like as a violinist and how he differed from most other violin virtuosos.

"Georges Soria said of father: 'He is a virtuoso who makes fun of virtuosity.' Father often said that he was more of a musician than a violinist. This was why he didn't let himself get carried away by the purely virtuoso aspects of playing the violin. This was why he wanted (throughout his life) to get out of the category into which he was forced by violin playing. This was why he devoted himself so deeply and with such pleasure to chamber-music and later to orchestral music. You can only see Oistrakh the violinist in connection with Oistrakh the musician. He himself had very clearly and simply defined the task of being an artist:

'I am trying to live up to my vocation as an artist and hope to open a rich world to many people, the rich world of music which makes everyday-life more beautiful. This is why I am living.'

Father seldom complained of difficulties, partly because it wasn't his way and also, this is the main reason, because he took life always as life is. But he never regarded his profession as an easy one.

'Man is accompanied by difficulties throughout his whole life and this is an absolutely normal thing; the circumstances change and with them the type of difficulties,' father wrote to Gidon Kremer. 'The young beginner has it difficult, but the same is true of the artist at the height of fame. The only thing that matters is that one should be prepared at all stages of one's musical existence and be ready to fight these difficulties. Achievements and the 'foundation stone' will always prove themselves later, they never get lost. This wealth is the most precious thing a man owns. It can never be devalued.

Bear in mind this motto: Through difficulties to joy, to recognition, to victory!'" David Oistrakh's art was characterized by high ethical standards and by a moral strength born by his contact with the public, the listeners, the people for whom he lived and worked. Just as Wilhelm Furtwängler, Oistrakh regarded the public in the best meaning of the word as 'God's judgement' as 'vox dei', 'judgement of mankind'.

"To characterize his violin playing in greater detail it may be useful to quote a few opinions. The first two date back to when the young musician returned to Moscow after his victory in Brussels:

'This is an extraordinary musician, who is in every aspect completely harmonious. What strikes one in his playing is the simplicity and extraordinary perfection which goes hand in hand with the complete mastery of the instrument.' (Abram Jampolski, 1937)

'David Oistrakh has once again proved his reputation as an outstanding artist. Noble simplicity, immaculate taste and a feeling for moderation, superb virtuosity which never degenerates to a purpose, by itself always remaining the means of realizing the artistic intention. All these properties make Oistrakh undoubtedly one of the best violinists of the day.' (Alexander Goldenweiser, 1937)"
Jampolski and Goldenweiser agree. The violinist and pianist recognize above all harmony and a feel for moderation in the playing of the young Oistrakh. Three-and-a-half decades later, in 1975, other statements are similar:

'To play with Oistrakh was the highest artistic pleasure. The wise simplicity, the extraordinary balance between the emotional and the rational, his exquisite taste as well as complete understanding of music of all styles and periods turned his performances into unforgettable feasts. This has always been so. I value these concerts higher than many symphony performances that I have conducted.' (Evgeny Svetlanov, 1975)

"The unchanging description of his violin playing over such a long period of time is remarkable. Regina Horowitz also pointed out in a review of the final years of the 1920s the balance between emotion and reason in father's playing."

There is an enviable consistency in the fundamental criteria of Oistrakh's artistic nature. Don't you see however a contradiction between the consistency of his artistic ego and his no less artistic self-renewal and development?

"This is only an apparent contradiction. The consistent force with which he mastered his art obviously demanded a nursing origin. This was father's restless work on himself. To use the words of Constantine Stanislavsky: It's not just a question of 'working on the part' but also of 'working on oneself'. By the way, we have already mentioned father's autodidactic method when we talked about his first years in Moscow. He had always mastered the art of listening and listening to himself. Not every musician can do this. Isaac Stern pointed out that his playing had a wonderful feeling of self-control. He always had this, whether he played a fast passage or a long and slow phrase."

The work bore its fruits. To mention some of them: Oistrakh mastered music in a universal way and this included the style (from Bach to Hindemith, from Vivaldi to Shostakovich), the national characteristics as well as the characteristics of certain types of violin music (from the miniature violin composition to the monumental symphony), and there was the extraordinarily natural way in which he opened up the world of sound of a composer with whom he wasn't yet familiar. We should also add the convincing power of understanding the nucleus of a tone poem and the equally strong power of its artistic reproduction.

"There are interpreters, among them important masters, for whom it always remains a problem to master a new composition, a new author or a new style. In this respect, however, father always succeeded with surprising ease. Naturalness is, in my opinion, the best word to characterize him as an artist and man. Just listen as an example to how he interprets the finale of the Violin Sonata by Franck. Simply, without the slightest mannerism in the tempi, the allegretto poco mosso sounds (when he plays it) without the slightest touch of 'sweetness' to the timbre. And what an extraordinary contrast he achieves, exactly through this simplicity in the passage where the fascinating proud, pathetic theme of the preceding third movement occurs again in the finale."

Examples of this naturalness and organic shaping of artistic intentions can be frequently found if one listens to the album Beethoven's Ten Violin Sonatas, which David Oistrakh and Lew Oborin recorded in Paris. They are a splendid confirmation of the previously discussed idea of the balance between the emotional and the rational in Oistrakh's violin art. Remember the Adagio Molto Espressivo in the 6th Sonata with its nobility and calmness and clarified purity of sound, or the Tempo di Minuetto of the 8th Sonata, the second theme of which is interpreted and felt by the violinist as a sad song without any side taste of sentimentality or hypocritical deep meaning. They used to say in such cases that he played as freely and unconstrained

as a bird sings.

"Howard Taubman, who discussed father's concerts in America for the *New York Times* stated: 'The violinist was playing a Stradivarius . . . The violin sounded as if he was born with it.'

There is a photograph with the amusing title 'Oistrakh, the violin maker' which appeared in several periodicals in the German Federal Republic. During an interval father is sitting in the stalls with the violin on his knees, you can see him cleaning it and then putting it right with a smile on his face. I liked this picture so much that I persuaded father to give it to me. It now hangs in my study."

Did your father have that typical passion for the instrument itself, which so many violinists have? Did he look after the violin? Did he have the habit of moving its bridge to obtain optimum sound effects?

"Father loved the violin, but without any eccentricity. It was a feeling of constant steady love. He didn't play around with the inner parts of the instrument, he left this to the experts or to the violin makers. He would normally take

*David Oistrakh - busy with his violin*

with him two violins and to be safe, two or three bows, on his many concert tours. I remember with what interest we both read the book about the history of the violin bow which Isaac Stern had given him.

Before father got his first Stradivarius he played for a long time a number of instruments which were hardly of average quality. I remember father telling us about his début in Leningrad. Already at the first rehearsal one of the orchestra players remarked to him scornfully: One doesn't come to Leningrad with such a fiddle (father called his violin 'Samovari' at the time). Father was not only able to get used to any new violin (how often had he not taken his student's instrument or that of an orchestra musician and played it with the same ease as if it were his own), but he was also able to make a medium quality violin almost sound as if it was a wonderful Stradivarius.

Father owned a so-called 'Jussupov' Stradivarius before the war. This was later replaced by another violin made by the great Italian violin builder, which also came from the state collection of valuable musical instruments. Father bought his own Stradivarius for the first

time in 1955 in the USA and after a time a Fontana (1714) in Paris, and he exchanged this for an even earlier violin which had the marking Marsick in 1966 and which was made in 1705; both instruments were also made by Stradivarius. Father played the Marsick until the end of his life. As you can see, he was even in this respect consistent. The only exception being the viola, not by Stradivarius but by Andrea Guarneri, which father and I used alternately. I didn't have to change 'brands' as I also use a Guarneri violin."

Surely David Oistrakh had a special reason for changing his violins. What was he trying to achieve? What did he expect of the instrument?

"Sonority, which didn't require any forcing of tone and which was still able to fill the large concert halls in which father played. This volume of sound was the main demand which father had of the instrument.

'I am playing on a new Stradivarius, which I have owned for half a year,' father wrote of the

*The master musician's two Stradivari*

Fontana. 'It sounds wonderful in concert halls holding 6,000-7,000.'"
A typical detail: when David Oistrakh was in Geneva in spring 1957 he had the chance of playing the violin of the great Paganini – an honour which only a few violinists shared. When asked for his opinion, he stressed the sonority of the violin:

'This violin made by Guarneri del Gesù appears at the first glance to be exceptionally large and almost a little too heavy. Its artistic quality is not immediately apparent but one only needs to touch it with the bow to be convinced that it has a marvellous sound: large, virile, dynamic.'
Strangely enough we are only talking of the volume of sound. Surely your father was also very conscious of the quality of sound, its colour, its timbre?

"It was because of the timbre that father was so interested in the Marsick. By the way, the name of the instrument is connected with the outstanding violinist Pierre Joseph Marsick, Professor at the Paris Conservatory and teacher of Georges Enescu and Jacques Thibaud; he played on it in the last century. Before the instrument returned to Paris and later to the Soviet Union it travelled around the USA, Switzerland and other countries."
How did the violin sound in David Oistrakh's hands? Do you think it possible to describe the sound of his violin?

"Many people have tried this, but I doubt their success. There is no doubt at all as to whether I could recognize father's playing solely from the sound of his violin. However, to translate the character of the sound into words is everything but easy."
David Oistrakh liked to play the viola. He loved its velvet timbre which reminded him of the sound of a deep feminine alto voice. He never became a dilettante when playing the viola. Weniamin Mordkovich, currently Professor at the Odessa Conservatory and previously a fellow student at Stoliarsky's wrote that their teacher always paid a lot of attention to viola playing when he gave violin lessons: 'He knew very well that someone who mastered the viola had a different appreciation of the sound of the violin and was able to hear the harmony of the accompaniment in all its richness.' 'To appreciate the sound of the violin in a different way' - a very interesting

*David Oistrakh as a viola player*

thought. One is reminded of it when one listens to the deep robust sound of David Oistrakh's violin just at the beginning of the Andante in the 3rd Movement of Prokofiev's 1st Sonata. You, Igor Davidovich, said that you experience this Andante as a musical portrait of Jaroslawna; I would like to add that Jaroslawna sings with a deep alto voice in your father's interpretation.

"Father never gave solo performances on the viola, the only exception being the *Harold en Italie* by Berlioz and the Mozart Duos for Violin and Viola and the Sinfonia Concertante; he played both parts at different times. Father had a particular weakness for *Harold*.

When father played in the USA for the first time, the critics stressed that he didn't misuse sonority and that he never tried to bluff them with this. Isaac Stern later writes of the noble, even sound which is produced by all parts of the bow and which never sounds forced or unpleasantly crass.'

The sound was even, rounded off and melodic, it was deep in the bass and crystal clear in the higher tones. I regard it as pointless to search for more or less perfect words which would show how the violin sounded in father's hands. If it is said: David Oistrakh was a great violinist, then the reason for it is not because his instrument sounded in such and such a way and not differently. Father was able to make the violin sing in full harmony with the requirements of each composition or any particular movement. One of the reasons for his greatness was that his violin transmitted the whole multitude of thoughts and feelings contained in the music."

The importance of the vibrato on the colour of tone of the violin is well known; how did your father use this means of musical expression?

"Father mastered vibrato perfectly and changed its amplitude and character according to the style of the work, but the main point was that he used even this technique only very sparingly.

'It is very uncommon nowadays for a violinist to abandon the vibrato voluntarily purely out of good musical taste. When it happens, it shows that the brain of the violinist functions as well as his fingers. This is the case with Oistrakh's work,' a critic wrote."

What was in your opinion more important to David Oistrakh's interpretation The lyrical or the intellectual element?

"Balance was the dominating factor, and in this respect I agree totally with Evgeny Svetlanov's words concerning the emotional and rational aspects. I am convinced that this balance ensured father the leading role among the numerous outstanding violinists."

You must admit, in spite of the superficial attempt to describe the contemporary performances as 'the age of the record' or as 'anti-romantic art', one cannot deny the increasing influence of the rational element in the interpretations which now count as modern. And I am throughly convinced that your father's interpretations were exceptionally modern.

"Yes, in father, restraint in expressing emotion dominated over impulsiveness and the clear structure of interpretation dominated over uncontrolled playing. We have already mentioned this. Consciousness overcame intuition and artistic stability replaced any form of lack of balance. Does this thought lead us away from the subject of his balance? Not at all. Whenever I heard father playing, it always seemed to me that reason didn't cool down feelings, but made them sharper and that the emotions controlled by his human and artistic ego impressed the listeners even stronger and in fact had a hypnotic effect. Do you know what I mean?"

Absolutely. I am trying to remember which piece of music and which interpretation could best explain how right you are, and the first which occurs to me is Oistrakh's virile restraint and at the same time deeply lyrical interpretation of the slow part of the 1st Violin Concerto by Shostakovich.

"And the lyrics of the Beethoven or the Brahms Concerto? You could give many examples."

I would like to discuss the Beethoven Violin Concerto in

greater detail. The Soviet press pointed quite rightly to the fact that the great German romantic school of conductors had degenerated in the last decade. This can above all be seen in the interpretations of Beethoven's works. The peak performances of Furtwängler or Klemperer are nowadays never attained. If you admit that there is a crisis with the conductors who concentrate on Beethoven and that this crisis is most pronounced in the German school of conducting, which is more Beethoven orientated than any other, then the question also extends to whether this crisis also involves the work of other reproducing artists. The cycle of Beethoven's Piano Concertos which were brilliantly recorded by Emil Gilels, or the Violin Concerto as played by David Oistrakh, remain as always outstanding examples of the interpretation of Beethoven's music.

"Wolfram Schwinger wrote in the Kasseler periodical *Musica*: 'In its musical shaping, one has never heard the Beethoven Concerto played in such a serious and satisfying way. A great violinist was playing – as great as when Furtwängler was conducting.'

I don't know which of my father's performances Schwinger was describing, but father loved and valued above all his recordings that of the Beethoven Concerto. He made three recordings: with the Orchestra of the Moscow Radio under Gauk, with the Stockholm Festival Orchestra under Ehrling and with the National Orchestra of the French Radio under Cluytens. Of all his recordings of the Beethoven Concerto, father loved the last one the most."

If Schwinger rates Oistrakh's interpretations so highly then this is last and not least due to the violinist's rare feeling for musical form and the pairing of attention to detail with the plastic understanding of the whole composition.

You can hear the desire for integrity in a number of his interpretations. Let's recall Beethoven's Kreutzersonate as interpreted by Oistrakh and Oborin. The first part gives the impression of a monolith. When the Presto begins after the introductory Adagio Sostenuto, the listener may have some doubt concerning the restrained tempo and as to whether the contrast effect is not going to suffer. Many artists emphasize here the contrast between reflection and energy, inhibition and forward urge. But we now hear with Oistrakh and Oborin a continuation of the exposition, the tempo remains measured as before, and – what is particularly important – remains solemn after the beginning of the secondary part. As a result of this, the first part gains integrity, although its exposition is not repeated.

"I would like to add something here. The chamber musicians succeed in an unobtrusive and yet clearly felt way in crystallizing the leading principle, which, according

*With André Cluytens, the conductor of the French National Radio Orchestra*

to Beethoven, loosens up each part of the Sonata with deviating secondary themes. These themes represent in their character thoughts in the middle of life's struggle. This principle is intensified almost to a 'Leitmotiv' in the Oistrakh-Oborin interpretation. I put this in inverted commas as I have the 'harmonious coordination' between the two artists in mind and not the thematic aspect of the whole Kreutzersonate. It is through this that the concept gains the monolithic form to which you referred in the Sonata's first movement."

What other characteristic points about your father's violin playing do you consider worthy of discussion?

"One has to talk of the wonderful feeling for rhythm in each piece he played. It is not just by chance that we find in his notes as a member of the jury in the Tchaikovsky Competition in 1966 the following remark about the performance of a Japanese violinist, Masuko Ushioda: 'Burning expression ... Individual initiative ... Conscious rhythm'. Paul Badura-Skoda said of father: 'This firm rhythm is typical of all great musicians. I always have to marvel at the firmness and certainty with which David takes the tempo and hangs onto it, without at the same time getting fixed and inflexible.' "

The feeling that Oistrakh knew how to find the only correct tempo is also shared by the Soviet pianist Bella Davidovich, who often played with David Oistrakh and who took part in his last tour to Amsterdam. He regarded the tempo not simply as 'moving speed', but above all as an expression of a certain state of mind. It is exactly because of this that the terms 'hesitating' or 'becoming faster' didn't just mean a simple Ritardando or Accelerando.

" 'I played Brahms' Concerto in D Minor in Oistrakh's home (of course, long before the appearance in Amsterdam). He follows my playing carefully in the score without interrupting me once; he comments only after I have finished.'

Father behaved in the same way in his class. He listened and never interrupted his students, for the simple reason that he met his students as artists and musicians.

Bella Davidovich continues, 'He criticizes the somewhat slow tempo of the exposition; he would like to hear the 1st movement of the Concerto played more dynamically and a little livelier ... But I discussed this with him and defended my point of view ... At the rehearsal in Amsterdam he gave 'his' and not 'my' tempo. The orchestral introduction in his interpretation sounds so convincing that I immediately give way, which means that I tune in to the whole process of making music in the most natural way.' "

Oistrakh's artistic attitude to tradition is also of fundamental importance – somebody else's tradition when he was dealing with the interpretation of a composition which he hadn't played before and his own tradition when checking his interpretation of a composition, even if he had played it quite often before. In 1953, David Oistrakh and Lew Oborin played Franck's Sonata in Paris. The composition, which had its own tradition of interpretation in the composer's home country sounded extremely fresh and with irresistible conviction.

" 'Franck's Sonata led to passionate discussion,' Bernard Gavoty wrote. ' ... Oistrakh, in fact, changed the superterrestial (seraphic) gentleness of the picture as painted by the author. Was Franck in reality an angel in ecstasy or a human being subject to all emotions? Oistrakh supports the second concept and I must admit that he enforced his interpretation with such rhetorical power that I had to give way to the irresistible splendour of his arguments!'

In disussing father's creative attitude to tradition I would like to point out his interpretation of the Tchaikovsky Concerto. It was of great importance in father's artistic career. He first played it in Stoliarsky's class, then in his first performance in Odessa and in Jelisawetgrad and afterwards at his début in Leningrad in 1928 and in Moscow in 1933 – on that occasion he presented his audience for the first time with three violin concertos in succession (in addition to Tchaikovsky's Concerto, Mozart's 4th Concerto and the Mendelssohn Concerto. Finally, he played the Tchaikovsky Concerto at the competition in Brussels.

'I remember that many of my elder colleagues advised me before the competition in Brussels in 1937 against playing the Tchaikovsky Concerto, since they apparently didn't like this Concerto in the West. The facts proved to be the opposite. Both first prizes went to competitors who played this Concerto,' father wrote many years later.

And how often he played the Tchaikovsky Concerto during the war and later ... The opinion of Leonid Kogan: 'Oistrakh's interpretation of the Tchaikovsky Concerto is in my opinion the peak of the interpretations of this work. Nobody has played the Tchaikovsky Concerto better than Oistrakh and probably nobody will play it better in the forseeable future.' "

In his search for a concept of the Tchaikovsky Concerto David Oistrakh overcame foreign traditions as well as his own with the usual consequence. He examined and changed his own interpretation several times. It became more and more mature as the years went by, deeper, emotionally fuller and more intensive.

"In his playing father undoubtedly realized the best traditions of the Russian art of violin playing: simplicity and the noblest creative shaping, the communication of the whole richness, the whole depth of the composition, the unconditional subordination of the virtuoso aspect

*A photograph which David Oistrakh gave as a present to the Tchaikovsky memorial house in Klin*

86

*Oistrakh plays in the Tchaikovsky memorial house*

in favour of the spiritual content of the Concerto, precision of expression, melodic purity of sound and wide animated tonal quality."

I would also like to point out the declamatory quality of Oistrakh's playing, the speaking intonation of his violin, the 'speaking style', as critics in different countries described it, the different traits of performing art, which is rooted in the tradition of Russian vocal art. Just remember Glinka, Dargomijsky's experiments and Mussorgsky's musical dramas.

Oistrakh belonged to the generation of interpreters who contributed to the basic principles of the Soviet style of performance. His activity as violinist and Professor at the Moscow Conservatory helped the Soviet violin school to its highest achievements: to world-wide recognition.

If your father worked so carefully on each composition and so systematically aimed at new solutions to their performance as well as the compositions he had repeatedly played before, then one could suspect that this attitude did not allow any 'loop-hole' for artistic spontaneity in the performance. Did this not happen at the expense of inspiration during the performance?

"Of course he experimented, mainly during the rehearsals, but his artistic fantasy didn't even switch off when he closed the score on the conductor's desk and put his violin away. His interpretation matured during his lessons with the students and in rare minutes of relaxation. But this happened as a rule before he stepped on the concert platform."

But this surely doesn't mean that David Oistrakh simply 'reproduced' a well-rehearsed interpretation again and again? Do you know, I have found myself several times in the situation of feeling that I am experiencing a new interpretation especially on an occasion when I heard your father play the same program two evenings in succession. I am not talking about changes in his interpretation as they happen over the years and decades, that would be an entirely different problem.

"In this lies the phenomenon of father's art. That his playing cannot be regarded as reproduction, as a copy or imitation of the original. His playing radiated the warmth of living marble and not the cold of a

*87*

frozen plaster replica. No one would dare to regard father as one of the actors of 'mimic performance', to use an expression from the theatre."

But you yourself have said that your father left all experimental ideas behind him as soon as he stepped onto the concert platform.

"The one does not exclude the other. When I said that father's interpretations matured before he presented a composition, I expressed it slightly differently and I didn't mean it to be taken word for word. However, I often wondered where father got his unending creative impulse from, which fed his inspiration even during the process of performing.

My answer to this question is: As a true musician the platform 'enthused' father and the process of performing on the violin awoke in him artistic inspiration. The pianist Frida Bauer declared: 'What we practised at his house and what we afterwards offered in our concerts was very different music. Even if only two or three people appeared at the rehearsal, Oistrakh virtually changed, you could suddenly notice that he was inspired.'

You quite rightly talked of father's repeat performances, and that with each performance a new interpretation was revealed, and sometimes a new appreciation of its entire shaping. I often had the opportunity of taking part in concerts with father which concluded our long tours. Each time. I was amazed by the freshness of his playing, I don't just mean his technique, although even that was exceptionally impressive, but something that was more important – the freshness of his emotions. Father's artistic exploration of the music didn't therefore come to halt on the platform. Furthermore, he always mastered one or two variants of interpretation of a whole work, as well as all the details. How can one describe such artistic ability?"

If I have understood you correctly, I would like to describe such an attitude to musical interpretation 'zonal'. Each precisely finished concept of a musical work (or its parts) does not change its valance within the limits of a certain interpretation range. A breach of this frame would alter the interpretation itself. It is in the nature of things, that the extension of the 'zone' depends on the musical style: it can be greater in romantic compositions, it must be smaller in the work of the Viennese classic. Fun-

damentally speaking, the performance of chamber musicians rests on this point, since each of them has the freedom of forming his own interpretation of the composition within the limits of a certain interpretation zone. When the frame of the zone is fully used, then this could serve as basis for collective interpretation as we experience it, with jazz for example.

Now an entirely different question: How did your father rehearse?

"I must disappoint you straight away. Father's laboratory was only accessible to himself. He didn't like to talk of problems, doubts and difficulties that occurred during the process of rehearsing.

Regina Horowitz wrote of father's early years: 'Dodik worked hard in those years. Although he never suffered, then or later, from the habit of some instrumentalists who play twenty-five hours per day.' I would personally like to add: There was no need for him to practise like that."

What was David Oistrakh's daily 'ration', and did a 'ration' even exist?

"First of all, father was a born violinist, and secondly, he mastered his instrument with complete perfection as the result of decades of concert activity. This allowed father not to have to 'practise' in the narrow sense of the word as one usually understands it: an endless repetition of each passage, scales and of études to develop his finger skill.

This had been so for as far back as I can think. One has to consider, however, that I experienced father's playing when he was already at the height of his career. Mother often said that she remembered another period, when father was just on the way to the top and still had to fight to achieve the high mastery which I mentioned before. There were, of course, many years of enormous and exceptionally purposeful work behind father's achievements.

Pawel Kogan, who arranged several tours through the Soviet Union for father in the 1930s, lived in the hotel next to him. Kogan and father were also for a long time neighbours in those Moscow flats. His impressions of the violinist's methods of practising: 'Just as at my first meeting with Oistrakh, it struck me with what amazing ease he obtained the perfect intonation on the violin, and with what almost playful ease he managed to disen-

*During rehearsal*

tangle even the most difficult knots. You never had the feeling of attending a rehearsal. There was no physical strain, no endless repetition of the same sequence of notes, passage or phrase. To put it simply, no sign of turmoil which usually accompanies the 'homework' of instrumentalists.'

A remark by Regina Horowitz agrees with this: 'The strongest and most powerful impression which he left behind after his rehearsals was the ease with which he practised. He did it all without stress and calmly. From the outside impression it seemed as if it all happened naturally.' "

Did the surroundings play a part when David Feodorovich worked, did they influence his productivity?

"The surroundings were of course not unimportant to father. He always liked to work at home. Perhaps this was the reason why he always liked to return to his Moscow home. At home, he practised new programs or with his accompanist, and rehearsed with Lew Oborin and Sviatoslav Knuschewizki. when it was necessary, father could practise in any situation, even in the presence of other people. This apparently cost him some self-control. I remember how father, after his first visit to the Music Festival in Prague, told us about Pablo Casals. Amongst other things, father admired the artist's ability to suddenly switch off from the environment in which he was, from the turmoil that precedes each concert and from the mixed and rather uninhibited audience, being able to concentrate on his cello without any effort."

I suspect the anatomy of David Oistrakh's hands also contributed to the success of his work?

"Father owned 'lucky' hands, which were by nature very elastic and flexible. He didn't need to 'train' them specially. I was often woken up in the morning by the sound of father's Stradivarius. He would be hardly awake and already grabbed the instrument while he was still in his pyjamas and was immediately able to play passages of legendary complexity."

Many violinists wouldn't even bother to practise regularly if they were equipped with such physical attributes and with such phenomenal 'violin apparatus'. However, David Oistrakh played the violin every day for several hours.

"Father was extremely industrious and full of restless thirst for knowledge. His repertoire was almost unlimited and was constantly extended. You could always find the scores of new compositions on his desk. I remember when father prepared himself for the cycle 'Development of the Violin Concerto', he had studied three monumental compositions in the one summer of 1946: the Concertos by Sibelius, Elgar and Walton.

At this point I must mention the letter which father received from William Walton shortly after the performance of his concerto:

'London, 26th February 1947
Dear Mr Oistrakh,
I was yesterday evening able to listen to the performance of my Violin Concerto. The quality of reception was unfortunately not very good due to the frequent interruptions and interference. However, I heard enough to convince myself that this interpretation was the best which the work has so far received, both by the soloist and by the orchestra. Would you please convey my sincere thanks to the excellent conductor and to the orchestras? I am particularly indebted to you, as you promoted the interpretation which will remain in my memory for a long time.
With best wishes, yours in sincere

admiration, William Walton.'

How many violinists of David Oistrakh's status and age would have been satisfied with only playing classic violin music from the eighteenth and nineteenth centuries! Father, however, played Bartók enthusiastically, interpreted the Concerto by Stravinsky (which he rather belatedly included in his repertoire), he also studied the Violin Concerto of the well known composer Ernst Hermann Meyer from the German Democratic Republic, at the age of fifty-seven. Meyer thanked him with the following words: 'First of all I would like to repeat that your performance of my Concerto was a great and unforgettable event for me – and not only for me, but as I believe for a great many people in the German Democratic Republic.' "

How did your father study a new composition?

Father read and played music from sight in a inimitable way. He had an incredibly quick reaction and the special gift of immediately finding his way in an unknown musical score, and sometimes even to anticipate what lay ahead.

Michail Goldstein wrote about the time when he together with father attended Stoliarsky's class: 'Once Nathan Milstein played a piece which none of us knew in Pyotr Stoliarsky's study: I. Dobrowen's *Fairy Tales*. Oistrakh liked it so much that he learnt it in one single day. We were all amazed, it was not just a question of learning by heart, but of 'shaping' a well-understood and perceived composition!

In my whole life I have never seen or met a musician who was able to play from sight as David Feodorovich did. In this case the term 'playing from sight' isn't even applicable. He read the score in an ingenious way and understood the character and style of the music at a glance, all its nuances, its tempi, the accent, everything that a musical score is composed of. This sometimes seemed to be witchcraft!'

Father kept this ability also in later years. I would also say that he developed it even further. Read Leonid Kogan's comment: 'Remarkable how he played from sight. He played in such a way as if he had played the composition many times, irrespective of how difficult it was.'

I could convince myself of this often enough and there were numerous examples of it. The most convincing being perhaps when father read and played Dmitri Shostakovich's 2nd Violin Concerto for the first time. Indeed, it was almost impossible to believe that father played it from sight. As I didn't believe my own ears, I recorded it on a tape. We can sometimes listen to this 'documentary tape'."

Did David Oistrakh's memory match the speed with which he understood and learnt a new composition; was his memory good enough to stand up to the permanent overloading of his repertoire?

"In all the years that I remember there wasn't a single case where father had forgotten the score of a work in his performances as violinist or conductor.

However, father never showed off with his memory. When he accompanied instrumentalists, he never conducted by heart and he didn't like it if a conductor accompanied his violin playing without a score in front of him. His urgent request which he once addressed to a somewhat obstinate maestro, to conduct the Tchaikovsky Concerto from the score, led to a funny situation. Father stepped out in front of the audience and to his surprise walked past the conductor's desk, where he came across a pocket edition of the score which was placed on a tiny bench behind the rostrum."

The lightning grasp of a new score (this is the way to describe Oistrakh's ability to play from sight) was followed by an uninterrupted search for a means of expression, to shape the philosophical depth of the music accurately. This was possible because of his excellent memory, which immediately assimilated everything permanently. It took time for all the details of his interpretation to settle down and to fit smoothly into his concept of the music.

"You are right. The process of absorbing a new composition was above all, for father, a development and refinement of his concept. He was always surprised when young self-confident musicians included compositions in their repertoire which they had only just begun to rehearse. This was to him totally inexplicable, since he was then only willing to perform a new composition when he had absorbed it completely."

Surely there must have been surprises and unexpected incidents in the life of a violin virtuoso?

Surely it sometimes happened to David Oistrakh that he was forced to accept compositions in his program that he had either never played before or perhaps hadn't played for a very long time?

"Of course, more than once. Shortly after the war, father got hold of the extremely virtuoso *Jewish Dance* by I. Achron. He studied and practised the piece in one single day. In 1968 father was in London and at short notice had to find something to put on a record, on which he had originally been expected to perform Mozart's Sinfonia Concertante for Violin and Viola with Paul Hindemith. Father chose Bruch's Scottish Fantasy (the playing time of the piece fitted the record apparently) and studied the piece in no more than half a day, although he hadn't played it for many years."

Regina Horowitz states in her memoirs that Oistrakh always played very calmly in his youth. He never got excited before a concert and he went to it as if he were going to a feast.' Did your father keep this calm state of mind also later in life?

"What he did keep was the festive feeling that each concert triggered off in him. As far as nervosity

was concerned, it was sometimes stronger, sometimes weaker." Weren't the continuous concert performances in the world's best concert halls and the continuous success with the audiences in different countries enough to neutralize that unpleasant feeling of nervosity which burns somewhere in one's stomach and is called 'stage fright'?

"Stage fright is an irrational feeling, as one doesn't get nervous because one hasn't sufficiently prepared, but simply because one gets nervous ... Look up any of father's letters written at different times. Also remember, as an example, the letters from Brussels in 1937, which we have already quoted."

David Oistrakh told me about an amusing incident, which happened during the performance of Walton's Concerto. The second movement of the Concerto ends with the double flageolet in the solo part. Out of fear that something could go wrong (flageolets are a delicate matter), Oistrakh wanted to be quite sure and during the rehearsal asked the two first violinists of the orchestra to join him in playing the flageolets in the evening. A very bad mistake! He of course forgot his fears during the concert. His flageolets would have sounded perfectly if there had not been the jumping bows of the two 'saving angels' in the orchestra, who were pale with nervosity.

"Father told me this story as well. He demonstrated in a funny way how his two assistants must have sweated the whole day with the unfortunate flageolet and how they told each other before the performance at which passage the bow had to be passed over the strings to produce a calm, clear sound."

The first recording was made by David Oistrakh, in those days there were no long playing records, only short playing records with 78 revolutions per minute. He played the Tango by Albéniz-Duschkin with Wsewolod Topilin and the violin transcription of the waltz in Tchaikovsky's *Serenade for Strings*. Since then the violinist always recorded his whole repertoire on records. He recorded over 250 small and large compositions, some of them two or three times. Oistrakh even played the Brahms Violin Concerto four times on records: with Konvichny, Klemperer, Kondrashin and Szell. How did your father behave during such recording sessions? Didn't playing

in a recording studio prove too much of a burden for him?

"Sessions are indeed a cross that some artists have to bear. The red signal light meaning 'everything ready' and the following short order from the recording studio: 'Tape running!' produces with many a stronger stage fright than in an overcrowded concert hall. Father was different in this respect. It always appeared to me that he was hardly worried by all these important moments which worried other artists: the emptiness of the studio, the necessity of making repeated recordings, the knowledge that the recording would fix what he played for ever, all this didn't worry him.

The Soviet sound editor Igor Weprinzew, who worked with Oistrakh a great deal, reports: 'Oistrakh was wonderful to record and was the ideal partner for every sound editor since he was familiar with recording techniques. He also understood every wish that I passed to him from the recording room. The contact between the editor's room and the studio was absolutely natural and unconstrained when working with David Feodorovich.'

*David Oistrakh in a record shop in Brussels*

The violinist knew how to create (in an empty concert hall or a studio) a mood which in no way differed from the festive atmosphere of a full concert hall.

It was not just I, but our whole team who, at David Oistrakh's recording sessions, had the feeling of coming close to very high, pure art – it was an indescribable feeling.'

In spite of this, father preferred direct recordings in the concert hall: 'In a studio, one never succeeds in putting oneself in that high artistic mood which one experiences on the concert stage,' he once wrote to the musicologist Grigori Schneerson. 'Provided one manages to avoid technical mistakes and uneveness, such a record has qualities which one hardly ever achieves in the studio atmosphere. I mean the living breath of the music, the dash, the sincere temperament, the contact with a well disposed audience, the footlights and the concert atmosphere, this brings out the artist.' "

Irrespective of what has been said, the recording process is by itself physically very demanding on artists.

"Did you know that father had the astonishing ability to maintain

Jean Rouart hands over to Oistrakh the Charles-Cros prize of the Academy for Musical Recording in Paris. On Oistrakh's left: Lilian Hochhauser, on his right: Vasso Devetzi and behind: Victor Hochhauser

his freshness, not only by keeping the elasticity of his hands, but also the freshness of the heart and the emotions. Each recording obviously made great physical demands, particularly if larger works such as a violin concerto were recorded. Sometimes one had to play several passages again because of a mistake

by the hornist, a missed entry by the woodwind instruments or the unfortunate creaking noise produced by the 'prong' of the double-bass. Everybody who participated in father's recording sessions, noticed that he played more and more perfectly with each rehearsal.

Father knew how to avoid appearing tired. Above all, as I have already said, he never allowed his exhaustion to influence the artistic verve of the performance. There is no doubt at all that father sank into his hotel bed totally exhausted after one tortuous day spent from early in the morning until late in the evening recording Mendelssohn's and Tchaikovsky's Violin Concertos as well as Vivaldi's Double Concerto with the Philadelphia Orchestra. However, neither Eugene Ormandy, who conducted the Philharmonic Orchestra, the orchestra players, nor Isaac Stern, who came to the Columbia studio in the evening, noticed the slightest sign of exhaustion. Father knew how much such recording sessions took out of him. Father took me with him to a recording session when I was sixteen. Glazunof's Violin Concerto and a romance by Beethoven were to be recorded with Kyril Kondrashin conducting, during the night. Mother was reluctant to let me go, but father insisted: Igor was preparing himself for a career as a violinist and must know how much sweat it takes!"

In one of his letters to David Oistrakh, Joseph Szigeti described listening to your own gramophone recordings as a 'Meeting with oneself'. What was your father's opinion of his recordings? Did he enjoy listening to them? Did he like them?

"Did father enjoy listening to his early recordings? You should really have asked me whether he had time to listen to them. Mother told me that on one of his tours to foreign countries father had by chance heard a recording he had made in his youth being played on the radio - he liked it. But I know how sceptically he accepted the idea of producing a record series entitled *The Young David Oistrakh*. When interviewed by a reporter from the *Stereo Review*, father replied: 'In my opinion the most recent recordings are the most important ones. I made several good records when I was younger. Now that I am older, I know more, and my recent recordings reflect my thinking and form of expression as they are today. I prefer them.'

Maybe this was the reason why father re-recorded several concertos. He for instance recorded Brahms' Double Concerto four times (with Sviatoslav Knuschewizki, Milŏs Sadlo, Pierre Fournier, Mstislav Rostropovich), the Tchaikovsky and Sibelius Concertos three times and the 1st Concerto by Shostakovich three times as well.

Father was very interested in recording techniques. He was pleased by the improvement of the studio equipment and valued high quality equipment and skilled technicians. He was always enthralled by people who knew their way about in the complicated interior of a modern stereo tape recording studio, who were able to repair a television in no time and who could explain the cause of a fault in a car engine simply by listening to it. He, for example, admired the craftmanship of a carpenter and had respect for every type of ability. Something that he never did and condemned in others was, as he described it, 'to do something with only 98% effort'." How high were Oistrakh's expectations of the quality of the recordings?

"Father considered an ideal recording to be one that gave the optimum illusion of a real concert performance. One must get the same strong musical impression, whether one is listening to a record or in a concert hall to a live performance. This was father's basic requirement. After listening to recordings he had made in Vienna he wrote: 'I am very very pleased with the recordings. They not only sound good, but they also convey the atmosphere of playing chamber music perfectly. Please give dear Mr Hans and his entire great team my most sincere thanks.' "

*95*

# The chamber musician

'Two women without whom he would have had a very difficult life.' That was the caption to a photograph of Tamara Iwanowna Oistrakh and David Oistrakh's piano accompanist Frida Bauer in a West German magazine. This was during David Oistrakh's last tour of the Federal Republic in March/April 1974. What was the relationship like between David Oistrakh and the pianist who accompanied him on the piano all the time?

"Father often repeated that he wasn't one of those violinists who play the violin part on the concert platform without caring what was going on behind their backs. It would have been out of the question for father to play with an ad hoc partner in his tours, as so many of his colleagues still do for a number of reasons.

Wsewolod Topilin was father's accompanist on the piano before the war. Abram Djakow accompanied all Soviet competitors at the Brussels Competition in 1937. In the years following the war, he let himself be first accompanied by Vladimir Jampolski and later on since 1960, by Frida Bauer. All these pianists were outstanding musicians and ideal partners for father.

'Oistrakh worked for many years with male accompanists,' Frida Bauer relates, 'and I can well understand his words which he once spoke in the Conservatory: 'If Frida were a man, I would perhaps play with her ... ' '"

What did David Oistrakh demand of his accompanists? Did he rehearse a great deal with his pianists?

"Father had high standards. He first of all wanted to see a creative personality in his accompanist. He rehearsed a great deal, discussed all details of the piano part and was always trying to achieve a uniform, integrated interpretation.

Regina Horowitz, who accompanied my father in the 1920s narrates: 'Oistrakh expected from me as a pianist above all that I should adjust to his desires of achieving uniformity of interpretation and a thoroughly polished performance of my piano part ... David Feodorovich, who already had a well-deserved reputation, used to consult me about the interpretation of each composition and he proposed several variants for me to choose from.'

The memoirs of Frida Bauer, his most recent pianist, bear witness to the cordial atmosphere during father's rehearsals: 'David Oistrakh asked me to play with him at a concert in Copenhagen in 1960. The concert was to take place two months later, but there was only time for two rehearsals with him: one before his departure for a long guest tour and the other on his return shortly before the performance in the Danish capital ... I wouldn't like to say that I was a newcomer as

*The trio:*
*Oistrakh-Oborin-Knuschewizki*

accompanist. I had already accompanied such outstanding musicians as the violinist Julian Sitkowezki and the cellist Daniil Schafran in Moscow as well as on tours ... In spite of this, I was very excited by Oistrakh's unexpected offer. The program included Beethoven's Kreutzersonate, which I had never played before. With his tact and high teaching ability, he managed to make me understand in two or three hours what was expected of me in the Kreutzersonate and in the whole program in general. Any doubts I had as to why I had agreed to play with this outstanding artist disappeared immediately. He had managed to 'charge' me sufficiently for my independent preparation, which lasted one and a half months. The concert in Copenhagen was a great success, proceeding calmly and without problems. People asked us afterwards: 'How long have you been playing together?' David Feodorovich was satisfied, praised me, but couldn't understand one thing: that it was he himself who 'caused' the success of his new accompanist.' "

97

The Austrian pianist Paul Badura-Skoda told us how he had rehearsed with Oistrakh – giving us a glimpse of David Oistrakh's artistic 'laboratory'. He wrote of the preparation for their first sonata performance at the Salzburg Festival.

'Since David Oistrakh liked to plan a generous rehearsal time, a whole week was set aside for this purpose. I was therefore expecting an extremely detailed rehearsal which examined every little nuance. How wrong I was. David's main aim was that we should tune in on each other (without of course neglecting the obvious precision in detail). Remarkably little was spoken. If, for instance, I began a movement quicker than he wanted it, he simply corrected the tempo by playing his entry a little slower. When we repeated it I already knew how he wanted it.'

"As far as the concert by father and Paul Badura-Skoda in Moscow is concerned, I can't remember that a whole week was set aside. Even if

*Oistrakh and Vladimir Jampolski in conversation with the composer Zoltán Kodaly*

*Concert with Frida Bauer*

father had wanted it, he never had that much time. Furthermore, he was convinced that both he and Paul understood one another extremely well already after the first concert. Father told us in confidence that one of his Mozart Sonatas which formed part of the program for a new record was recorded almost without any rehearsal."

Paul Badura-Skoda used this secret. In order to stress how much the two were working on the same 'wavelength' he wrote: 'In the end it reached a point where David made the following proposal a few minutes before the recording: "Paul, we need another sonata, would you like to record the G Major Sonata?" I was very surprised. Without rehearsal? "Well yes, but we rehearse it in front of the microphone." It was not surprising, that it was this last recording which turned out to be our most harmonic and spontaneous interpretation on records.'

What was your father's opinion concerning the dynamic aspect of cooperation between pianist and violinist?

"This obviously always depended on the type of composition (a sonata for violin is one thing, a violin piece with piano accompaniment is something quite different). If you talk in general terms, one has to point out that father was very sceptical when he met pianists who tried to play too loudly."

How can this be related to his desire for a pianist who didn't just

*With George Szell*

accompany his violin playing, but who as a musician together with him tried to bring out the nucleus, the basic substance of a musical composition?

"Father's desire to achieve a dynamic level in the piano part didn't originate from his intention to reduce the creative, musical role of his partner. We were however just talking about dynamic balance and since father never increased the sound of his violin, he would never have agreed to play louder just at the pianist's request.

"I would like to add: David Oistrakh expected a joint interpretation from his chamber-music partners whilst at the same time having a surprising fine feeling as chamber musician, all instrumentalists and conductors pointed this out. George Szell wrote to Oistrakh: 'There is no musician today that I respect more than you. Nobody with whom I feel more "at home" when I play, and with whom I feel so strongly that we are one heart and soul.' "

Could David Oistrakh's feeling for chamber music have not perhaps been sharpened by his participation in so many chamber-music ensembles and above all by his long and fruitful cooperation with Lew Oborin and Sviatoslav Knuschewizki?

Many artists perform as chamber musicians sometime in the course of their lives. For some this was the quickest way to solo concerts, for others (who have already crossed this 'Rubikon'), it is an episode, an interlude in their career as soloists. There are not many soloists of repute and in whose life chamber music was of such essential importance as for David Oistrakh.

"I would say that it was part of his creative personality, of his whole musical consciousness. I must in addition mention the violinists Joseph Joachim and Ferdinand Laub, who led excellent quartets in Berlin and Moscow in the last century, or Alfred Cortot, Jacques Thibaud and Pablo Casals who formed a piano trio in our time.

The trio Oistrakh-Oborin-Knuschewizki was created shortly after the beginning of the war. I would like to stress that each member of this trio was already a mature artist recognized in the Soviet Union and enjoyed an intensive concert activity."

You can multiply their experience of playing sonatas. I say this on account of the duo performances Oistrakh-Oborin and Knuschewizki-Oborin. Musicians of the older generation remember with pleasure Oborin and Knuschewizki's incomparable interpretation of the Rachmaninof Cello Sonata in which the musicians surpassed one another in the art of producing a flowing sound and of making their instrument sing. Their performances of sonatas by Chopin, Grieg, Debussy, Beethoven and Shostakovich were extremely interesting. Lew Oborin told us that the first composition which he played together with Oistrakh was Greig's C Minor Sonata - in 1935 in Ankara at a previously described guest tour of Soviet musicians: 'We both enjoyed playing together and we thus decided to continue to as soon as we got home. Our joint regular concerts started in about 1937.'

"The artistic contact with Lew Oborin was of great importance to father. He was only one year older than father, but had already received a high distinction in 1927, the 1st Prize at the Chopin Competition in Warsaw. He remained the older colleague to his trio partners. Father sincerely admired Lew Oborin's pronounced sense for the piano, his pianist's thinking. He wrote of him: 'The contact with this great musician, a man of refined culture, has greatly enriched me. The joint playing of works of the great masters of the past and present gave us many happy hours.'

Since we have dealt with the pre-history of the Oistrakh-Oborin–Knuschewizki trio, I would

100

like to add that father had also played with Knuschewizki. Thinking back, Lew Oborin remembers:

'Our trio with Sviatoslav Knuschewizki was formed in 1941. Oistrakh and Knuschewizki had played previously with C. Igumnof, I was engaged for a recording of Tchaikovsky's Trio. The record seems to have never been released (only the tape exists), but our trio began to continue as a permanent chamber-music ensemble.'

The piano trio Oistrakh-Oborin-Knuschewizki took active part in the capital's concert life in spite of the extremely difficult situation in the first years of the war. Father once wrote:

'I remember the first years of our joint work. It was during the war. We met in a cold flat for a rehearsal. The first concert of our trio took place in the Tchaikovsky Hall at the beginning of 1942. We had to have a heating lamp close to our music stands so we could warm our hands during the interval. We couldn't complete the concert: an air attack alarm forced us to go down into the cellar.'

After the war you could regularly listen to the performances of father and Oborin and also of the trio. In spite of the intensive solo activity of each of the three partners, in spite of the commitments that each of them had as Professors at the Con-servatory, they rehearsed together very often. These rehearsals took place in our house as a rule. I obviously didn't miss a single one. It was a feast for me each time when Lew Oborin sat down at the piano and father and Sviatoslav Nikolayevich took their place on the two sides of the Viennese double desk. I was very proud that Lew Oborin allowed me to sit next to him, follow the score and turn the pages. I must admit that I sacrificed my own teaching lessons to attend these rehearsals without father knowing. They awoke in me the love for chamber music. I knew almost the whole repertoire of the trio by heart."

How did the partners actually rehearse? Did the relationships between their artistic characters and the long period in which they worked shoulder to shoulder have an effect?

"The atmosphere at the rehearsals was always friendly, full of mutual respect and good natured humour. Although they were sometimes joking, I could hear a great deal of interesting and valuable statements. They never had arguments or disagreements. The rehearsals of the three musicians characterized true creative art in which all three took an equal part.

Of course it sometimes also worked out like this: after having got to know a piece which they had never played before or only once or twice and had in general agreed on how to interpret it and how to get around the dangerous 'cliffs', exactly in the moment when father wanted to begin with refining the details and to attempt a deeper interpretation, a voice sounded from the piano: 'What really went wrong?' Oborin, with his extraordinary competence and everlasting desire to acquire new compositions looked questioningly at his partners. In such cases in was Sviatoslav Knuschewizki who, with self-sacrificing loyalty to music and with his soft yielding character, formed a quiet pole, a 'centre'. Father wrote:

'He was a sort of 'balance' in our trio that harmonized any opposing views when they occurred. His art 'cemented' the trio.'

The interrupted rehearsal continued and the musicians were soon completely under the spell of the composition, especially Oborin, and the music making didn't seem to want to come to an end.

And how they liked to start a rehearsal with the performance of a work which they had played at their latest concert, as if they wanted to check themselves once more!"

The high standard of the trio can be explained by two factors: Oistrakh, Oborin and Knuschewizki were true musicians and obviously related to each other as artists. This was above all apparent in the simplicity, clarity and harmony of their interpretation. It however always appears to me that in addition to this unity one must mention the rare ability which characterized each of the three – to give way to one another, to subordinate the ego to the demands of the music. The critic Hans Petzold wrote in the *Leipziger Volkszeitung* on the occasion of the trio's concert in Leipzig:

'We often experience in chamber music by outstanding soloists, that the one or the other remains the soloist and tries to play himself into the foreground. The opposite was the case with the Soviet guests: each of them subordinated himself to the whole, a simple servant of the composition. A more ideal music making collective than this is hardly thinkable.'

Did the trio undertake many guest tours?

"There was a certain discrepancy between the trio's great skill and the relatively low number of their guest tours. This, however, can be simply explained by the tremendous demands on each of them, since their main activity was that of soloist.

The trio performed in Vienna in 1945 together with other Soviet musicians. During the time after the war it played in England and twice in the German Democratic Republic. I can remember in detail the preparations of the trio for the England tour of 1958. Father got so excited, no comparison to his solo performances! But then he was even happier when he read the enthusiastic press comments. *The Times* wrote:

'Beethoven's Triple Concerto

was enchanting in this performance due to the clarity and infinity of conception, especially in the slow movement. One experienced the interpretation of the piece by Brahms as a romantic tragic *Lied*. In their interpretation of Tchaikovsky, the multitude of their individuality as artists, the passion and the lyric's expression came out perfectly in their playing.'

A further voice from the Paris press in 1953, when Western Europe heard the Oistrakh–Oborin duo for the first time: 'There is a trust between these two artists which the audience immediately notices. As the two have already played together for twenty years one can immediately see what a fantastic understanding links them together. Precision, feeling and ease are paired in their playing.' (Marcelle Schneider)"

The artistic cooperation in the trio lasted for more than twenty years – until the death of Sviatoslav Knuschewizki in 1962. Didn't the question then arise for Oistrakh and Oborin to find another artist to continue the famous trio?

"I think I can say with certainty that such a thought did not occur to father or to Lew Oborin. The bond between the three musicians was far too great for them to imagine having somebody else instead of Svet, as people called Sviatoslav Knuschewizki, as cellist. Who could take his place at the cello, that could sing in such an expressive and extraordinary way, with the virile timbre that entered deep into the soul? A young cellist, or a mature one, or one of his students? The trio had no name - what was there for the other two members to have to maintain now that the third was no longer with them?

'I always have to think of Svet,' father wrote, 'It is impossible to get used to the idea that the life which overflowed in him has ended. The sound of his cello will always be in my ear.' "

Almost everything important composed for piano trio was in the repertoire of the Oistrakh - Oborin - Knuschewizki ensemble. The trio also played with well-known Moscow instrumentalists, quintets and string sextets. What do you consider the trio's artistic peak performances?

"We have already mentioned these in our conversation. The peak performances were based on the ideal combination of the three artists' personalities into the one single whole. If one has to pick out individual interpretations by the trio one could choose Tchaikovsky's Trio, Dvořák's *Dumka*, Rachmaninof's *Elegiac Trio* and Shostakovich's Trio, in spite of the difficulty of such a question. I would however like to repeat that in giving this selection I still have in mind the sound of other compositions such as Schubert's two Trios for instance."

It would perhaps be putting it a little too straightforward to suggest that certain types of music are connected with certain emotional spheres, in other words, that they trigger off certain emotional vibrations. It has often been pointed out that the piano trio in most cases produces dramatic feelings irrespective of whether one is dealing with the lyrics, philosphical reflections or with concentrated tragedy. It is remarkable that the three compositions which you mentioned confirm this view entirely: Tchaikovsky's Trio has the subtitle *In the Memory of a Great Artist* and is dedicated to Nikolai Rubinstein, Rachmaninof's *Elegiac Trio* was to a certain degree an obituary for Tchaikovsky, and Dmitri Shostakovich, who designated his Trio to Iwan Sollertinski the well-known Soviet musicologist, allowed himself to be inspired by the tragic and heroic pathos of the great patriotic war. It is not just by chance that this Trio is recognized as being complimentary to Picasso's fresco *Guernica*.

"Father often remembered the day at the end of 1944 when he heard the Trio for the first time in Leningrad. It was first performed by the composer and the members of the Beethoven Quartet Dmitri Zyganow and Sergey Shirinsky. Lew Oborin and Sviatoslav Knuschewizki were also present. The music moved them to such a degree that they studied the Trio shortly afterwards: it was heard for the first time in Moscow in April 1945. I heard their interpretation several times, I was each time impressed at how the three musicians penetrated the philosophical content of the music. It was amazing how they interpreted complicated pictures so that they almost assumed visual significance. The song of the violin and of the cello in the Passacaglia didn't leave the listener unmoved and one had the impression that the world itself was bursting into pieces. The theme of the first movement, which is taken up again in the finale, rang out in its emotional transformation as a symbol of hope, as a grandiose requiem which announced the victory of life over death."

Did your father prefer any particular chamber music?

"He could hardly have answered this question himself. Ignoring the violin sonatas and the trios, he played many quartets and quintets by Schubert and Brahms, Tchaikovsky's Sextet *Memories of Florence* and Schubert's Octet. In all these cases we are dealing with outstanding music. It can hardly be said that father preferred a certain piece. You could perhaps pick out Tchaikovsky's Trio from all the compositions which father played; father often said that he got very excited when he performed this Trio.

'My heart bleeds each time I reach the subsidiary theme in the first movement,' he once said. I can remember very clearly how this Trio sounded when it was performed by father, Oborin and Knuschewizki. A superb, unique interpretation! Fortunately – like many others – it is preserved on record."

I read in a note about the famous Budapest Quartet, that its members, the brothers Alexander and Mischa Schneider, Joseph Roisman and Boris Kroit, had very little contact with one another outside rehearsals, that they kept apart when they were in New York and on other tours and addressed each other formally – although they played music together for many years.

"The members of the trio were closely linked by warm human bonds especially father and Sviatoslav Knuschewizki. Their relationship was nothing like the formality in the Budapest Quartet.

'I can't remember when we first met,' father wrote of Knuschewizki, 'but we immediately called each other by first names. The inner bond was firmly established.'

It was different with Oborin. Father and Lew Nikolayevich had been addressing each other for years in formal manner and only reluctantly became more familiar in speech. However, the musical contact suffered in no way because of this.

I would like to conclude our conversation about father as a chamber musician by quoting his own words:

'I love chamber music very much. It not only gives the listener much pleasure but above all the musicians who are performing it.'"

# The conductor

It was only late in his life, after his fiftieth birthday, that David Oistrakh began to conduct. For how long had he thought about this additional artistic activity?

"The heart's desire to stand at the conductor's desk (it's not exaggerating when I say 'heart's desire') was with father for many years. I have already told you that when he was a child and taken to the Odessa opera, he was always attempting, together with Pribik the conductor, to give the entrance cue to the orchestra. If the boy wasn't allowed to go to the opera with his mother because of his mischief with the violin, he would build his own little theatre at home. Stage design, costumes, lighting, all the things that children are normally interested in about theatre performances didn't interest him much. He would take the piano score of the opera that was being performed that evening (he loved *Carmen* and *Prince Igor* most of all) and began his 'performance' exactly in the minute when the curtain went up in the opera. He'd sing the whole opera alone: the solos, the choir, the orchestra – all the time trying to conduct the 'enormous body of sound'."

Your father was presumably even

then such an unselfish person that he thought little about the audience success and the applause?

"I don't know if there was applause. He certainly had an audience: father's grandmother, his sole, but faithful admirer at the time. It was also her job to arrange a buffet, as the little boy drank tea after each act.

Father used to talk about this jokingly, but I am sure that his 'home-made' theatre meant more to him than just a childish way of passing the time."

Just like his frequent visits to the Odessa opera. I don't know if you share my opinion, but it always seemed to me when I thought about the reasons why David Oistrakh became a conductor, that he was longing for a greater range of sound than even his own violin could give him. He was in love with the orchestra, he couldn't stay calm, just like Hector Berlioz who couldn't stay calm when he heard an orchestra playing; he would have arranged his own *Soirées de l'orchestre* just like the French composer.

"I would like to take advantage of this opportunity to say that father valued Berlioz very highly and liked to listen to his composi-tions."

I find this attraction quite easy to explain in view of the inner similarity between the two musicians. I remember one evening in Pärnu, the Estonian town, David Oistrakh spoke with great warmth about Berlioz whose music we had just been listening to in your house.

" 'The strongest unforgettable musical experience in my early childhood,' David Oistrakh wrote, 'was when I heard the symphony orchestra in the opera for the first time. The feeling of a "miracle of sound" will never leave me.' "

From his earliest youth, Oistrakh had desired 'to play with the orchestra', initially subconsciously, as with the 'miracle of sound', later however, more and more conciously and distinctly. This wish later developed into the intent of being artistically active and to express his own ego in music. However, Oistrakh's interpretations were that much more individualistic the less he tried to force his own personality on the performed piece, as Kurt Blaukopf pertinently mentioned at the time.

"Many of the violinist's admirers asked themselves the question, when he started to conduct, to which branch of art he would finally decide to go: to play the violin or to conduct. Few people could regard the second activity as the natural consequence of the first. They assumed he would neglect the violin. I can remember exactly how angry father was when in 1968 he read in a Paris newspaper that he was supposed to have said in an interview to a certain Mr Kaufmann that he wanted to part with the violin. He published a denial in the newspaper with the help of some of his French friends and especially of Georges Soria, the impresario of the Soviet artists in France.

He said, with ironical reference to the article in the Parisian paper, in an interview with K. Adam entitled 'Violin or Baton' in 1968: 'I will remain faithful to the violin as long as I can play and no bad arthritic bone in my little finger puts an end to my activities as a soloist.'

As a violinist I know that the violin is merciless to violinists, it demands sacrifices every day. In spite of this, it was not exhaustion that induced father to pick up the baton. The best proof of this were the violin performances in his last fifteen years which didn't throw the slightest shadow on his fame as the

106

most outstanding violinist of his day – they in fact established it even further."

But surely love for the orchestra was not the only cause?

"Father said something about this point: 'Conducting is more than a pleasure for me, more than just a relaxation from a habit; it widens one's point of view, provides new challenges, enables one to discover new worlds! And what can be more beautiful than discovering something new even in one's old age?' "

Although David Oistrakh always tried to enlarge his violin repertoire and to contribute to the wider distribution of works by Soviet composers, it was quite understandable that he, the musician of great format, felt the limitations of his violin repertoire which blocked his path to the unlimited wealth of music. This is the reason for the joy which he expressed in many letters during the 1960s about his breakthrough into the macrocosm of great music: 'My concerts as conductor in La Scala were brilliantly successful. The hall was overcrowded each time and I got general recognition. I am of course very happy, although I have to work like a devil and I am very tired. The satisfaction I get from this work has a much better effect on me than any medicine (surely only a temporary effect and one with "limited liability").'

David Oistrakh wrote this to a friend shortly after he had started to work again following the interruption of his artistic career due to his heart attack.

'I don't feel too bad at the moment and I am again giving concerts,' he wrote to Yehudi Menuhin. 'I derived tremendous pleasure from two performances in which I conducted Mahler's 4th Symphony and Brahm's 3rd Symphony. I literally bathed in the indescribable beauty of these two chefs-d'oeuvre.'

But David Oistrakh gave the best formulation of his feelings at an interview when he explained that conducting gave him the feeling of having swum in a beautiful river with beautiful banks, but that having now reached the open sea, the shore has stepped back and given him a view of the infinity of the elements.

"One can only marvel at how father carried his heart's desire with him for so long as until 1960, the date of his official début as a conductor. Since I know how much artistic pleasure conducting gave father, I can understand how much will-power he had to have not to step much earlier onto the conductor's platform."

What finally stimulated David Oistrakh to start conducting? He had surely never been taught . . .

" . . . If you ignore the really important conductors with whom father appeared as violinist during that period. These were: Oskar Fried, Otto Klemperer, Karl Böhm, Hermann Abendroth, Herbert von Karajan, Charles Münch, Dimitri Mitropoulos, Eugene Ormandy, Alexander Gauk, Eugene Mravinsky, Evgeny Svetlanov, Gennadi Roshdestvensky, Kyril Kondrashin . . . perhaps it would have been easier to list those conductors with whom father did not appear on the concert platform or in the recording studios of almost all the country in the world."

Oistrakh had other teachers, the orchestra musicians. Their contribution to music culture, which at a glance appears modest, is in reality very important and was valued very highly by Oistrakh when he began to conduct.

" 'It was once in Pärnu,' Regina Horowitz remembers, 'where I was the unintentional witness of a friendly improvised lesson. I had attended Oistrakh's lessons before, but this one was remarkable because this time David Feodorovich was the "pupil". A Moscow orchestra player was "teacher", and he explained the advantages of some of his gestures as a conductor and the uselessness of others.'

This interesting side of father is very typical.

I am of the opinion that the affection which father enjoyed from all orchestra musicians in different countries substantially contributed to the success of his career as a conductor. You once mentioned in our discussions that the orchestra musicians are the most critical judges of soloists and conductors. The orchestra feels immediately what sort of a musician it has before it. It virtually x-rays him and draws its own conclusions. An orchestra can play technically perfectly and correctly but without feeling and then everything is lost. No orchestra remained indifferent under father's baton. He had a great feeling for tact and knew how to use friendly words. If something didn't turn out right at a rehearsal, he knew how to loosen the atmosphere with a joke. I often heard the opinion of orchestra musicians that this conductor radiated kindness. They were unanimous about this."

I don't think that it was just patience and tact in David Oistrakh's approach to the orchestra. It was more likely the charm of his personality as an artist and the peculiarity of his style which made the orchestra players and the strings in the first row surpass themselves by trying to copy David Oistrakh's violin.

Charles Bruck told me that his teacher Pierre Monteux always advised him not to conduct for the public, but for the orchestra musicians. This got rid of all mannerisms and all poses and the understanding was 100%. David Oistrakh conducted for the orchestra player.

" 'The orchestra players of the French Radio and TV have never played so well!' a critic wrote in the Paris *Figaro*. 'How could they deny their great colleague their very best, who also gave them his best?'

It is true that the orchestra sounded different when father stood on the rostrum. The basses gained depth and had an unusual intensity. I read press reviews in which his orchestra was compared with that

108

of Fürtwangler, Barbirolli and Bernstein."

Did Oistrakh pay attention to the scores of the strings during the rehearsals? Did he mark them?

"Yes, he regarded it as his duty to mark the appropriate strokes. This took him a long time at first, but as the programs were repeated it was only a question of marking the bowing which was tried and tested as well as his own bowing."

What music did Oistrakh conduct most frequently?

"Mozart, Weber, Schubert, Brahms, Tchaikovsky, Mahler . . . Father said in 1970: 'My repertoire as a conductor concentrates mainly on the classic and romantic school as well as on contemporary Russian composers. I am particularly attracted to Prokofiev and Shostakovich.'

Father's interpretations as conductor increased the listener's understanding of the romantic works of Weber, Schubert and Brahms, which were particularly dear to him. It is characteristic that in our time, which is occasionally called the age of rationalism, the interpretation of the romantics becomes for many musicians and particularly for the younger ones a matter of distaste, although they are

at an age which should be open to the romantic. However, the manner in which father conducted Weber's *Oberon*, Schubert's 2nd or Brahms' 2nd Symphony was fascinating by the remarkable freshness of feeling and by the natural way in which the musical thought flowed."

It was a brave decision of David Oistrakh to conduct the Brahms in Paris. Brahms is a composer who is not a favourite of the French audiences. However, the way that Brahms' 2nd Symphony sounded under David Oistrakh's baton can be read in the following press review:

'In his sincere effort to transmit the music as well as possible, he made the Symphony appear in a light which was completely free from the "taboos" which so often darken it. To put it another way: instead of dramatizing the Symphony, he transmitted its gentleness, its brilliance, its "forest air" and he didn't even avoid letting the intimate expressions of the sensitive poet, which Brahms was, come through in the careless peace of the second movement.'

Brahms is a sort of guiding star in David Oistrakh's career as a conductor. It shone for him already in 1960 when he accompanied you at

the recording of Brahms' Violin Concerto and again at the Vienna Music Festival when he performed the Brahms Cycle in four programs.

"The performance during the weeks of Vienna Festival in 'Brahms' town' was the greatest my father ever had as a conductor. It was proof of his recognition as a conductor.

'The Great Hall of the Vienna *Musikverein*, the place for the great Viennese concert events since the days of Brahms, Bruckner and Mahler, has rarely in the last few years experienced such enthusiasm as after the four concerts of the Brahms Cycle which David Oistrakh conducted in the frame of the festival weeks in 1968', wrote the journal *Fono-forum*.

As a listener and participant in the cycle I can confirm that the critics weren't exaggerating."

How did David Oistrakh prepare himself for his appearances as a conductor?

"Father studied the scores, didn't even part with them during holidays, marked them with symbols and comments and listened to many recordings of the compositions with different interpretations."

Couldn't his listening to other conductors' interpretations become

*Studying a score*

a burden which influenced his own interpretation and by this the development and expression of his interpretation?

"When I had done something wrong as a child and was scolded by my mother and then when father (unaware of mother's words) had told me off and corrected me in a different way, mother complained: 'This is how you undermine my authority in Igor's eyes.' 'If authority is so easily undermined then it simply does not exist,' father replied.

It is impossible in art to make abstractions from everything that has preceded - reproductive art is no exception. Only someone who hasn't got his own concepts is afraid of others. I repeat that father listened to many recordings, he certainly learnt a lot from them, but he passed everything he had heard through the prism of his own artist's personality. The important point is that the depth and seriousness of father's interpretations, irrespective of whether he used the violin or the baton, primarily relied on the exact reproduction of the score and the exact obeying of the composer's will.

'David Oistrakh attempts to be an honest transmitter of music,' we can read in the already quoted contribution ... 'Violin or Baton?' ... by K. Adam. 'The fact that a "rest" is no less music to him than for instance the moving song of the strings in the Coda of the first movement of Brahms' 2nd Symphony. Oistrakh doesn't want to conduct his interpretation of Brahms, but Brahms himself.'

Another opinion, which is even more valuable since it comes from the outstanding conductor and musician George Szell. He writes in a letter to father:

'I am happy that your Brahms Cycle in Vienna was such an outstanding success. I had heard of it before your letter reached me and I also read about it in the papers. Franz Walter the critic wrote about your performance in the *Journal de Genève*: "When one hears such a performance one no longer thinks about the interpretation or reception - one just feels that that's the way it must sound and not differently! This is undoubtedly the highest praise that an intelligent critic can give." '

A few more personal impressions which father's way of conducting had on me: I often didn't hear him in the hall but on the concert platform where I played the violin with him conducting. I couldn't imagine a more ideal accompanist than father. It was extremely easy to play with him since he conducted as simply and naturally as he played the violin. In considering other aspects of his style as a conductor I would first of all like to mention his excellent feeling for form, his feeling for harmony of proportions, the precise polish of all details of the score and the plasticity of the lines which finally lead to the culmination and to a resolving conclusion. Finally his ability to make both audience and orchestra feel the character of the composition already after the first few bars. Father's way of conducting combined gentleness with willpower and strength."

Could your father have been a chief conductor of an orchestra as far as his character is concerned?

"Oh, no. I was just talking talking purely of artistic strength. Father himself admitted that his character lacked the necessary complex of qualities which is essential for a successful activity as chief conductor. He would never have applied for such a post."

Did your father ever say which orchestras were easier and more pleasant to conduct - top orchestras or medium orchestras?

"Father always insisted that the 'easier and more pleasant' are not suitable terms in this case. Conducting outstanding orchestras was according to him a more pleasant but more difficult job, since they played in such a way from the first rehearsal that it was totally superfluous to study the score with them. Knowing how to fill three or four full rehearsals, that is the main problem as one has to concentrate only on problems of interpretation,

without for one moment forgetting that on the same day not only 'barbeaters' but great musicians will stand on the same rostrum, many of which can also be found in the orchestra."

The opera made many strong artistic impressions on David Oistrakh in his childhood. Did he remain faithful to his love of opera?

"Undoubtedly. Mother can confirm with what pleasure and self-indulgence father abandoned himself to the music at an opera performance. His greatest operatic experiences were: the Moscow first performance of Shostakovich's *Katerina Izmailovna* in the Stanislavsky - Nemirovich - Danchenko Music Theatre, Tchaikovsky's *Eugen Onegin* at the Bolshoi Theatre, Verdi's *Othello* under Karajan in Salzburg, Puccini's *Turandot* with Birgit Nilsson playing the main part in Milan, Verdi's *Simone Boccanegra* with the young Abbado conducting.

It was suggested in several countries that he should conduct an opera himself. The problem in each case being lack of time. In order to study an opera one has to stay in one city for at least two weeks uninterruptedly. Furthermore one would have to conduct it even after

*Igor Oistrakh with his father conducting*

its first performance for several more evenings. One of the offers was so tempting that father forgot all difficulties and gave his consent. We however know the sad ending of the performance of *Eugen Onegin.'*

I would like to conclude our conversation about Oistrakh the conductor with his own words, which as always originate from his modesty and sense of humour: 'As a violinist I have many rivals, but as a conductor - none at all!'

111

# The teacher

April 4, 1975 in the Great Hall of the Moscow Conservatory. The program reads: Memorial evening for Professor David Feodorovich Oistrakh. Violinists - David Oistrakh's students, 1st Prize winners of international competitions: Igor Oistrakh, Valeri Klimnow, Semjon Snitkowski, Viktor Pikeisen, Rosa Fain, Oleg Kryssa, Gidon Kremer, Oleg Kagan, Liana Isakadse, Michail Sekler, Olga Parchomenko, Jean Ter-Mergerjan (the last two were ill). All stars in the violinist's sky! What an extraordinary multitude of artistic individuality! A worthy crown for the forty years of teaching activity of the great violinist David Oistrakh.

What did your father tell you about the beginning of his work at the Conservatory?

"Not really very much. He got the offer to teach at the Conservatory from the director, Professor Alexander Goldenweiser in 1934. Goldenweiser relied on father's abilities and entrusted him with a violin class at the Moscow Conservatory where famous violin teachers and violinists were teaching: Abram Jampolski, Lew Zeitlin (the director of the unique symphony orchestra without conductor which was called Persimfans) and Konstantin Mostras. Father played repeatedly in sonata concerts with Goldenweiser whom he greatly admired and whose stories about meetings with Lew Tolstoi in Jasnaja Poljana he enjoyed listening to. Father became a lecturer at the Conservatory as early as 1934, Professor in 1938 and has held a Professorial Chair since 1950."

What was the relationship between Oistrakh and his elder colleagues like?

"I can remember more clearly the times when father's fame as a virtuoso and teacher wiped out the age difference between himself and Abram Jampolski for example, the creater of a whole school and teacher of many Soviet violinists. However, I know from father that their friendship, which I witnessed in the 1940s and 1950s, went back to a much earlier date. Certainly, father's high opinion of Jampolski, Zeitlin and Mostras contributed to this in no small way. As I told you before, father already visited the classes of these professors in his first years after moving to Moscow and in addition to the art of violin playing also acquired some of the secrets of their outstanding teaching skills.

In 1937 Jampolski was a member of the jury at the International Eugene Ysaye Competition in Brussels and was one of the judges who gave David Oistrakh the 1st Prize."

What was David Oistrakh's attitude to his work at the Conservatory? Didn't it become a burden for him since his concert activity increased continuously?

"This question can hardly be

answered with a yes or a no. I have myself after all taught for seventeen years at the Conservatory and I would be dishonest if I said that this work didn't demand much strength and time, which one really needs for practising on the violin. The students differed greatly and so did the feelings which teaching them created. Sometimes I left the class depressed as I thought that all my efforts were wasted. However, already on the following day a student produced an interesting interpretation of the Brahms Concerto or of an Ysaye Sonata and the mood immediately improved."
Your father was presumably also sometimes subject to such variations in mood? In a letter he confessed:

'The Conservatory bothers me as much as it can - the continuous turmoil with the competitions, with the selections and everything connected with it robs me of any possibility of working in peace in a concentrated way.'

"The problem of competitions,

*Teacher among teachers: the Professors and specialists of the Moscow Conservatory violin classes, represented by Dmitri Zyganow, congratulate David Oistrakh on his 60th birthday*

which has just been mentioned, is important but probably less so in comparison with the continuous work at the Conservatory. We will presumably come back to discussing competitions, particularly as they didn't decrease from 1958, when the words were written which you just quoted. Father complained to me in a letter in 1963: 'I am nowadays harassed in the Conservatory. At 3 p.m. tomorrow, the Competition for Paris starts, to be followed by the examination for the Competition for Genoa.' All this doesn't exclude father's positive conscious attitude to teaching which not only helped the many candidates who crowded into his class (he never complained about a shortage of students), but also helped himself. He often spoke and wrote about this:

'The mature musician has to communicate his experience to the younger generation. That is his sacred duty. The teaching activity is a sort of 'artistic laboratory', which is in my opinion of great value to the concert artist. In dealing with talented young people and carefully following the development of young musicians one finds the answers to questions which are posed during one's work.

113

Sometimes you can see that the student has consciously or unconsciously solved a problem about which you yourself have more than once worried. New experiences gradually build up in this way and this has a favourable effect on one's own art in the end. The standard of our young violinists is so high that frequent contact with them also gives the teacher new impulses. Youth is very sensitive. It watches the work of its teachers with a critical eye and if you don't want to be left behind you have to advance intensively and consistently.

I am convinced that, If my performances matured from 1934 on, it was also partly due to my teaching activity.'"

On this occasion David Oistrakh once more expresses his ideas very

*The teachers of the Music Conservatory during the war. From left to right: Lew Oborin, Alexander Gedicke, Constantin Igumnov, Wissarion Schabalin, Nikolai Miaskovsky, David Oistrakh*

precisely. Always with the great modesty which was so characteristic of him. The fact that this modesty was not just an act can be seen from the many notes which he made during international competitions where he was a member of the jury. In contrast to the varied contributions at interviews he wrote these notes entirely for himself. Oistrakh didn't keep a diary – he hardly had time to note down all the appointments for performances and their programs. His notes at competitions

are therefore of particular interest. In them we find more concrete information and confirmation of those general ideas which you have just mentioned. Let me give a few examples. At the Queen Elisabeth Competition in Brussels in 1959 Duchamps (from France) played Lalo's *Spanish Symphony*. Listening to the fifth movement Oistrakh notes: 'Good tempo. I am now convinced that my own tempo is correct.' The next competitor played Beethoven's Violin Concerto, but not too well. Oistrakh writes: 'The first movement. A Woodcutter. Fell asleep. Woke up. Thank God I didn't hear a few pages.'

However, even here the judge (who had won the laurels in the same competition about two decades earlier) noted down a few interesting details for himself and kept them in mind: 'Take note.'

Since we have now again returned to the subject of competitions we should first of all answer the question, how important competitions really were to David Oistrakh.

"I agree. Particularly as the words quoted about the turmoil of the competitions could give the impression that he was an opponent of international competitions. No, he wasn't an opponent – neither when he himself took part in competitions, although it meant an extraordinary nervous strain for him (I remind you of his letters from Brussels in 1937), nor later when he sat with the jury, although even that took a lot of energy and valuable time."

I recently read in Genrich Neuhaus' autobiographical notes that he fell ill after every competition in which he was a member of the jury. *'Cela donne à penser,'* concludes Neuhaus.

"Father was not unaware of the fact that the increased number of competitions and a students participation in two, sometimes three such events, would not always help his studying at the Conservatory. It could even inhibit it. This was the 'turmoil' which he was fighting against. Father furthermore disagreed with the theory that an artist's career is entirely determined by his success at competitions."

The value of international music competitions has been discussed for a long time in many countries. Many participants in such discussions take part in competitions, others refuse to do so. Father would never tolerate it when musical competitions turned into sporting events.

" 'I basically don't suppport the idea of musical competitions,' he stressed in one of his letters, 'as I consider the "sporting" element as foreign matter in art, which could lead to its downfall. The only permitted form of competition in the area of artistic presentation is competition with oneself, the fight against one's own deficiencies, against one's usual mistakes which are natural and unavoidable. This form of competition is in essence noble and in addition valuable and pleasant.' "

Since even the most pronounced opponents of competitions are unable to suggest a rational system for determining young talent, it seems that competitions are for the time being the only method. However, according to David Oistrakh's opinion, they should be used carefully. He had particular respect for certain competitions such as the Moscow Violin Competition:

" 'The International Tchaikovsky Competition is one of the most difficult that I know,' he wrote. 'This applies not only to the complexity of the program but also to the stylistic variety of the compositions in it.'

He also asked his students to take

*Oistrakh before the draw of the participants of the 2nd International Tchaikovsky Competition 1962*

advantage of the competitions:

' ... Not only to gain external success but also for their own future artistic development, about which one never has the last word (fortunately for true art!).' "

Obviously none of the many Oistrakh students were sent to a competition if the teacher wasn't convinced that it was of value to the student. We here again return to Oistrakh the teacher. How did he work with his students?

"In a very calm and considerate way. Father had many different students in his class, not just prize winners. In spite of this the atmosphere never changed. Father didn't seem to get tired of teaching. He was always alert and awake as were his receptivity and friendly humour, which were occasionally coloured with a touch of friendly irony. He above all always remained in top violinistic shape. I was often amazed when father picked up the violin after six or even eight hours teaching. He showed the students how one or another passage should be played with great mastery and without previous rehearsal."

Not all teachers use the instructive method of playing themselves, as they are afraid that the students could slip into mere imitation.

"Father wasn't afraid of this. His open violin case always lay on a table in the classrooom. He liked to play during the years when I was at the Conservatory. This performing in the class was always effective. Particularly when it was a question of technique, such as bowing or fingering."

Many people imagine the teaching in David Oistrakh's class to have been a sort of academy of the art of violin playing, a sort of master class. Surely he didn't avoid trying to improve the playing technique of his students?

"Obviously problems of pure musical interpretation dominated in the class, but father was always trying to ensure that absolute technical perfection would free his students from all technical worries during playing. In order to achieve this perfection, not a single technical mistake was overlooked."

And what, in his opinion, were the main technical demands which had to be fulfilled before one could turn to the finesse of interpretation?

"Irrespective of which type of style and music the piece belonged to, father's main demand was always exemplary intonation, perfection of rhythm and a soft natural unforced tone quality. According to father's opinion, these are the three pillars on which violin playing is based."

I here remember again the notes which your father made at the competitions. When he listened, he applied the same rules as when he was teaching. Because his notes contain several interesting thoughts and observations let us quote some of them; first some critical comments:

'Right and left hand are not well synchronized.'
'Bad balance of the bow.'

'Each note overemphasized.'
'Uninteresting sound.'
'Dirty. Everything blurred.'
'Too much glissandi.'
'Too much sighing and rustling.'
'Very square playing.'
'Primitive phrasing.'
'Colourless and impersonal.'
'A good violinist, but rather dry playing.'
'Pathos, but without greatness, without power.'
'Professorial playing. A scientific collaborator.'
'Play it back! Wipe it off the tape!'

"Father was exactly the same in class: if, for example, he advised more use of the lower positions in the playing of Bach's works or to be as sparing as possible with the vibrato in Mozart, then it wasn't always possible to separate the technical and the interpretory elements. Everything formed a complete indivisible unity maximizing the penetration into the musical content. This is also shown by his positive complimentary notes at competitions, even when they are taken out of context:
'Powerful.'
'Daring, active.'
'Sovereign!'
'Great initiative.'
'There is technique in the music.'

'Rhythmical, conscious rhythm.'
'Very lively phrasing.'
'Warmth and feeling.'
'Precise, interesting.'
'Mature, playing full of style.'
'Exemplary behaviour on stage.'
'Good self-control.'
'The playing forces one to listen.'

I would particularly like to comment on his note 'There is technique in the music.' There is in addition an outstanding part of a letter: 'Take care in your work and observe the sound and technique in the cantilena. Let me warn you about the usual tendency for superfluous glissandi, make an effort to solve technical problems not just in a straightforward manner, always look for the possibility of playing the material as full of music and meaning as possible.' "

Let's go back to the teaching in Oistrakh's class. Did he listen to the musical pieces which a student brought for the first time? What was the most important thing for him?

"Father's principle, which I also acquired as soon as I began to teach, was based on the following: never to rob the student of his courage with a flood of comments, but to let him play the whole piece and to listen to himself; to strengthen his faith in his own ability to reproduce the whole work (even if much didn't succeed at that moment), and finally not to hurt his pride as an artist."

If you consider that Oistrakh's classes were always well attended – in addition to his own people (students and aspirants) there were also 'foreigners' present (violinists from other classes, musicians from other countries and cities) – you can understand how much depended on not robbing the student of his inner composure.

*Lesson with Stojka Milanowa*

" 'It was a very modest man who sat with his violin on the small settee in the class,' remembers Leonid Kogan, Professor at the Moscow Conservatory, who often attended Oistrakh's lessons. That was certainly true and because of that we didn't take much notice of the visitors to our class.

Grażyna Bacewicz, a Polish violinist and composer whom father had known since the Warsaw Competition in 1935, told us about his unusual method of teaching; in doing so she described her impressions of his lessons at the Conservatory:

'A young French girl came to the lessons, her nervosity was quite noticeable. David politely asked how she was, looked to see if her hands were warm and joked a little.

Even a bad physiognomist would have noticed immediately that the young violinist's nervosity disappeared with each of his words. She was already quite calm when she began to play.

The task was to play an old Italian sonata.

I waited for the moment when David would interrupt the violinist (Flesch always used to do this), but this moment never came.

The student played the whole sonata to its end, David listened with the greatest attention. When she had finished he said: 'Great, wonderful, you are making tremendous progress. You improved the intonation, enriched the dynamics and the chords don't sound as dull as before, etc.'

The joy visible on the girl's face increased with each minute. Because the very flattering comments lasted for quite a long time her happiness grew immensely. As soon as the girl felt she was a true violinist, David began to criticize:

'I have discovered a few weaknesses,' and he then proceeded to analyse the sonata bar by bar.

He talked about the style, phrasing, rhythm and demonstrated after each remark how to eliminate the mistakes of which there were thousands.

The violinist followed every word intently, but her happy mood didn't leave her as the master's tone didn't lose any of its warmth in spite of the substantial corrections. You got the feeling that the challenge to overcome these 'unimportant' mistakes would not only give the violinist the greatest satisfaction but it would also increase her faith in her own ability.

What an ingenious method, I thought, above all unartificial, stemming from Oistrakh's character, and entirely natural. Well, this method is extremely difficult in spite of its simplicity. To be able to employ it, one had to have King David's kindness and wisdom.'

Problems of good taste were always in our class. Father dismissed exaggerated glissandi (portamenti), the everflowing of temperament. He dismissed everthing that broke the framework of ideal harmony which characterized his own playing and therefore appeared to him to be so simple to achieve."

David Feodorovich's thoughts about the individuality of the musician are important in relation to this:

" 'I don't consider the term "individuality" as something original or special. Individuality is the most natural thing in the world. It is the "truth" of life, simplicity, kindness, which in its heavenly harmony is radiated by her majesty MUSICA in unique beauty.' "

What can be said about the effect your father had on his students?

"I find it difficult to answer this question. I can only say that father impressed us all with the weight and charm of his personality both as man and musician. It was not by chance that the relationship between the professor and many of his students such as Viktor Pikeisen, Valeri Klimow, Semjon Snitkowski, Gidon Kremer, Oleg Kryssa, Oleg Kagan, Liana Isakadse, went beyond the usual teacher-student relationship. They communicated with each other as musicians, colleagues and friends. This comradely relationship was based above all on father's faith in the student."

A faith which extended equally to professional as well as human abilities. When Oistrakh set his students certain tasks, which were

*Oistrakh and students Valari Klimow, Viktor Pikeisen, Igor Oistrakh*

so complicated that additional stimulus was intended, when he tried to stimulate the creative potency of each sutdent by supporting his desire to play a certain piece or to compose his own cadenza to a certain classical concerto, this was when he believed in the professional ability of his student. He relied on his own personal qualities when he allowed himself to praise his student verbally or in writing. Behind this trust lay the conviction of the experienced teacher: The student will not fail, even in difficult passages, nor will he despair, on the other hand he will neither get too big headed. It was also important that the relationship between student and teacher lasted a long time as David Oistrakh had met many of his students long before they studied at the Moscow Conservatory. Wherever he appeared, as a guest performer in the Soviet Union or in foreign countries, talented young violinists were always introduced to him. Oistrakh was always prepared to listen to them and give them advice and recommendations.

"Forgive me for interrupting you, but I would like to add that father, who didn't think much of child prodigies, was at the time fascinated by the playing of the little Vitja Pikeisen whom he heard in Kiev. He said in conclusion: 'I predict a great future as a violinist for this youngster.' He wasn't wrong. Pikeisen was the only student whom father really taught before joining the Conservatory (in the Gnessin School of Music). He holds the record as far as the number of years under father's tuition is concerned: fifteen years! Pikeisen was the five times prize winner at international competitions (he for instance won the 1st Prize at the Paganini Competition in Genoa) and was one of the violinists who have brought honour to the Soviet violin school in and outside our borders.

Father's remarkable ability to discover talented musicians long before they passed through his school is shown by the many comments he made at competitions. When he heard the Turkish violinist Aila Erduran in Brussels in 1955 he commented: 'nineteen years old. Gifted girl ... A child of nature. An unpolished jewel but

*119*

devilishly talented. She still has many faults but it is impossible to ignore her.'

You talked earlier of father's long acquaintance with many of his students. Although this fact was partly responsible for the atmosphere in our class, it was not really decisive. Something else was decisive: the steady, I would even say moving attention which father paid to his students, joy at their success, sadness at their failure. He knew and treated his students as if they were his own children and

*With Viktor Pikeisen*

loved them like a father. He was fully absorbed with them and they regarded his house as 'theirs'. 'He inspired his students as artists and they loved him as a human being,' the Czech violinist Alexander Plocek wrote in his memoirs."

Extracts from David Oistrakh's letters confirm this. Written from all possible countries in the world during demanding tours, they bear witness to his concern for his class in general and for each student in particular:

Tokyo, 1955, To Igor Oistrakh:
'I am very worried as to how my candidates for competitions are getting on, above all Linie Vitja and Klimow. How are they working? Tell them something about my concern.'

"I would like to point out that neither of them needed my admonitions. Both Viktor Pikeisen as well as Valeri Klimow worked to their best ability and conscience and soon afterwards won at the Tchaikovsky Competition."

A few more extracts from letters:
New York, 1970. To Oleg Kagan:
'I have unfortunately received hardly any news of what is hap-

pening in the class. I have only had letters from Gidon (Kremer) and Peter Guth. I know the results of the competition in Riga and have heard about the elimination test for the Tchaikovsky Competition in Moscow.

I am worried about your problems, whether everything is alright, whether you are playing, where you are playing, etc. I can't wait to get back to Moscow, I worry about everyone and everything.'

Amsterdam, 1972. To Ljuba Kormout:
'I am nervous because I haven't seen my students all autumn. If only you knew how sad their little eyes become as soon as they hear that I have to leave them again . . .'

"It also happened quite often that father, having arrived back in Moscow after a long tour, interrupted his concert activity and devoted himself entirely to the students (for instance in 1962 after his American tour).

Another trait which distinguished father as a teacher and which we can't ignore is his objective judgement of his students as well as of concert artists in general.

'He was as just as a prophet,'

Alexander Plocek said, who quite often sat next to father in the jury. 'He also knew how to value the playing of a violinist whose style differed from that of the Moscow school provided of course that the performance was convincing and that it showed true talent. Oistrakh was a noble character. I still remember that he knew how to comfort those violinists for whom the competition was prematurely over.'

*During a student evening David Oistrakh's class ask for their teacher to come on the stage*

Leonid Kogan talks about him with the same enthusiasm: 'I remember David Feodorovich at the Tchaikovsky Competition and the young violinists who had been eliminated in the the last round. He spoke so politely and with such passion that I had tears in my eyes. He explained to them what they had to do in order to perform more successfully the next time. He didn't spread honey on the wound and spoke with them just like a father. I shall remember Oistrakh's speech to the new generation of violinists for a long time.' "
There is also an extract from a letter from Oistrakh to his friend the physician and Professor Krakowski concerning this:

'How much it costs me to comfort those who failed in the competition! I imagine this to be similar to the sad duty of a doctor who has to tell a patient's close relatives that nothing else can be done for him.'
This sympathy didn't however stop him from judging the achievements of his violinists in an unprejudiced way. He was of course very happy at his students' success and at the achievements of Soviet participants in competitions. This never barred

his sight from the failure of his 'protégés' and from the successes of their rivals.
The most dangerous competitor for the Soviet participants at the Queen Elisabeth Competition in Brussels in 1955 (Viktor Pikeisen, Igor Politkowski, Marina Jaschwili and Julian Sitkowezki, the first two being students of Oistrakh) was from the start the American Berl Senowski, who then went on to win the 1st Prize. David Feodorovich immediately remarked: 'An extremely dangerous rival!' which didn't stop him from having a high opinion of Senowski's playing. Now a note after the first round: 'First class violin playing. Very mature, an exceptionally pleasant sound, wonderful phrasing, very lively and full of style.'
This note concerned the performance of an adagio by Bach. He simply wrote: 'Marvellous!' about the following fugue.
Several violinists who were quite rightly fighting for the first places in the Tchaikovsky Competition in Moscow in 1966 were involved in a bitter battle. Two of them were Oistrakh students: Oleg Kryssa and Oleg Kagan. Their rivals were: the American Erich Friedmann, the Japanese lady Masuko Ushioda and

*121*

- the most dangerous - Victor Tretyakov, a pupil of Juri Jankelewitsch, Professor at the Moscow Conservatory. David Oistrakhs' note after Tretyakov, the future victor, had played the program in the first round was: 'This is perhaps the most attractive and the most sincere talent which I have ever come across in the Soviet Union.'

"Many foreigners also studied under father's guidance. Very many young foreign musicians would have wanted to be trained at the Moscow Conservatory and particularly in father's class. The students who entered class no. 8 for the first time were very excited. Already after a short time they would feel like that French girl whom Grażyna Bacewicz described in her memoirs: they felt at home with the circle of friends formed by father's students. Their nervosity disappeared. They listened to their teacher's every word, followed each of his instructions, didn't miss one of his concerts and, above all, they made great progress in their violin playing."
Which of these students would you like to mention?

"Preferably almost all who studied with father at different times. Particularly the Rumanian violinists Jon Voicu and Stefan Georghui, the Bulgarians Bojan Letschew and Stoika Milanowa, the Czech Václav Hudeček, the Pole Kaja Dańciewska, the Iranian Ali Forough, we have just mentioned the Turk Aila Erduran, Gustav Schmahl the violinist from the German Democratic Republic, Peter Guth the Austrian, Michele Boussino and Danielle Arture (both French), Evelio Tieles the Cuban, the Dutch lady Emmi Werhej." When and where did your father meet Václav Hudeček?

"Father and I were on a tour in London in 1968. Victor Hochhauser, an old friend and impresario for our English concerts drew father's attention to a talented young violinist from Czechoslovakia who was giving his début in London. Father was enchanted by Václav's artistic ability and admired the way in which he mastered the instrument. Václav's parents asked father to teach their son.

The fact that Václav didn't disappoint father - the teaching was more in the form of consultations - proved the high standard of his talent and application as shown in many letters and statements.

I can also add that I met Václav at the 30th 'Spring in Prague' in May 1975. I took part in the final concert in which father, at the request of the organizers, should have conducted Beethoven's Ninth. Bach's Concerto for Two Violins with Orchestra was included in the program after Beethoven's Symphony under Arvid Jansons' baton, for the first time in the history of the 'Springs'. I played the concerto with Václav Hudeček and we dedicated our performance to my father's memory. The joint performance with Václav gave me great artistic pleasure.

During the autumn of the same year a week of Czech music took place in Moscow. Václav Hudeček played on the stage of the Kremlin Congress Palace, whilst one could at the same time see (on the wall behind the stage) a film showing fragments of a lesson given by David Oistrakh to the violinist from Prague. The effect was extraordinary, one got the impression that the performance was an expression of gratitude which Václav paid his teacher.

Almost all his students nowadays show their gratitude. Before we quote some of these, let's listen to the words of Vladimirovna

Kollegorskaja, the permanent pianist of our class:

'I have been incredibly lucky. For 31 years - from 1943 till 1974 - I was the permanent accompanist to David Oistrakh's students. I witnessed his many successes as interpreter and teacher. Oistrakh could not be equalled as a violinist and he also gave everything he had when he taught. He worked with enthusiasm and great devotion. Whatever he said was of extraordinary value for young people. Although David Feodorovich was reserved and laconic, he could literally with just a few words shape the view of his class about the interpretation of a specific composition. When he held an instrument in his hand everything became quite simple. During the many years of my work with David Oistrakh his voice never sounded irritated. The atmosphere at the lessons was always uninhibited and friendly. I have learnt a great deal from David Feodorovich as a musician. I am most grateful to him for this. I treasure his interpretations in my memory.'

Inna Vladimirovna performed with many of us students as well as with father himself quite often outside the Conservatory. She played with Valeri Klimow and Viktor Pikeisen, with Liana Isakadse and with me, she accompanied us at the elimination battles as well as on tours. A faithful travel companion in our musical creative work, our friend, our adviser, our ally.

And now let David Oistrakh's students have a word:

Viktor Pikeisen: 'The years when I studied in Oistrakh's class are for me the most memorable in my life. It is impossible to talk of Oistrakh exclusively as a teacher since the different aspects of his manifold artistic activities were organically interwoven. The most important thing that David Feodorovich taught us was to always start with the content of the music when interpreting it. He was an enemy of any liberties in a performance. He taught us truth in art.'

Valeri Klimow: 'The enthusiasm for David Oistrakh's art lived in me already when I was a child when he played in our home town of Odessa with my father conducting. Alexander Klimow was director of the local symphony orchestra at the time. It is in the nature of things that my later impression of Oistrakh the teacher surpassed my earlier enthusiasm. To be more accurate it multiplied it. In my opinion, Oistrakh's most important advantage as a teacher was that he conversed with us students in the language of music. Any detail which he had to specify could induce him to take the violin and play with great inspiration. He sometimes played large passages, sometimes whole sonatas or movements in concertos which his students were studying. How sad that these pearls have never been recorded. It is sometimes said that teachers who often play in class suppress the student's individuality. Quite on the contrary to this, Oistrakh awoke our creative will through his playing.'

Igor Politkowski: 'Oistrakh's pedagogic school was not only a fantastic source for "all secrets" of violin playing, it was a whole university, through which one passed as man, violinist, artist and musician. Sometimes I left the extremely interesting lessons at the Conservatory in a great mood, sometimes I was dissatisfied with myself, but I always left with infinite gratitude for David Feodorovich and was above all convinced that the teacher's advice could be carried out. I stress "advice" because Oistrakh never insisted that his interpretation was the only "true" version. He always allowed the student the possibility of finding his own technical solution or his own interpretative conception.'

Liana Isakadse: 'I had the luck to study in Oistrakh's class for seven years, five years as a student and two years as an "aspirant". However, I first met David Feodorovich when I was ten years old. He heard me play at a competition which took place during the world festival of youth and Moscow students. He followed my development after that with a watchful eye. He was interested in all details of my life, cared not only about my artistic problems but also about my personal ones in an amazingly and surprisingly gentle and unobtrusive way. He cared for me like a father.

The first point which Oistrakh made to me, when I joined his class in 1964, was that I should try to think myself deeper into the interpretation. I only played spontaneously at the time and David Feodorovich had to spend a lot of time with me before I was able to change my intuitive playing into conscious playing. As soon as I began to split hairs he demanded

*David Oistrakh hands over the gold medal to the victor, Gidon Kremer, during the 4th International Tchaikovsky Competition in 1970*

directness from me which he was not prepared to suppress in any way.'

Gidon Kremer: 'A man goes and still remains. Oistrakh is with us every day – with his observations, his attitudes and his smile. He accompanies us in our search, in our experiments and in our problems. There is no eternal life, but perhaps the values of life which will never

be lost lie exactly in this sort of presence, the link with the next generation, the continuation of spiritual life. The constant factor was the unique pleasant atmosphere which David Feodorovich always managed to create. I remember with what excitement I played Beethoven's Kreutzersonate for the first time in the class, a lot went wrong, David Feodorovich's conclusion was quite clear: 'If that is your conception, then it is certainly strange to me.' Even in this moment, when he undoubtedly saw the student's confusion, he demanded an independent, original, but in respect of style musically faultless interpretation. How much wisdom and generosity was in his words: "I would do it differently, but you are right so often . . ." Only a truly generous man could speak this truth to someone and be so happy about his successes.'

Oleg Kagan: 'Today I see myself as clearly as twenty years ago in a queue of violinists which had built up at the stage entrance of the great hall of the Latvian State University in Riga. We are all excited. I am also. To ask David Oistrakh for his autograph. . . Another memory: I, a student of the 9th class in the Central Music School of Moscow, play for the first time in the Hall of Columns in the Trade Union House. A concert for young people. Suddenly I am told that among other masters of the art, David Oistrakh will perform. I was just as proud to appear in the concert and to turn the pages for David Oistrakh's accompanist Frida Bauer. When Boris Kuznetsov, my past teacher, introduced me to David Oistrakh, I asked with embarrassment how one can pull the bow right to it's end during a "piano" without one's hand quivering. . .

I joined David Oistrakh's class for the first time in 1964. The most valuable thing which we students could learn from him was the radiating love of music, the desire to communicate it to everybody. It was no means by chance that the "small première" of the Violin Sonata by Dmitri Shostakovich took place in our class at the Conservatory and was naturally attended by its composer. "Let us remember today," David Feodorovich said to the students at the time, "For we are all witnesses to the birth of an ingenious composition. . ."

Nobody ever wanted to miss David Feodorovich. The feeling of radiating goodness and joy and of being together with him accompanied me all the time.'

Oleg Kryssa: 'When I played to David Feodorovich for the first time in Kiev, I stood out of fear, not in front of the piano but behind it, but only a few words were sufficient to make me forget my excitement. I heard him play in class, also observed him closely and was amazed by the natural way in which he played, the absence of any forced false way, his taste, his exemplary sense for each musical style and the convincing culture.

The teacher demanded exactly the same of his students. If the performance of one of his students lacked one of these fundamental components, David Feodorovich could lose his balance. No, he didn't raise his voice, he didn't make accusations, he simply took his violin and by caricaturing the performance succeeded in making everybody loses the desire to defend the interpretation they had just heard.' "

Let's continue our discussion about Oistrakh the teacher with a conversation about the relationship between him and one of his students, namely yourself, Igor Davidovich. But I would first of all like to quote David Oistrakh's advice which he gave to all young violinists on their way. In order to stress the neccessity of a deep and serious attitude to music he said:

'I would like to tell our young friends: Keep and develop this attitude. Try to know more. The limitations of ones horizons, a narrowing of ones interests leads to a decline, even of a strong talent. Avoid any way of restricting the repertoire. I hope that the brilliance of virtuoso pieces doesn't rob you of the sight of many treasures of deep musical thoughts which are sometimes dressed in less exciting apparel.'

*125*

# *Father and son*

'We played three concerts in London, one in Oxford and one in Manchester. The day after tomorrow we are playing the sixth and final concert in the Albert Hall. In spite of the size of the halls, they are all overcrowded. We have performed a wide range of music from Bach to Sarasate.'

Your father wrote this from London in 1961 were he appeared together with yourself. The newspapers published many reviews, of course, when you were together on other occasions:

'Igor Oistrakh's interpretation of the E Major Concerto by Bach was full of youthful strength and overflowing energy and this was counterbalanced by the more refined interpretation of the A Minor Concerto which David Oistrakh presented.'

'The difference in the playing of the two Oistrakhs, if there is such a thing, doesn't lie in the style but in the age difference of 30 and 52 years.'

"I remember saying at an interview at the time: 'We feel neither the differences nor the similarities which others discover in our playing. When we play together, we are not father and son but musicians'."

What was the relationship between yourself and your father like in other respects?

"It was always the same and always different. It was the same because I loved father very much and he loved me no less (as I well knew). It was different because the father-child relationship changes with the child's age. I am also a father, and I am learning this truth for a second time. The relationship was the same because of the consistency of father's teaching and educational principles based on the trust and respect for my human individuality (I experienced this from my earliest years!). It was different, because I didn't always obey."

It probably wasn't always possible for your father to care about your education during his many tours?

"Of course, mother had to carry the burden of my education, my school work and my musical training. This wasn't simple, since I was anything but an exemplary boy and it cost mother a lot of patience. But father never forgot me, wherever he happened to be. I owe them both eternal thanks, to mother as the good spirit of our house and to father, whose love I always felt."

Oistrakh senior was determined to make a musician, a violinist out of Oistrakh junior.

" 'Everybody in Brussels knows of Garik's existence and his musical ability after my press interviews', David Oistrakh wrote after his victory in the Eugene Ysaye Competition. 'I am just about to leave, to play Tchaikovsky with an orchestra (a phenomenal orchestra). Before I go I want to post the letter with the promised surprise for

Garik – his picture in a Brussels paper. They all know about him here and expect him at the Eugene Ysaye Competition in ten years time.' "

Did the son immediately agree with the father's wish?

"I must admit that I didn't immediately agree. But I should stress: father obviously wanted me to play the violin, but only as a part of his effort to inject in me a general respect for work and to teach me how important it is to acquire knowledge right from childhood and youth. I would like to quote three letters from father, which I particularly treasure and which were all written during the war.

'Dear Garinka,
Many thanks for your letter. I would be very happy if you would write more often. I am glad that you are now learning harder, as mummy tells me. You realize that nothing makes mummy and me sadder than your laziness and naughtiness. If you would realize how important it is for your future independent life to acquire as much knowledge as possible now in your

**127**

childhood, in your youth, where everything that you read, see and hear is absorbed by your memory consciously as by a sponge and then stored for ever, then you would take mum's, dad's and your teacher's admonitions more seriously. They have already trodden the road which you are only just starting to walk. Mummy and I had school friends who were very different, some were hard working and others lazy. We could observe how differently their life developed. The lazy ones spent their childhood perhaps happier and freer from worries, but when they grew up, life grabbed them very hard since they were unable to cope with any serious work . . .

I had many friends as a child. Those who learnt well at the time and therefore turned into good musicians, doctors and engineers also remain my friends. What happened to the others nobody knows, nobody asks about them, one simply doesn't need them. Imagine how annoying this must be for those boys who were lazy, since they had chosen such an unenviable life.

*David Oistrakh with his son Igor*

Think this over seriously, Garinka. Don't forget that you are robbing yourself worse than the worst thief could do on days when you do less, learn less and practise less. Appreciate your mother's sacrifice through which she gives you the best years of her life; you must try to learn to read each wish in her eyes. Aren't you ashamed that she sometimes has to cry? Garinka, little son, I would so much like to have a son whom I can love very strongly and in whom I have a growing friend and comrade. You have surely seen how my relationship with you improved as soon as I noticed a change for the better in you and even as soon as I just see some indication of a conscious attitude to work, discipline and to the fulfilment of duty. Write to me in detail and at length what you think about my letter and how you intend to improve the present situation. I kiss you from my heart and expect your letter.          Your papa'

The second letter is addressed to mother, but it contains a few lines which affect me directly:

'I am very happy that Garik is getting more independent. If only he would work harder and be more keen to acquire knowledge. Tell him that I would like to love him very much but he has to change a little bit for that and if he would try to achieve this before my return I would be very happy. Do you hear, Garjuschenka, trust mummy's and granny's words. Believe the advice your father gives you and train in yourself the desire and ability to behave in a disciplined way – at home, at school, in play and in earnest, in your relationship with friends and relatives. If you want to be respected (you are only little, but you have a right to be respected), then you must also show care, respect and love to those surrounding you, mummy, granny, your teachers, etc. I would like to converse with you as if you were a big boy, because you are already big and now in the hard times of war you have to age almost at once by three or four years. Young people of your age achieve miracles of bravery as partisans and support their family by helping in industry, etc. This does not mean that from time to time you can't turn back to being the little boy, even I do that, and then we will play soldiers together. I write all this to you since I recently have thought a great deal about your future prospects and how to teach you true human qualities. When I return we shall talk about it in greater detail. I now kiss you from my heart and wish you good health.'

And now a few lines from a letter which father wrote to me in the same year (1942). He was supposed to be flown into the encircled city of Leningrad to play to its brave inhabitants, who had to suffer the horror of the blockade. Father wrote how happy he was to play for the people of Leningrad and to bring his heart close to them, and he stated:

'One has to work a great deal to have the ability of creating miracles by giving people joy. You can believe me, Garjuschenka, this work pays dividends. First of all it brings you yourself joy and later you share it with those around you.' "
Was you father also your first violin teacher?

"I got my first lessons from the excellent teacher Valerie Merenblum. In the widest sense of the word, however, father was and always remained my teacher."
When was the first time you felt the desire to play the violin?

"I was six years old when I started to play the violin, but after two years I reached the conclusion that the sound of my violin gave me little pleasure, particularly in comparison with the magical sound of father's violin. I changed to the piano. The war interrupted my music lessons. The meeting with Pyotr Stoliarsky proved 'fateful' and I again returned to the violin." Did your own impressions of Stoliarsky agree with those which you received from your father, his elder student?

"When you get to know people better, people about whom you have heard many good things, disappointment frequently occurs. I was spared this experience with Pyotr Stoliarsky. He really was a remarkable man and a wonderful teacher. He unfortunately only taught me for three months, but even this short period was sufficient to guide me onto the right path. He had an exceptionally sharp fingertip feeling for teaching. I have told you this before and if I repeat it, it is only to stress that I confirm from my own experience what I had heard about Stoliarsky as a child from my father and his friends. All Stoliarsky needed was a short discussion with a child to form an infallible judgement of his ability. One sometimes thought that he only had to look into the eyes of a

*Igor plays to his parents (1938)*

child to determine whether a talent was sparkling in them.

When Stoliarsky's pupil became famous in the 1930s, he wrote (already an older man): 'No, the years can do nothing to me, I shall train talents with new energy and enthusiasm so that their music can sound proudly throughout the whole world.'

After the outbreak of war Pyotr Stoliarsky moved to Swerdlowsk. There, he virtually collected almost all the children who knew how to move a bow over the strings and taught them in exactly the same unselfish way as in Odessa many years earlier, when the little David Oistrakh had attended his class.

Stoliarsky didn't seem to feel the worries or problems of war nor the burden of age. He was a virtuoso of his subject, a fanatic apostle of art. When father later acquainted me with Salomon Hurok, I learnt that every activity which corresponds to a person's mission can be done with such virtuosity. I often compare these two men and discover much in common between them."

What influence did Stoliarsky have on you?

"He succeeded where no-one else had succeeded before, in convincing me that I shouldn't just play the violin because my parents wanted me to, but because it was stimulating and interesting. I was eleven at the time and that is not exactly the best age to learn to play an instrument properly, particularly the violin. Father's letters and concerts in Swerdlowsk, which he visited from time to time, influenced me in no small way of course."

Did your father teach you during the time after the war when you attended the Central Music School at the Moscow Conservatory?

"Before I answer this question I would like to say a few words about this school. Several outstanding Soviet musicians had the idea of creating such special schools for musically gifted children. Amongst them were Alexander Goldenweiser and Pyotr Stoliarsky, who since 1933 had managed such a school in Odessa, the school which was later named after him. Later these 'ten-year music schools' were created in Leningrad, Kiev and other big cities. The best Soviet music teachers taught in them. The combination of music lessons with lessons on all other subjects was of great convenience for the students as they didn't then have to attend two schools – the music school and the usual general school. Each 'ten-year music school' is combined with a boarding house where able children from distant cities and villages can live.

The music school in Moscow is an excellent training place for young talents. It is sufficient to point out that during my time it was attended by such famous musicians as the conductor Gennadi Roshdestvensky (we started to play violin sonatas together in the school, he was a brilliant pianist), the violinists Igor Besrodny, Eduard Gratsch, the pianists Jewgeni Malinin and Lasar Berman.

I myself had lessons with my first teacher, Valerie Merenblum, to whom I am very grateful. When my father wasn't on tour he of course had the opportunity to listen to my violin playing. Even if he was working in the adjoining room I never forgot his presence and this put a particular responsibility on my shoulders. Sometimes I even thought that this was the reason why I later in life didn't suffer so much from stage fright. In 1945 father for the first time showed faith in my violinistic ability. To be honest before that, I was above all stimulated by the presents which he brought back from his world tours. But this time I didn't even allow him time to change on his return and I begged him that he should listen to me immediately. Father wasn't expecting anything special from me and was amazed when I played Lipinski's Concerto. I can even remember that he had tears in his eyes."

Did your father always agree with the program of work which you were given at the school?

"Father valued Valerie Merenblum highly and was on the whole not only in agreement with the repertoire but also with her teaching instructions. I intentionally make the reservation: on the whole.

I remember that mother occasionally had to step in and support me. According to her, I needed her support when father advised me to learn a complicated piece which was, in her opinion, much too difficult for a child. However, I was no longer a child and furthermore I loved it when I was given difficult tasks. Father knew this only too well." Can you remember what pieces these were?

"But of course. For instance the 1st Concerto by Vieuxtemps, which I was to play in the seventh class at father's urgent request, also the Violin Concerto by Ernst, which particularly inspired me and advanced me a great deal. I rehearsed it in the summer holidays. When I returned to the school in the autumn everybody was pleasantly surprised, nobody had expected such progress from me."

You left the school in 1949 and afterwards studied under your father's guidance for nine years, first at the Moscow Conservatory and then at the Aspirantur. Did your father work more intensively with you than with other students?

"As a rule I didn't have more but fewer lessons from father than the other students. He quite often taught me at our house. I was always the last one. One student followed the other, nobody looked at the clock, I listened and waited for my turn. This continued until the evening and since I felt sorry for father, I asked him to take a rest and postpone the lesson to the next day."

What demands did the father have on the son?

"Well, also in this respect there was nothing to laugh about. I can't remember that father ever made such demands on his numerous students as he did on me. I can't forget an incident in 1949: one week before I was supposed to travel to my first international competition, to Budapest, father returned from a tour. He listened to my playing and criticized the intonation, the rhythm, the whole interpretation. However, a week of hard work under his efficient direction bore its fruits."

The fruit was the 1st prize in the competition. And how did you work when you had grown up and started to play on your own?

"Father's demands remained the same, even after I had become a prize winner and after I had performed both in the Soviet Union and in foreign countries. I was sometimes angry with father because of that; however, I am now extremely grateful for the strict standard which he expected from me."

Were you an obedient student of your father in every respect?

"I always tried to be one, but I didn't always succeed. Although I was always conscious, even in the days when I resisted, what a great luck and joy it was to work with such a teacher as David Oistrakh."

Were you sometimes 'obstinate'?

"Already during my years as a student and even at the Aspirantur I lived a life that had little in common with that of a usual student. I already gave many concerts and had a considerable repertoire. It was therefore only too natural that I had my own ideas about violin playing, the principles of interpretation, about the use of the vibrato and the problems of tempi."

In what way did these views coincide with those of your father and in what way did they differ?

"We were agreed on the general aesthetic principles of violin playing: to open up the artistic pictures which are expressed by musical symbols with the greatest accuracy possible. But we were both very different characters. Father was balanced and wise, I was effervescent and inclined to exaggerate conflicts. Secondly I had been through a modern violin school, a point which I often laughingly stressed in conversation with father: 'You have studied with Stoliarsky, I however have studied with David Oistrakh.'

This of course influenced our interpretations. When we played Vivaldi, Bach and Mozart, as far as the interpretation was concerned, we felt no particular differences, as they occurred in our performances of compositions of the post-Mozart epoch, particularly in the works of the Romantics.

If I think about it today, I don't feel that our divergencies were all that serious. I note that in matters of taste, similarly to father, I trod the road from Brahms to Beethoven and, after passing my fortieth birthday, on to Mozart and Bach."
You briefly mentioned among other things the problem of tempi. As we know you play some pieces or movements somewhat faster than your father did. I would like to mention as an example the finales of the Mendelssohn, Lalo, Sibelius and Tchaikovsky Violin Concertos. You could of course object that in his youth David Oistrakh also played the finales rather fast, for instance the finale of the Mendelssohn Concerto.

"Of course we differed as far as tempi are concerned, but I feel that this was only partly due to our age difference. The difference in our characters was decisive. The artistic individuality which led to a different attitude to the interpretation of each individual composition. For example, father played the finale of the Sibelius Violin Concerto in a pronounced monumental way which always sounded convincing. I, however, played it with fanatic spontaneity. But our divergence was only relative, even in this respect. The following lines by Otto Klemperer, who is well known as a convinced supporter of moderate tempi in the performance of classic scores, are characteristic. After he had got to know the recordings of the Beethoven Sonatas by Natalja Serzalowa, my wife and myself, he wrote:

'Your interpretation is excellent and close to life. It fully satisfies me. I congratulate you and your wife, in whom I see your equal partner. I recently heard Beethoven's 7th Symphony performed very badly (everything much too fast) and feel that your recordings are good medicine for me.' "
Was your attitude to your father's playing always the same?

"As the years passed, I understood his profundity better and better. Nothing ever prevented me from admiring father's playing. In particular the ideal harmony of all proportions of his performance: the dynamics, the tempi, the colours."
On one side admiration and on the other the search for your own road in art?

"Yes, I am convinced that that was the only true solution. It was already absolutely clear to me that it would be useless to try to imitate somebody in art, even if the model was David Oistrakh in person. Copies are of little use in every type of art."
Presumably, your father didn't insist on imitation?

"Of course not, although he frequently tried to convince me. 'Why do you want me to play this in exactly such a way?' I asked father. 'Because I myself have played the piece the way you play it and because I have dismissed this interpretation a long time ago', he replied. But I wanted to make all these discoveries myself and to choose the best variant on my own."

*133*

Surely the main reason why you had this urge for self expression in your youth was because you were David Oistrakh's son.

"Father understood this very well and often said to mother (as I obviously only found out much later): 'Igor must be given more freedom for his artistic development.'"

How did your father react, when in 1959 after discussing your concerts in Paris, the critics wrote: 'Igor is no longer his father's son'?

"Intelligent as he was, he knew that I was going my own way. It was more a question of tolerating my 'breaking away' than agreeing with it. In any case our relationship wasn't darkened by any shadow.

'I am very happy that everybody tells me about your successful concerts in Paris and Belgium,' father wrote in the same year (1959) from Brussels. 'I think that your two last tours will strengthen your artistic status even further. I therefore congratulate you. The Paris press reviews have been translated in Moscow and mama and papa were radiant with joy.'

If I now go through father's letters I can see particularly clearly how much he loved me, how he was longing for me if we hadn't seen each other for a long time, how concerned he was about me and how happy at each of my successes:

'Tokyo, 1955. Loved ones,
Today is the 26th of February and in one hour Garik's concert in the Great Hall will start. You know that I am with you in all my thoughts, and would therefore like to write you a few words at least.
According to local time, it is now one o'clock in the morning (the time difference is six hours), I have already played my concert today (the third one). The concerts start early at 18.30 in Japan, so I have been free for some time. By the way, I have also played Lalo.
I am impatiently awaiting a telegram, which I hope you will send me immediately after the concert.'

'Moscow, 1958. My dear little son,
How wrong it is that we not only can't see each other, but apparently can't even phone each other during the next ten days.
As you know, both mother and I are very much longing to see you and are sad to be separated from you for such a long time.
We were very happy to read the press reviews of your successes last year.'"

When did your joint performances with your father begin?

"I played with father for the first time in 1947. He was in Moscow and we performed Bach's Concerto for Two Violins and Orchestra, which we later often played together. However, the regular performances with father, the joint tours and recordings started much later, at the end of the 1950s. We played in many cities in the Soviet Union and in other countries. Our repertoire included concertos by Bach and Vivaldi, Mozart's Sinfonia Concertante for Violin and Viola (each of us had studied both solo parts), furthermore trio sonatas by Benda, Bach, Leclair, Tartini, compositions by Haydn, Spohr, Wieniawski, Ysaye and Sarasate. Our modern repertoire: Honegger's Sonatine and Prokofiev's Sonata, both for two violins."

Which of these joint performances do you remember in particular?

"The question is difficult to answer. Each was in some respect unique and for some reason memorable for me. Our performances were very different. We played works for two violins, for violin and viola and I played with chamber and symphony orchestra

134

with father conducting. If you mean concertos for two violins, then I could talk about our performances in October 1961 in France. We made a record in Paris, which won the Grand Prix of the Year from the Académie du Disque. The record contained duos by Spohr and Haydn, Honegger's Sonatine and Prokofiev's Sonata.

A review contained the following comment: 'Hardly anyone could produce a better interpretation than the two Oistrakhs, whose enthusiasm, technical perfection and absolute coordination are fascinating.'

In those days many critics called the two Oistrakhs 'King David and Prince Igor'."
It was sufficient to recall the sounds of your two violins, for example in Haydn's Duo in B Flat Major, to feel the pleasure of this music, which you transmitted with so much feeling, with such pure clarity and transparent intonation for anyone to agree with the French critic and in fact describe David and Igor Oistrakh as the king and prince of music.

135

# Personality

# Character

" 'I know that the world has become a much poorer and less interesting place since his death; he was a golden human being.' (Isaac Stern)"

Similar obituaries to David Oistrakh can be quoted by the dozens and hundreds, in the press, and in letters to you and your mother. The world has lost a wonderful musician and a great HUMAN BEING – this thought repeats itself in all its variants in the statements of old and young, famous and average musicians, as well as those who knew Oistrakh personally and those who were only familiar with his art. What was David Oistrakh like as a human being? Which of his qualities would you regard as particularly typical?

"This question is not easy to answer. For a start, father's character was anything but simple and one-dimensional. Some of his traits seem to contradict each other. Secondly, it is not up to me, his son, to use those 'epithets' which his colleagues used. Thirdly ... However, I will try to give my own impression about father as a human being. He had a noble character, and that was the determining element of his nature in my opinion. He was noble through and through."

The memory of David Oistrakh's last summer, the summer of 1974 is still fresh in my memory. He had only just recovered from his long heart illness (or been cured?). He was sitting for hours at the desk of the violin jury in the stuffy overcrowded Great Hall of the Conservatory. The days of this 5th International Tchaikovsky Competition were hot in every respect. Every day, sometimes between two eliminating examinations, he would drive to the hospital to visit his sick wife.

'I am so ashamed that I still haven't replied to your two wonderful letters!' David Oistrakh complained in a letter to Mr and Mrs Krakowski. 'I think that you might forgive me for this disgusting behaviour if you knew what torture this whole competition was for me (and also for my health) right until the finish which only took place yesterday.'

Tamara Iwanowna could tell many stories, how David Oistrakh behaved as a gentleman to her in the difficult times of war and in the 'years of wandering'. However, out of modesty, a trait which both man and wife shared, she kept silent about all this.

"One of father's knightly traits was logically a highly developed continuously practised sense of duty. Take the 5th Tchaikovsky Competition for example. I think that father should have refused to serve as a member of the jury, but it was not in his character to refuse anything: his sense of duty to his students, the Conservatory and to the Soviet violin school prevented him from doing this. He was a permanent chairman of the jury since 1958, the time of the first Moscow competition.

Take another example: you mentioned father's relationship with mother. It was of course an incredibly warm one; however, the knowledge of his official social commitments won. In London in 1972 there was a festival week of Soviet music. You could read on the posters that father would par-

ticipate in the final concert. He was at the time still on tour in France. Evgeny Svetlanov was to be conductor at the London concert. He later wrote in his *Word about Oistrakh:*

'He seemed very excited and troubled when he came to the rehearsal from Paris. There was a good reason for this. He had left his wife, Tamara Iwanowna, seriously ill in Paris and David Feodorovich was deeply worried. Did David Feodorovich do the right thing by flying to London at this time to conclude the musical week? As husband, he should surely have remained at his wife's bedside, but would it have been right for him to miss such a performance which had enormous artistic and political importance? As a Soviet artist who did not just belong to himself and his family, it would have been wrong. This is why he didn't refuse. If you could only imagine how beautifully he played on this evening ! ! ! ' "
Cancelling a concert - such a thing didn't exist for Oistrakh, and in this his sense of duty found clear expression. There are two types of artist, whom one can perhaps characterize as follows: the one who cares more about the audience, the other more about himself. The one

finds a thousand reasons to delay or cancel a concert, he sometimes even insists that this is done out of interest for the audience to whom he only wants to present himself when he is in 100% good form and in the best shape as far as nervous and violinistic conditions are concerned. I personally think that such claims are nothing other than a cover up for the 'star ego'.

"I would like to tell you what father thought about this and how he educated me in this respect: the audience has bought tickets, has got prepared for an artistic event and this musical event must not fail to occur - unless one is lying in bed with a temperature of 40°C.

Of course, father (like every other artist) would have been only too happy to be in his best form before every concert. But nobody can claim to be that. Since this is the way it is, one has to accept that each concert has a certain risk, each performance is basically a battle, the result of which can never be exactly predetermined even after the most careful preparations.

You can remember that we talked about stage fright. Am I wrong to suggest that it springs from that feeling of the inevitable with which each of us wakes up on

*139*

the morning of a concert? The evening comes, you have to put on your tails and walk out onto the floodlit stage. That is the 'categoric imperative' of life as a virtuoso. 'It must be!' as Beethoven would have said.

Thinking of father, I feel that his sense of duty to his listeners was as strongly developed as his feeling of realizing the will of the composer in his interpretations." The word 'goodness' crops up in almost all people's memories of Oistrakh. 'The terms music and goodness were always interwoven in David Oistrakh's view,' Kyril Kondrashin wrote. 'These qualities enveloped everybody with their atmosphere, everybody with whom he came in contact.'
But this was by no means a tribute which he paid to 'goodness' in an abstract sense. Oistrakh could also hate: every type of hypocrisy, opportunism, sanctimoniousness, not to speak of injustice and force. Nevertheless, he was always trying to find something positive and not negative in his surroundings. He tried to stress people's best and not worst qualities, to note successes and not faults, achievements and not failures in the performances of his colleague violinists. It is

*With Viktor Goldfeld*

therefore not by chance that Oistrakh had many friends and never enemies. Who were his friends actually?

"Of course all the great Soviet musicians and many musicians from other countries were among father's friends. We shall have more opportunity to discuss meetings with some of them in detail. But what was much more informative for an understanding of father's character was his friendship with many people who could never be regarded as famous:

'He was a great master, got to know glory and admiration when he was quite young but kept his simplicity and accessibility right to the end of his life. Not everybody is given this!' Kyril Kondrashin wrote in a letter to my mother. He remained Dodik to the friends of his youth, such as Viktor Goldfeld, Michail Goldstein, Regina Horowitz and Ilja Schweizer. As Regina Horowitz wrote, neither the past decades nor his world fame were able to let his friendship rust.

His letters bear witness to his friendly devotion to the friends of his youth. Wherever he was in the world, no matter how overworked he was, he always found time to congratulate his friends on their birthday and to share his new impressions with them.

'I was yesterday in the little town of Berlington,' he wrote to W. M. Goldfeld from the USA, 'I found Radio Moscow for the first time and listened to the violinist Prizker, student of Professor W. M. Goldfeld at the Minsk Conservatory. What luck! She played Tchaikovsky's *Meditation* very well.'

When father came to Odessa, Charkow, Kiev or Minsk, he would never leave without a 'meal of friendship'. It would usually start after his concert and go on far into the night. As father afterwards told us, they exchanged memories on these occasions, there was humour and jollity, everybody felt uninhibited and at ease."

Which of your father's foreign friends would you like to mention?

"Surely it was only natural for father to get most excited before concerts in a country in which he had never been before. He knew that he had no friends there, that he couldn't have any. He had many friends and admirers in countries where he had already performed. It

*141*

would be impossible to name them all. On the other hand it would be impossible not to mention some of these friends.

Jerry Gross for example, a surgeon from Cleveland and a first-class violinist who died during Oistrakh's lifetime. Father felt his death as the loss of a very close friend. This acquaintance, which quickly changed into a friendship, had no medical reason and was purely musical. Jerry adored music, he played the violin very well and was proud to have a few lessons with father whom he literally adored.

When father had a heart attack in London in 1966, Jerry immediately flew to him from America.

*With Jerry Gross*

Not only father, but our whole family loved this charming, intelligent man. He was an authority in his subject and his son also became a surgeon. However, we hardly ever talked about anything other than art during those many evenings which we spent with him in his house in Cleveland or at our place in Moscow. We played quartets in the night at Jerry's house – father never had to be persuaded to play, Jerry seemed to shine from within when he took the violin. Father emphasized that Jerry had always had the great advantage, as violinists do, of not falling into workmanship of professionalism, because he was and remained an amateur."

In what language did the members of the quartet talk to each other?

"German to start with and later Russian. Gerry learnt to speak Russian so perfectly that he was able to recite Pushkin, Lermontow and Yevtushenko off by heart.

'When God created the world for you,' Gross wrote to father, 'It was not his intention that you should work like three horses, two dogs and one donkey.' "

It is said: Tell me with whom you are dealing and I will tell who you are. This is enough reason in itself

142

to name David Oistrakh's friends when talking about his character. In addition, it was in his dealings with each of his friends, that certain traits of his nature became apparent. Jean Rouart, Director General of the firm Le Chant du Monde, and the writer Georges Soria, Manager of the Literature and Arts Agency, both members of the Communist party, great friends and propagandists of Soviet art in France, Ljuba Kormout, Classical Manager of the record company Ariola-Eurodisc in the German Federal Republic (Ljobochka, as David Oistrakh called her in his letters), Jelisaweta Lotar, the Russian interpreter in Paris, the couple Victor and Lilian Hochhauser, the English impresarios and Walter Legge the important German musician, Oistrakh was linked with each of them by many years of friendship and he gave each of them a piece of his soul. But to convince oneself of this, one has only to read some of father's letters addressed to these friends.

"I was once asked how my father could carry the 'burden' of his fame. He couldn't stand it when he was described as the 'first' violinist. There is no such thing as a first one, there are always several first

ones, he used to reply."

How did Oistrakh react to his fame? I often ask myself this question. I found the answer in the memoirs of Paul Badura-Skoda:

" 'A really great man doesn't have to show off or insist on his own importance. His greatness is part of himself, partly even unconscious to him. David's modesty was the natural outcome of his

greatness, also of his goodness and of his childlike purity as a human being. It was far removed from that false and artificial modesty with which some artists try to decorate themselves. He of course knew exactly who was and that he was better than almost all his colleagues, but he never made any fuss about this.'

'It is easier to live with me in

friendship than to quarrel with me,' father remarked in one of his letters, and this is true. This was in no small way because father had very high standards had demands on his own person and judged himself objectively. He often told me, 'If you are in a situation of conflict with somebody, try to find the cause of it in yourself first of all.' " However, even when David Oistrakh wasn't the cause of friction, he always tried not to blame anybody. Paul Badura-Skoda also relates how a technician had forgotten to switch on the 'pilot', the synchronizer of sound and picture at the recording of a television film in which both Oistrakh and Paul Badura-Skoda performed (they recorded a sonata program in two parts). As the devil wanted it, this was only discovered at the end of the performance, approximately two hours of concentrated work were lost. The producer was near despair, irrespective of some other aspects, he was threatened by a considerable financial loss. It was already very late and there were no other days available.

" 'It's much better that this "pilot" should fail and not the other one to whom we all entrust our lives when we walk up the gangway into the plane,' David Oistrakh said with a smile on his face.

The tension broke immediately, lighting engineers started moving, the Jupiter lamps went on again, the order 'Let's go!' was given, and one-and-a-half hours later everybody was breathing much slower.

Humour, gentle and non-aggressive, was one of father's outstanding features. His friends, colleagues and orchestra musicians of many countries knew that. The prospect of dealing with such a conversation partner was always enjoyable.

The natural character of father's humour is witnessed by many notes which he made as a member of juries during competitions. A girl competitor, who stood out as a violinist very early in her life and who expected laurels, didn't justify the hope people had for her. David Oistrakh listened to her playing and commented: 'She hasn't progressed further than the rhythm of the walz.'

He commented about her performance of Kreisler's cadenza to the Brahms Concerto: 'She plays it from bar to bar as if on hire-purchase.'

About the playing of another violinist who performed Paganini's 24th and last Capriccio: 'This is not her favourite composer. I would prefer it if she would play the 25th Capriccio.'

How often didn't humour help father in tricky situations, particularly when it was a question of getting rid of troublesome reporters. One of them once asked why he had made the superhuman effort of performing three violin concertos in one program. Father replied that he had the modest hope that he would play at least one of them well." At the beginning of our conversation about your father's character you used the words 'not one-dimensional'. What did you mean by this? Which traits in his character appeared to you to oppose and exclude one another?

"His gentleness in conversation and the unshakable will, the stubbornness (I could almost say obstinacy) when it came to music, violin playing and interpretation. This obstinacy was based on his fanatic conviction that he was right. 'I am not asking that you agree with me unconditionally, I don't want to force anything on you,' father stressed during lessons with me, 'I am only telling you something about which there can be no doubt.' "

144

# At home and on tour

David Oistrakh performed in many countries and he played in almost all of the world's important musical centres. We have so often mentioned the extraordinary tightness of his timetables on his tours, that I hardly dare to ask the question whether he found time to get to know the towns and countries and to form an opinion about their nature and their people.

"Pictures, slides and films taken on his tours piled up in our flat after each concert tour. When he went to Spain for the first time, he travelled specially to Barcelona to visit a bull fight, although he knew in advance that this spectacle wouldn't give him much pleasure. As he himself said, he did it 'for the camera'. Yes, he loved filming and taking photographs and enjoyed letting his friends see what he had seen. But he also needed the illusion of stretching time. He was always hoping that the films would help him to intensify his impression. In this way he always forgot the fact that even watching films takes time and time got shorter as the years went by, not only to record the impression but to then experience what he had caught on

*The Oistrakh family*

145

film. This could have been the reason for father's laconic words which (according to mother) he often used: 'I am not a tourist but an artist.' It would be best to let his letters speak for themselves:

1955. In New York for the first time:
'New York is a rather large village, which however I have hardly seen – no time. For the time being, my only optical impression is Wolodja's back.' [He means the back of his accompanist W. Jampolski – the author]

1955. In Boston, in the middle of the American tour:
'I get to know the cities on the whole by the postcards which I have sent you. There isn't enough time for a visit.'

1961. In London, joint concert of David and Igor Oistrakh:
'When we are not at the rehearsals and recordings, Igor and I see nothing – we sit like moles in our hotel room and work. But the satisfaction is naturally enormous.'

1968. In New York. David and Tamara Oistrakh are again on a long tour of the USA: 'We have just

enough strength for work. Constant rehearsals and travels from city to city. The rest of the time we sit at home and forget in which town we happen to be. You just won't believe it if I tell you that I haven't been out a single time to walk up 7th Street!.

1969. In Tokyo:
'Although we are now in Japan for the third time, we still haven't seen anything. Concerts and travel take up all the time.'

Father always had eyes and heart open to new impressions. Until the end of his life he kept this open mind and receptivity for nature, architecture and painting. It was totally strange for him to become blasé or oversaturated. Father felt the true joys of discovery when he saw the beauty of New Zealand, he wrote enthusiastically about

*David Oistrakh on tour: in Athens, Leipzig, Japan and on the Niagara Falls*

Hawaii, where he made a short stop on his way to Australia, was fascinated by the Niagara Falls and the countryside near Karlovy Vary. One of his most lasting impressions – in Barcelona – he described as follows:

'I was able to admire real Spanish song and dance late at night in one of the popular taverns. Many foreign tourists sat at the tables, handsome boys and youthful girls danced and sang accompanied by a guitar quartet. I enjoyed the view from a box and always had the feeling that I was watching a scene from the second act of *Carmen*. The performance was thrilling, sometimes ecstatic. How much inner expressiveness, grace, burning temperament, what a multitude of rhythmical figures! The ability to improvise and the stamina of the young artists appeared unlimited! However, when the songs were over and the dances had finished, the 'artists' once again turned to their professional activity – they served the guests and brought the light country wine to the table in mugs. They were waiters . . . ' "

And the endless meetings with professional artists? Didn't David

Oistrakh's receptivity and ability to experience everything diminish as the years went by?

"Oh no! In his letters to me, to mother and to friends, father described what he had seen, the visit to the houses of Goethe and Schiller in Weimar, the Kabuki Theatre in Tokyo, the concerts of the New York Philharmonic under Leonard Bernstein in the recently opened Lincoln Centre for Performing Arts. In Vienna in 1945, he heard *Boris Godunov* under Josef Krips; in 1956, (we have just been talking about this) Mozart's Requiem under Bruno Walter; 1954 in Stockholm, he heard *Rigoletto* with Jussi Bjorling as the duke; in Tokyo in 1955, he admired Prokofiev's *Cinderella* in the production of the Kaitani Ballet; in 1962, he enjoyed the famous Budapest String Quartet in New York. If you only take the violin evenings of his colleagues and the many concerts which father attended, there would be enough not only for one lifetime for many music lovers, but for three lives. But that would be the subject of a separate conversation, since each of these events would merit more than just a brief reference."

Andres Segovia once said: 'Each time I wake up in the morning, I ask myself where I am, just like the actors of the romantic school asked the same question when they recovered from a faint.' David Oistrakh's life was that of a restless traveller, how did he manage to live with this? Did he ever ask himself: Where am I?, or was he resigned to the fact that he was always there where his toothbrush was, to use expression well-known to virtuosos who have travelled a lot?

"It is difficult to get used to a nomadic way of life. I am judging this from my own experience, although for the time being I can't claim to have made such extensive tours as father. By the way, father was not even thirty when there were the first signs of homesickness in the letters which he wrote during his tours. As the years went by, his homesickness increased more and more.

'Oh God!' he once complained. 'How fed up I am with travelling through the world! One's whole life is spent with strangers and strange hotels.'

Neither the wealth of the many impressions nor his successes with the public, nor his meetings with friends, nothing was able to relieve his homesickness."

Perhaps it was because your parent's marriage was warmed by their steady sympathy for one another. When we speak of great musicians, we easily forget many aspects of their human existence and part of this is their family life. Although each creative artist knows how important the atmosphere at home and firmly established family links are for inspiration to remain on a steady level.

"Father loved mother very much and I understood this better and better with the years. 'Only by your generosity and by your true love can it be explained that you protect our great ardent and irreplaceable love for one another and that you maintain this holy feeling in an ocean of passion, disappointments and hopes, in truth and lies, in tears and joys,' he wrote in one of his letters to mother. 'You are so dear and close, unique and unrepeatable to me, because life doesn't repeat itself and you form a large part of my life, its real heart.' "

But didn't David Oistrakh always travel together with Tamara Iwanowna from the middle of the 1950s?

"He didn't want anything more than to travel with her, not out of egotism ('I will have it easier this

way'), but for an entirely different reason. One can read in a letter:

'I would so much like to take you away from our little house to distant interesting places and I wish that we both together could absorb the impressions which await us. We shall share everything, discuss everything together, we shall be two of us.'

Father, of course, had it much easier physically and psychologically when mother became his travelling companion, but the homesickness remained, except that both of them now felt it."

Do you have any thoughts about the reasons for this homesickness?

"We are all probably the same in our family, we just love our home. Mother spent a great deal of love, care and effort to make our home comfortable. Father always eased up when he came home from his grinding tours."

Does this mean that during those few days and hours which he spent in the Moscow flat he liked to be alone or would have liked to be alone?

"Oh no! Father liked to read, in particular books about music and specifically the *Conversations with*

*Stravinsky* by R. Craft. He loved serious literature or rather aesthetic literature (in one of his letters to mother he describes the impressions obtained from such books as Knut Hamsun's *Pan,* Freierman's *Dingo* and Leonid Andreyev's tales) as well as historic works (E. Tarle's *Napoleon,* which he read in two days). But father never liked to be alone for a long time. Loneliness depressed him. He wanted people around him, and father's friends loved to visit us. They chatted excitedly over a cup of tea or a glass or wine, listened to his stories about meetings with musicians and afterwards the very latest record was put on, and everyone got lost in the sounds of the music."

Were you yourself not one of the reasons for your father's homesickness? Didn't concern for his son also draw him home?

"We have already talked about this. But I also remember the times when father didn't find me at home on his return, as I was performing in some other part of the world. This always made us sad. We sometimes didn't meet for months. But 'grandfather' David Oistrakh still needs introducing, a gentle and

150

caring grandfather. When my little son Valeri was born, father wrote in a letter: 'With the appearance of the little one, our whole family will live an even more turbulent life (if that is at all possible). It means a lot of problems and excitement.'
Father called his grandson Kusenka* lovingly, and when the little one said 'grandad' for the first time, father's enthusiasm knew no limits."
But David Oistrakh couldn't see his grandson more often than his son, was that not so?
"Oh, father had a wide range of tricks. During a long tour of the USA with the orchestra of the Leningrad Philharmonic, father envied Gennadi Roshdestvensky, who brought a little record player with him as well as lots of records which immediately got him intoxicated listening to them. Mother objected to carrying a record player or tape recorder to the USA. However, father suddenly remembered that he had in his suitcase a tape with a recording of Valeri's voice. He wrote in the next letter: 'We hear Kusenka's voice every day, which gives us the greatest pleasure and,

the main thing, mother doesn't complain any longer that we carry a little tape recorder with us.
I kiss you all. Grandad.'
Mother was a matching counterpart to father as granny, the 'fresh baked' grandad.

*With his grandson Kusenka*

'We think a great deal about you, mother in particular, whose thoughts always centre around dried plums, fruit, baby jackets, baby shoes and similar objects. I get the impression that she is always with you in her thoughts, with each of your breaths and every activity. I blame her for this, because she herself needs rest and relaxation. Well, I shall look after her.' "

*Diminutive of Kusja

151

# Relaxation and hobby

Anybody living as tense a life as David Oistrakh needs regular relaxation. Did he know how to relax on holiday? Did he enjoy his relaxation or just tolerate it as a mere necessity?

"Rather the latter, and even that only since the 1950s. Father complained so often that man sleeps for one third of his life despite being surrounded by so many interesting things for which there simply is not enough time.

I already told you that father didn't like the Datscha. He went to a sanitorium from time to time, but the idle life as a patient was a burden on him. Mother received some very acidic letters from father in Kislowodsk* (or as father wrote it with its full name 'sour water'). We travelled with father several times for a holiday in the south and I could there convince myself how much he felt a stranger outside his home and away from his rehearsals."

He probably preferred to combine holiday with violin playing?

"Of course, once he had tried this out, he began to talk of a holiday several times a year. My parents spent their vacation in

*Russian: *kislaja woda* – sour water

Pärnu (Estonia) every year since 1953. I also spent the summer there until 1960. The pleasant climate of the small Baltic holiday resort, the hospitality of Mr and Mrs Valmet, who put their large house entirely at our disposal, pleasant company – everything there appealed to father.

'I'm happy that you like our beloved corner in Estonia, where you can breathe freely and see the most beautiful sunsets. Where one can also work quietly and productively,' father wrote to N. I. Krakowski.

Irrespective of the country in which father happened to be, he always said that there was no more beautiful place on earth than Pärnu with its golden sands. He was always happy to return there. Surely everybody needs such a corner to dream in, for physical and mental relaxation."

You were talking about pleasant company. Who were they? Was it a permanent circle?

"The circle wasn't permanent, but rather more the atmosphere in Pärnu. David Oistrakh's preference for Pärnu was no secret and the place soon changed into a sort of violinists' spa. The company of musicians was much more agreeable to father than the many hundreds of autograph hunters. The door of our house in Pärnu was open to everybody who didn't want to recover from music (there are unfortunately people like this among musicians!)"

David Oistrakh's dramatic traits can be expressed in this. Everybody felt uninhibited and free in his house. The famous musician as well as the young violinist, the professor at the conservatory and the student, the well-known soloist and the simple orchestra player, the students from David Oistrakh's class and the students of another teacher (there was no 'class interest' here!). These surroundings were the air that David Oistrakh breathed. He was not only an interesting talker but also a good listener. He was always ready to help with advice and action. It made him happy to help someone, a pleasure which he was never prepared to give up.

"Father loved to listen to music in the evenings. From Moscow he took a tape recorder, a record player and a mountain of tapes and records. He enjoyed so much wonderful music throughout the summer and heard so many interesting stories, and those who came to our house also heard many interesting things. Father talked about his foreign tours and meetings with musicians. Music – and I want to stress this before we talk about father's hobbies – was always the subject of his greatest enthusiasm.

'I can't imagine a greater happiness,' father wrote, 'than to spend an evening listening to a recording of *Tristan* under Fürtwangler with the score in my hand.'"

I only had the opportunity twice or three times to be your guest in Pärnu. I remember one evening when I heard Berlioz symphonic poem *Harold en Italie* (Oistrakh was to conduct it the same year) and the Oratorium 'L'Enfance du Christ'. When I heard *Harold* in the wonderful recordings with William Primrose and the Boston Symphony Orchestra under Charles Münch in the unique atmosphere of David Oistrakh's home in Pärnu, I felt a strange illusion. I felt as if I had been suddenly transferred into the previous century to the Hector Berlioz circle in his little house in Montmartre, which looked as if it had been painted by Utrillo. I felt as if I had been transferred to the period of the composer's life which a biographer described as 'recollected in tranquillity.

"I often thought how interesting

*153*

life in our Moscow flat would have been, if we had had a little more time for friends."

I can remember well seeing David Oistrakh on the beach at Pärnu playing chess, or met him on a walk with a friend. He was frequently accompanied by Arkadi Raikin, the famous Soviet actor and Director of the Leningrad Miniature Theatre, who also loved Pärnu.

"I saw them most frequently standing up to their hips in water in a place where not quite so many people would point at them: 'That's Raikin! That's Oistrakh!' The sun warmed the shallow bay of Pärnu which both artists liked so much and they stood there for a long time talking to each other. I greeted them and swam further out where one's feet couldn't touch the ground. After swimming and having got tired, I returned to the beach and found that the lively discussion was still going on. They never ran out of material for their conversations and they didn't run out of humour either!

'Don't you swim?' father was once asked.

'Of course not,' was the immediate reply.

'But you were surely born in Odessa on the Black Sea and grew

*Father and son play chess*

up there.'

'Well, this is it,' he replied. 'In addition to swimmers, Odessa has also produced a few tolerable writers and artists.'

Father had one other passion: playing chess. Like every other activity to which he devoted himself, he took chess playing seriously from the earliest days.

'He wasn't one of those who sacrificed themselves completely for music, neither as a boy nor later as an adolescent,' Goldstein remembers. 'Strangely enough, he always found time for childish

games and pranks, later for chess and tennis and when he had grown up for driving, which he mastered completely as well as filming. He did nothing half-heartedly. He took everything seriously and whatever he did, he did really well. That was remarkable.'

I can only confirm this. Let's take driving for instance, which gave father so much joy. He was able to drive from Moscow to Pärnu and from Pärnu to Riga in his car. In France, he was happy to be able to drive a hired Simca to his heart's content. He regretted not having a car in Karlovy Vary, since he wanted to see more of the delightful countryside of Western Czechoslovakia than was possible for a mere pedestrian. Considering father's weight, neither driving nor chess playing did him much good.

'Mother and I continue our endless discussion: What is better, to play chess or to walk? For the time being (as always) each of us sticks to his own opinion.'

To 'sticking to his opinion', father sat at the chess board for hours on the beach at Pärnu, where he was happy with any partner, and also in his Moscow flat with I. B. Schweizer, N. I. Krakowski and P. Badura-Skoda. Father took part in a number of single and team competitions; he didn't miss a single important competition as an observer, provided that he happened to be in the town where the competition was taking place.

Father met in Amsterdam, soon after his victory in the Brussels Competition, the stars of the chess world. This meeting impressed him very much. After his concert there appeared 'among the innumerable guests who had come to congratulate me, Flor Lasker with his wife, and Max Euwe with his wife. I was happy! These are my Gods after all! Euwe said he knew that I was a chess player and asked me to greet Botwinnik. I was afraid that he could see in my eyes, what a greenhorn I was at the time.'"

Did he pass his greetings on to Botwinnik?

"Apparently so. They had met before. Michail Botwinnik reports: 'We met in 1936. David Feodorovich was a little older. We had both won fame in international competitions at the time: Oistrakh as a violinist (Brussels, 1937) and I as a chess player (Nottingham, 1936). David Feodorovich was ahead of me in overall evaluation, since he didn't play chess all that badly whilst I had never held a violin in my hands.'" In the summer of 1937 David Oistrakh had the chance to meet Emanuel Lasker in Astafjewo, who was living in the Soviet Union at the time. The revered senior master – he was about seventy at the time and one of the most famous grandmasters in the history of chess playing – played one game after another with Oistrakh, without taking the cigar out of his mouth. He played absolutely seriously, without a shade of condescension towards the amateur. David Oistrakh revelled in this pleasure. The depth and seriousness of Lasker's playing fascinated him.

The climax of David Oistrakh's career as a chess player was his competition against Sergey Prokofiev in 1937, but we will come back to this game later. Chess playing enabled David Oistrakh to meet many people. In a letter to Krakowski, who was also a great chess lover, Oistrakh describes his meetings and discussions with Mark Taimanow, regetting the lack of success which this able chess player had against the American Robert Fischer and analyses the game absolutely professionally.

In another letter to Krakowski, he wrote of his disappointment about the game between Boris Spasski and Robert Fischer (1972) and commented, not without humour:

'The chess world is searching for truly exciting events, but it can only find them in the skyscraper on Wosstanje Square or near the Kursker railway station [by this David Feodorovich meant Krakowski's flat and his own flat – the author]. A special reunion in the form of special embracing is guaranteed. The final game takes place at the flat's door (as at our last party). Checkmate is not declared, it would not be noble to threaten the highest powers.

The 'chess plebs' are waiting for

blood to be spilt, but only blue blood.

The most important rule: whatever the result of the game, it is counted as a draw. Just imagine what sort of an inducement this is for daring sacrifices, fairy-like combinations, etc.'

I would like to add that father remained faithful to his love of chess for his entire life. When he wanted to characterize his lack of time, which he felt more and more, he used to say: The chess periodical remains unopened."

If I think back to Pärnu, I recall another picture: David Oistrakh on a tennis court during stormy weather. Didn't he try to get you interested in this sport right from early youth?

"I played singles and doubles with father as early as 1939/40. Father wasn't a bad tennis player in his youth. Tennis was the only bait with which one could lure him out of our Moscow flat to our Datscha in Shodnja.

He was a complete sports enthusiast. When it was a question of sport, irrespective of whether he watched an interesting football game or ice hockey match on TV or whether he himself was playing chess or tennis, father was always passionately involved. Whoever his opponent on the tennis court was, the game always had to be scored, even if he lost.

There is a letter about this: 'If only you knew how boring this year

*David Oistrakh and Gustav Ernesaks, chief conductor of the Estonian State Malevoice Choir, as tennis players*

is! The weather is dreadful, cold, raining, the tennis court has already been put in good order but is deserted. Nobody feels like playing. I once exchanged balls with Boris Jewgorow, your previous partner and a little boy. This lasted fifteen minutes and the greatest tribute was paid to the wood. I want to make up for this as it is annoying me.'

This youngster later became a

cosmonaut. As far as father's tennis playing is concerned, it didn't improve with the years, in contrast to his violin playing. He commented about this jokingly in the same letter:

'I practise a little. The first few days, my game was just as 'woody' as before and that spoilt my enjoyment as I now thought that it was all over. I am now slowly getting into form again, but not that impressively.' "

With this we touch on the question of whether he practised a lot during his vacation and whether he worked during the summer months. One can, for instance, read in one of his letters:

*Playing billiards with singer Alexander Baturin*

'Tamara Iwanowna and I spent a lovely summer in Pärnu, the weather was wonderful and bathing a pleasure. There wasn't one bad day during the one and a half months. However, the weather wasn't ideal for practising, but I don't regret this as I needed absolute rest.'

"Father never played the violin without interruption for many hours, neither in the winter nor in the summer. However, he only rarely allowed himself to relax completely. Father used to study new programs in the summer and repeated the pieces which he hadn't played for some time. After he had started to conduct, he spent a lot of his time in Pärnu studying music scores. If you are going to talk about the practical value of this work, it was certainly very valuable in Pärnu. This circumstance had no less a favourable effect on father's condition and mood than the beauty of the surrounding nature and the pleasant company.

In one of his last letters to Krakowski father confessed: 'I learnt everything new that I have studied during the last twenty years at the home of our warm hearted and modest elderly friends, the Valmets.'"

157

# Meetings

In his creative period which lasted for over half a century, David Oistrakh met many outstanding musicians: composers, instrumentalists, conductors and singers. Before we begin to talk about these meetings in detail, we should recall your father's general attitude to such contacts.

"One can assume that father must have long ago got used to being surrounded by more than average people, since many that fate brought him in contact with as well as many of his friends were outstanding musicians. In spite of this, he never tired of enjoying each new talented acquaintance, irrespective of whether it was a student at the Conservatory or a performing violinist - he was always sincere and enthusiastic.

There are people who think and hide, as though they were wearing a suit of armour, when they meet the great ones of their subject. However, father blossomed when he met great musicians. They appeared to increase his creative potential. He began to talk in a more exciting manner, played more interestingly and was willing to devote himself to them entirely. Father had a highly developed feeling for tact and a cordial rela-tionship with his friends.

The meetings which we shall discuss, as a rule concern people who were close to father's mentality, his character, his human and artistic individuality and his ethical views. It is only natural that these meetings with friends should have a special mention."

## Nikolai Miaskovsky

One of the most important first performances in David Oistrakh's life was that of the Nikolai Jakovlevich Miaskovsky Violin Concerto. Miaskovsky was one of the 'seniors' of Russian music. Do you know anything about this?

"I was seven or eight years old at the time. I remember a few things, but none of the most important points and some aspects have escaped me. I still remember that father was greatly attracted to Miaskovsky's personality, he had never met him before. He must have been impressed by the kind character of the com-poser, his modesty, his love of joyful optimistic themes, which characterized his compositions at the time. Above all, he enjoyed the music of the violin concerto which Miaskovsky had composed shortly before. However, we can better reconstruct the events of that time by looking at father's letters.

When Miaskovsky had finished the score of his Violin Concerto, he wrote to father:

'Nikolina Gora, 7 August 1938. Dear David Feodorovich, I have been informed, to my great pleasure, that you are prepared to tackle the most thankless task of familiarizing yourself with my experiment in producing a Violin Concerto. Please be pitiless when you judge my work, since, although I have tried to shape the music as attractively and richly as possible, I cannot guarantee the specific technical aspect of the composition.'

Father later told me that Miaskovsky was worried about many aspects connected with the violin part: the configuration, the triads, the length of the cadenzas - which the composer later shortened - and the bowing, which he himself considered to be his weak point.

Miaskovsky closed his letter with

the following résumé: 'I will consider all your comments with the greatest appreciation.

Should you like the concerto to such an extent that you would be prepared to study it seriously, it would be highly desirable if we could meet for a discussion and consider all doubtful points . . .

All the best! with sincere thanks

*Nikolai Yakovlevich Miaskovsky*

for your attention. Yours, N. Miaskovsky.'
I can't remember if father answered this letter."
Oh yes, Igor Davidovich, your father did answer Miaskovsky's letter, it can be found in the composer's archives:

'Shodnja, 12 August 1938.
Dear Nikolai Jakovlevich, I have just received your letter and the Concerto (violin score and piano extracts), which I awaited with the greatest interest and impatience. I immediately liked your Concerto tremendously after playing it for the first time. My love for your excellent composition grows stronger every day. At the moment, my enthusiasm for the Concerto is so great that I play nothing else. In addition to this, I find the music deeply searching and extremely attractive, the Concerto is very varied and rich, as far as using the violinistic possibilities is concerned. I will make every effort to communicate the Concerto as well as possible. I would very much like to meet you to discuss a few details, which are of course of no real significance, but should be clarified. In sincere admiration, D. Oistrakh.'
"Father went to Nikolina Gora,

near Moscow, where Miaskovsky lived, several times in August. After the first meeting, the composer wrote to him:

'Nikolina Gora, 15 August 1938.
Dear David Feodorovich, I am very happy that my Concerto made a good impression on you. I am eager to meet you (he means the next meeting. I. O.) As I already mentioned in my previous letter, I will be in Moscow on the 18th and 19th. Yours, N. Miaskovsky.'"
In autumn 1938, Miaskovsky's Concerto was completed and Oistrakh had studied it. There remained some time before its first performance in January 1939. David Oistrakh played the Concerto in a Moscow club and performed it in the Conservatory at a meeting of professors of string instruments. During this time, he also a wrote an essay about this Concerto and described the composer's new work. Amongst other things he said:
'N. J. Miaskovsky's Violin Concerto is undoubtedly one of the most interesting compositions of its type. It not only enriches the Soviet but also the whole of international violin literature. The composition shows high mastery and deep, moving honesty. The intimate

warmth that Miaskovsky knows how to dress in the language of music is worth emphasizing. As far as mood is concerned, it is a very jolly, light hearted Concerto . . . The musical pictures appear to be inspired by bright childhood memories.

The simplicity of the musical language, the melodic and harmonic clarity, the broadly flowing cantabile and the clear structure are the main characteristics of this Concerto.'

The first performance of Miaskovsky's Violin Concerto was a great success. The composer was delighted. The press acknowledged father as a violinist who had given life to a new Soviet composition. He also performed this concerto later quite often. It is characteristic that in his contribution to a discussion of the violin part of Miaskovsky, he stressed the technical possibilities for expression but didn't say a word about his own part in its preparation – frankly, he had edited the whole solo part.

In 1946, I was witness to a meeting between father and Miaskovsky in Prokofiev's Datscha near Moscow. Both composers had written violin sonatas and performed them for the first time.

I particularly remember the first impression that Nikolai Yakovlevich's appearance made on me, when a man of very noble artistic stature approached us from a romantic copse. For a moment I thought I saw Tchaikovsky before me."

Oistrakh's 'discovery' of Nikolai Miaskovsky's Concerto and a year later of the works of Aram Chatschaturjan received a lasting response from listeners.

" 'One can quite safely describe the performance of these concertos in the Great Hall of the Conservatory as musical feasts,' Leonid Kogan remembers. 'They were startling performances. I will never forget the smiling faces in the audience, the encores of the finales of these concertos which Oistrakh played with such ease, perfection and greatness, almost in a playful mood, that we were all deeply moved. It was an experience for life. I am very happy that I witnessed these extraordinary performances.' " It only remains to be added that the relationship between David Oistrakh and Nikolai Miaskovsky remained very warm and full of mutual respect.

Miaskovsky's works are unfortunately seldom performed in the West. Oistrakh was one of the first great Soviet violinists who publicized his compositions. David Oistrakh's effort is nowadays continued by such outstanding musicians as the conductor Evgeny Svetlanov and the pianist Sviatoslav Richter.

## Sergey Prokofiev

Oistrakh and Prokofiev. A friendship which lasted for a quarter of a century. What a tempting subject for a biographer, who would prefer to make the work and life of these two musicians the subject of his studies . . .

". . . and no less rewarding for our conversation. I heard from childhood on how enthusiastically father talked about Prokofiev's music, his piano playing and himself in person. We once bought a tape recorder and started to 'fish' for transmissions of the composer's works on the radio which we then recorded on tape.

In the 1930s, when we moved

162

into a new house in Tschkalow Street, we discovered that Prokofiev also lived in the same building. Other celebrities were also our neighbours: Valeri Tschkalow the pilot, Samuil Marschak the poet, Genrich Neuhaus the pianist, Kukrynisky the caricaturist. On my way to school and coming back, I often met Sergey Prokofiev walking slowly; sometimes he came to visit us. I of course didn't participate in the conversation, but I noticed that he and father talked vividly and that they always had something to say to each other.''

You have already said that David Oistrakh knew Prokofiev's music before he met the composer and that he played the 1st Violin Concerto in 1926, before finishing at the Odessa Conservatory.

"One has to add to this that father, although he was not the first one to perform the Concerto, had never heard an interpretation of this work before. And also: together with the 1st Concerto, father studied Prokofiev's *Five Melodies* which he later performed frequently.''

Just as he did the 1st Concerto. Here, for example, is a comment by Evgeny Svetlanov who conducted the final concerto of the week of Soviet Music in London in 1973 in the Royal Festival Hall. David Oistrakh played the solo part.

'Prokofiev's 1st Concerto can hardly be counted as one of those compositions which contains a great deal for the soloist to show off. There is in the fragrant, sincere and intimately lyrical music of this Concerto, the final sounds of which fascinate the listener and lift him up to unlimited heights, a virtuoso movement, the Scherzo. After the sounds of the magical D Major finale had faded away, the audience sat completely mesmerized for a time and then a storm of applause broke out. Strangely enough, people say the English are cool, reserved and prudish – the overcrowded Royal Festival Hall didn't let Oistrakh leave the platform, and we repeated the Scherzo – a unique case in the history of this composition by Prokofiev.'

How did your father's personal acquaintance with Prokofiev begin?

"It started with a rather embarrassing incident which father told us about with good natured humour later on. The composer gave a guest performance in 1927, one year after father had played in his diploma exam in Odessa. There were two piano recitals in the opera house.

Father later wrote: 'It was the first time in my life that I received such a strong musical impression, not so much from the music itself, which I had in the meantime got to know and love much better, but from its performance. Prokofiev's playing amazed me by its simplicity, no unnecessary movement, no feeling unnecessarily exaggerated. Nothing one could possibly describe as 'showing off.'

Father was expected to perform the Scherzo of Prokofiev's Violin Concerto at an evening arranged in honour of Prokofiev by the musicians of Odessa. One can hardly blame the eighteen-year-old for trying to 'impress' the composer, and by so doing making a fool of himself. Prokofiev sat in the first row.

Father told us: 'His face got darker and darker during my playing. He didn't take part in the applause which followed; he took one large step to the platform and without paying any attention to the noise and the excitement of the audience asked the pianist to let him take his place. He then turned Father could only be glad that Prokofiev wasn't present at his exam at the Conservatory . . . But

163

to me with the words: "Young man, you are playing it fundamentally in the wrong way," and began to explain the character of his music to me. The scandal was complete.'"
I can imagine David Oistrakh's state . .

"Yes, unenviable as they say. this incident didn't affect their later friendship in any way."
Did your father ever remind the composer of this incident later in his life?

"Father would never have done this if Prokofiev hadn't mentioned it himself. Many years later, they were talking about their youth, they remembered Odessa and Sergey Prokofiev talked of his concerts in this town.

'To my surprise,' father wrote, 'he was able to remember everything down to the minutest detail: the exact content of the program, the number of encores and also the 'unhappy young man', to whom, as Prokofiev himself said, he had really given a piece of his mind.' 'Do you actually know who this young man was?' When he found out that it was me, he got very embarrassed . . . 'What are you saying!' and I could convince myself how human and gentle he could be.'"

*Oistrakh plays Sergey Prokofiev's
1st Violin Concerto with the
composer conducting*

You, Igor Davidovich, had it a hundred times easier to penetrate Prokofiev's composition than your father. You got to know his music at a time when it was already well known and in addition you got to know it through the prism of your father's enthusiasm. However, in his youth, how did he feel about Prokofiev's music, which in those years was dismissed as 'exclusive' and 'unapproachable'?

"Of course it took time before father understood the full magic of Prokofiev's Violin Concerto. 'I don't want to claim that the music captivated me immediately,' he later confessed, 'it contained a lot of unusual elements for the taste of those days as far as the character of the material and its construction were concerned. However, the more familiar I became with the new unknown composition, the more I liked it. The melodic theme, the fantastic strangeness of the harmonic accompaniment, the new technical inventions and above all the light colouration of the whole music attracted me.'"
David Oistrakh later became the interpreter of all Prokofiev's violin

concertos, he played both his concertos, the two sonatas for violin and piano, the sonata for solo violin, and together with you, Igor Davidovich - the sonatas for two violins.

"I often read in the press, which discussed father's playing, that the stability and fruitfulness of his artistic contact with Prokofiev represented a continuation of the tradition of friendship between violinists and composers, as for example between Ferdinand David and Felix Mendelssohn, Joseph Joachim and Johannes Brahms, Leopold Auer and Alexander Glazunof. It is quite justifiable to include Sergey Prokofiev and father in this list. He was the first violinist to perform the composer's 1st and 2nd Violin Sonatas.

I shall never forget that summer's day in 1946, when father took me to Prokofiev's Datscha near Moscow for the first time, where the recently completed F Minor Violin Sonata was to be performed (I have already mentioned this once when we talked about the meetings with Miaskovsky). The composer had invited father to Nikolina Gora the day before. How happy I was that father took me with him. At the time, I was just prior to completing the Central School of Music final examinations, I was already playing Ernst's Concerto and therefore found Prokofiev's words very hurtful: 'Perhaps Igor would like to walk along the river . . .' I was always the child to him, whose bows (on greeting me) he always returned most politely when we met in the yard of our house. Father supported me and I was allowed to stay.

Sergey Prokofiev told us the names of the movements of his Sonata and then played it without interruption. When he had finished, he said that he dedicated this new composition to David Oistrakh.

'The impression which the music made was extraordinary,' father later remembered, 'we had the feeling of being present at an important event. Indeed, one can say without exaggeration that there was no work for decades that could equal its beauty and depth in international violin chamber music.' "
This opinion was certainly not an exaggerated one; it agrees with the laconic but eloquent note in Miaskovsky's diary: 'Heard Prokofiev's new Violin Sonata - an ingenious composition.'

"Father was excited by the fact that the Sonata was dedicated to him and he felt the urgent desire to study and perform it as soon as possible. He frequently travelled with Lew Oborin to visit Prokofiev, and listen to the composer's directions. Just as at the time when father rehearsed Miaskovsky's Concerto, he now didn't want to play any other music. I can't remember father ever taking such a lively interest in a composition as for Prokofiev's Sonata in F Minor.

On the other hand, Prokofiev entrusted father with the editing of the violin part before publishing the Sonata. 'On Sergey Sergeyevich's request I am sending you his Sonata,' wrote L. Atowmjan, composer and musician, to Oistrakh. 'He begs you to help him with marking the bowing.'

The first performance of the Sonata took place on October 23, 1946 in Moscow. Shortly afterwards, father could congratulate the composer for receiving the State Prize for the Violin Sonata."
And how did Prokofiev's 2nd Sonata for Violin and Piano in D Major originate?

"Although it is known as the 2nd Sonata, it was in reality composed in 1943, that is before the 1st Sonata. Furthermore, it was not originally thought to have been written for violin, but for flute.

'As far as the Flute Sonata is concerned,' Prokofiev wrote in 1944, 'violinists were interested in it. Together with David Oistrakh - one of our best violinists, I recently composed the violin variant of the Sonata. The work proved to be simple, since it turned out that the flute part can easily be adjusted to violin technique. The changes in the violin part were small and mainly connected with bowing. The piano part remained unaltered.' "

Which of these two sonatas did your father prefer, which did he play more often?

"Father was quite certain that the two sonatas were very differently constructed. He had a high opinion of the F Minor Sonata, talked about its chamber-music character and the smaller emotional amplitude in contrast to the D Major Sonata. He played the F Minor Sonata more often. He played it virtually incomparably.

'S. Prokofiev's F Minor Sonata,' father wrote, 'is a tremendous epic work in which the picture of the past of our great country lives again and in which the composer's thoughts about his people's fate take form. I am deeply convinced that this work, because of its purposeful content and its extraordinary mastery in the realization of its purpose, the beauty of the musical pictures (it is sufficient to be reminded of the slower part), can be counted as one of the most outstanding violin sonatas of world literature.' "

I didn't know these words of David Oistrakh, although I can imagine how he felt about the F Minor Sonata, since he played it so marvellously.

"I must say that my own opinion of the 1st Sonata comes very close to that of my father. The Sonata also arouses thoughts in me, which are connected with the Russian past. In the first movement I even imagine quite concrete pictures and figures: the Russians under the yoke of the Tartars (remember the heart moving violin passage in the pianissimo, which Prokofiev at the time explained to father as the howling of the wind in a cemetery); in the second movement, a bloody battle; in the third, the picture of a Russian woman which reminds me of Jaroslawna, a figure in Borodin's opera *Prince Igor*, and finally in the finale, with its changing rhythm which reminds one of the finale of *Alexander Newski* (in my opinion, the Sonata has altogether the same atmosphere as Prokofiev's Oratorium), Alexander Newski's arrival at Pskow. All this is of course very relative, but I am talking of subjective impressions, I am trying to clothe my associations with words, which is not easy."

Prokofiev frequently conducted his own compositions. Did your father have any opportunity to be accompanied by Prokofiev?

"Father played the 1st violin with Prokofiev conducting at a Prokofiev evening. Prokofiev's best qualities as a conductor, which father used to stress, were simplicity and naturalness in interpretation, the ability to give the orchestra musicians the feeling that they themselves were playing and that they weren't playing under a dictator. These qualities of a conductor later became guidelines for father's own way of conducting."

Prokofiev's 5th Symphony was one of the first symphony scores which Oistrakh put on his conductor's desk. He clearly felt the special character of the creations of the great Soviet composer, was an outstanding interpreter of his works and at the same time knew the difficulties of Prokofiev's music for the orchestra musician.

' "Nothing must be left out, no arabesque of the melody, no modulation,' David Oistrakh wrote. 'It demands a fine and detailed expression, subtle but not artificial charm and an attentive understanding structuring of each intonation. And the decisive point: it does not allow any form of artistic discretion.' "

Although these words concerned Prokofiev's violin compositions, they can be applied to the interpretation of all his works. In addition to music, Oistrakh and Prokofiev had a second passion - chess. Both could have rightly said that they were the best chess players among musicians.

"However, neither father nor Sergey Sergeyevich ever claimed to be the best musicians amongst chess players! As a chess player, Prokofiev belonged to the 'Performance Class I', father also. They played innumerable games together in our house as well as at Prokofiev's. Furthermore, they often met at chess competitions in the Soviet Union as well as at international competitions and both got very worked up as fanatic Botwinnik fans, when Botwinnik beat Capablanca in Nottingham in 1936 for the world master's title. Both kept their love for chess until the end of their lives."

Paul Badura-Skoda, also a chess

*"The best chess players amongst musicians: Prokofiev and Oistrakh"*

enthusiast, who, as he himself said, lost against Oistrakh most of the time, once repeated Oistrakh's story about his chess battles against Prokofiev. Oistrakh said that it was embarrassing for him to win the last game, since he knew that in such a case Prokofiev wouldn't sleep the whole night but would analyse the game.

"In 1937 there was an interesting competition between father and Sergey Prokofiev in the Central Building of Creative Musicians in Moscow. The conditions were of a peculiar type: whoever won the prize would join the audience; the loser was obliged to give a concert.

How seriously the two 'rivals' took the contest can be shown by Prokofiev's interview which he gave to a correspondent: 'Whether you believe it or not, this chess competition has somewhat retarded the progress of my work on the opera *La Duenna.*"

The Oistrakh-Prokofiev battle took place in an overcrowded hall, in which there was neither a shortage of famous artists nor of well-known chess players. Even Botwinnik turned up occasionally. He had met Prokofiev in 1936 during the Chess World Championship in Moscow. The composer

*167*

was a member of the audience at the time, but had rather mixed feelings: 'On the one hand he was sympathetic with me, the young Soviet world champion, on the other hand, he couldn't wish the ex-world champion Capablanca to lose, with whom he had formed a chess friendship in Paris.'"

Michail Botwinnik must have experienced a similar dilemma of feelings at the competition Oistrakh versus Prokofiev.

"I don't know on whose side Botwinnik was, however in an analysis of the possibilities of both players, he gave father the advantage:

'It was a fight between two characters. The passionate Prokofiev, who was brought up in the spirit of the pre-revolutionary Russian chess school (he played the king's gambit and other openings and dived almost senselessly into the attack) and the cautious cold-blooded Oistrakh, a modern chess player (he preferred close openings, took no risk and had an adequately high technique).' "

Prokofiev's works and personality became an essential part of David Oistrakh's own life. He always recalled his friendship with Sergey Prokofiev with the greatest gratitude, he regarded the dedication of the 1st Violin Sonata as one of the most precious presents which he ever received during his whole life.

"As far as Prokofiev's attitude to father is concerned, it is expressed in the composer's dedication on the first sheet of the score of his 1st Violin Concerto in a laconic way:

'To the outstanding artist, the fear inspiring opponent and the very dear human being David Feodorovich Oistrakh from the composer. 1939.' "

## Dmitri Shostakovich

"When I met Dmitri Shostakovich, he and father had already been friends for years. In spite of this, as I clearly remember, father got happily excited each time we went to Shostakovich's house. This was also the case in 1948. Shostakovich had invited father to show him his recently completed Violin Concerto. By the way, father awaited each new composition with great impatience, irrespective of whether it was a piece for the violin or something else. He adored Shostakovich as a genius, followed the development of the musician since the time when the unique individuality of the nineteen-year-old composer of the 1st symphony first rose as bright star in the heavens of music. Father was deeply impressed after the first performance of the Piano Trio in Leningrad, which the composer played with Dmitri Zyganow and Sergey Shirinsky in 1945. He soon took part in the shaping of this composition – together with Lew Oborin and Sviatoslav Knuschewizki.

One day the telephone rang and Dmitri Dmitriyevich invited father to introduce him to his Violin Concerto. Father had dreamt of this day for many years. However, I would like to discuss the details a little later."

How close Shostakovich was to Oistrakh can best be seen by the fact that he dedicated two violin concertos to Oistrakh and David Oistrakh was the first to play his Violin Sonata.

"Dmitri Shostakovich and father belonged to that generation of musicians which one could describe as the creators of Soviet musical culture. Their friendship proved itself in a human and artistic contact which lasted for decades. But if I consider what brought the composer and violinist together and what their mutual attraction was based on, I would neither like to put the long years of their acquaintance first nor the fact that they admired each other. The main links between them were similar traits of character, a complete abandonment in art, the artistic 'maximalism', an organic uncompromising attitude and their extremely developed sense of duty."

One should add the mutuality of their artistic nature. I want to point to the fact that both knew how to hit the heart of things with enviable consciousness (Shostakovich in the composition and Oistrakh in his violin playing).

"I didn't mention this, since the similarity between their artistic natures, father's and Shostakovich's, were the result of the similarity of their characters, a similarity which was fed by the ethical potential of personality.

'I got to know Shostakovich's music fairly early,' father told the well-known musicologist Grigori Schneerson. 'We were all enthusiastic about his 1st Symphony, a marvellous composition which hasn't lost any of its artistic importance today and which is fascinating with its extraordinarily precise formulation and daring discoveries as well as spiritual content. I am convinced that this composition from Shostakovich's youth, which has belonged to the repertoires of the world's best orchestras for the last fifty years, will never lose its attractiveness, will never fade from the consciousness of people who love music.' "

Did your father mention Shostakovich's pre-war compositions?

"The 5th Symphony and the opera *Katerina Izmailova* were his favourite works from Shostakovich's creations of the 1930s. Father attended the Moscow first performance of *Katerina Izmailova* in 1934, he often told me about the strong impression which this performance made on him. In the already mentioned discussion with Schneerson, father said about this opera: 'The tremendous dramatic impulsiveness, the pointed nature and the precision with which the actors are drawn, the wealth of the harmonic and melodic language and the tragedy of the final part of the opera moved me deeply. Years have passed since then. I have since heard the opera again in different opera houses. However, the first experience could not be wiped from my memory and stays with me like an unforgettable meeting with a person who is dear and precious to oneself.' "

I am not quite sure when Oistrakh met Shostakovich. The composer explained that the acquaintance began in 1935. We have already quoted his enthusiastic verdict on Oistrakh the winner of the second union competition.

"The personal contact between my father and Dmitri Shostakovich, whether it began in 1935 or earlier, grew stronger on the occasion of their visit to Turkey with a group of Soviet artists. 'On this journey, when we all came closer to each other, I got to know many outstanding traits of Dmitri Dmitriyevich: his great kindness, his human warmth, his extraordinary modesty,' father related. 'Shostakovich was an excellent travel companion, understanding and attentive. One could say a lot about this. He was born with this trait.'

The 7th (*Leningrad*) Symphony was one of the deepest Shostakovich experiences which father ever had as listener: 'I heard the 7th Symphony in 1942 as an excellent performance of the Orchestra of the Bolshoi Theatre under S. A. Samosud in Kubyschew. It was the first presentation of this work, which deeply moved the listeners as well as the orchestra. Everybody felt joy and sadness, everyone was proud of our nation which resisted a well-armed, hating enemy. We were also proud of the fact that there was an artist in our country, who in these difficult times and with inspiration knew how to shape the terrible events of war. Already in those days when we nervously listened to the tragic news from the front, Shostakovich's music predicted victory over Fascism. It was a lyrical expression of the nation's patriotic feelings and its confidence in the triumph of light and humanism.'

Shostakovich's Piano Trio was also an exciting event for father, even more so, since father was listener as well as trio player."
He played it a year before Shostakovich showed him his Violin Concerto, at a musical evening which the composer gave in the frame of the festival week 'Spring in Prague' with the composer and the Czechoslovakian cellist Miloš Sadlo. It is quite possible that the joint performances with Oistrakh's masterful playing stimulated Shostakovich to compose the Violin Concerto, which he later dedicated to your father.

"I suspect that father's art was already well know to Dmitri Dmitriyevich before the joint performance in Prague. But back to that memorable day in 1948, when father and I listened to Shostakovich's 1st Violin Concerto in his flat for the first time: Dmitri Dmitriyevich sat down at the piano and played the score with a virtuosity which itself would have been admirable (how he played the whole score of the Scherzo without leaving out a single note of the violin part remains an enigma to me even now) if he had not been so deeply moved by the music. All external superficial aspects disappeared into the background at once. The tragedy of the images conquered one as much as the lyrics of the whole structure."

"The first performance of this Concerto did not take place until 1955 in Leningrad. Did the relationship between your father and the composer develop any further between 1948 and 1955?

"Contact was never broken. I can for instance remember that Shostakovich asked father in 1955 to make a recording of Prokofiev's Sonata (which father already knew) on his own tape recorder with Lew Oborin. This was to be done with eight-handed piano accompaniment. Father agreed of course. At this time he was also rehearsing with his friends the so-far unplayed 4th Quartet by Shostakovich. If the contact between the two befriended musicians wasn't regular enough, then the reason for it lay only in father's permanent tours.

Father had a special relationship with Shostakovich's 10th Symphony. I quote: 'I am deeply impressed by the 10th Symphony. There is nothing in it that wouldn't convince me ... The symphony is saturated with high ethical values, deep humanity and the sincere feeling of a great artist and patriot. Its strength rests on its immense drama, the pointed conflicts and the overwhelming beauty and closeness to life of the pictures.'

I still remember that father, when he returned from the Moscow first performance, immediately listened to the Symphony for the second time – he had recorded it on tape in the Great Hall of the Conservatory. He was deeply moved by the music of the 10th, which remained his favourite composition for ever. Father later conducted it frequently."

Shostakovich's 10th Symphony induced David Oistrakh to repeat the question, why the Soviet violin repertoire was growing only relatively slowly?

'Why do we violinists only have at our disposal a relatively small selection of compositions by Soviet composers, of creations which were composed with their hearts' blood, were filled with it, inspired and truly dramatic? Why has our repertoire so few compositions by Soviet artists, which reflect our epoch and the feelings of our contemporaries which would give a great artistic challenge to violinists?'

This was surely a challenge directed at the composers. However, Oistrakh already knew Shostakovich's Violin Concerto and knew that the composer was working on a second version. He performed this new version on October 29 and 30, 1955 in Leningrad.

'We prepared ourselves very carefully for the first performance by rehearsing about a dozen times in the presence of the composer. We tried to put our whole ability, our heart and soul into Shostakovich's new composition. And I was very happy that the public accepted the concert very warmly. So it was a happy launching.'

Shostakovich was not only enthusiastic about the presentation of the concerto which Oistrakh and the Symphony Orchestra of the Leningrad Philharmonic performed under Eugene Mravinsky, but also accepted changes that would have to be made to the score, which were dictated by the sound of the composition:

'Dear Dodik,

I send you the score. I have edited it, but I cannot guarantee a high standard of work. Anyway, I have improved points which I noted.

I did not manage to produce a new orchestration of the beginning of the finale. However, I think that it would not prove difficult for the conductor to conduct using the score (with the violin solo). I thank you once again for the great pleasure which you have given me. I wish you much success. Give Tamara Iwanowna and Igor my kindest regards. Yours, D. Shostakovich.'

"Father started his first tour of the United States in the same month. He had given careful thought to the program of the violin evenings and symphony concerts, but one thing was, right from the beginning, beyond any doubt: he would play Shostakovich's Concerto in the USA. To make one's début with a new composition in the program in the United States was just as daring an undertaking as father's youthful decision years ago to include Prokofiev's Concerto in his diploma examination at the Conservatory.

The first performance of Shostakovich's Concerto under Mitropoulos in New York was a triumph. We have already talked about its success with the press, audience and musicians. Father received the following telegram from Shostakovich:

'Moscow, 30th December 1955.
Dear Dodik,
I thank you from my heart, and I send you and Tamara my good wishes for the new year. Please also give Dmitri Mitropoulos and the members of the orchestra my sincere thanks and best wishes for the new year. I embrace you. Shostakovich.'

Father received similar telegrams from Shostakovich almost after

*171*

each performance of his compositions in different cities in the world."

What did your father think about the 1st Concerto?

"What father liked about the Concerto, as he himself wrote was: 'the surprising seriousness and depth of its artistic contest, its absolute symphonic thinking'.

He found in this Concerto the same philosophy as in the 10th Symphony, and this found its impression much earlier, already with the 5th Symphony, the Piano Quintet and the Piano Trio."

Shostakovich, however, projected such philosophical music for the first time into a type of composition where this was most unusual: namely in a solo instrument concerto, which must surely have been very attractive to your father. There is a good reason why he introduced his contribution about the new composition, which you previously quoted, with the following words: 'I had the honour of being the first to perform D. Shostakovich's Violin Concerto. This position offers the violinist an extremely interesting and attractive challenge. It is, if one can put it this way, a task full of content which offers the violinist great possibilities not only to display his virtuosity, but also to transmit deep feelings, thoughts and moods.'

"In his verdict about Shostakovich's new composition, and above all, of course, in his interpretation, father represented the musical content of this Concerto as it appeared to him in a definite way, but it was not generally recognized at the time. He said in particular that the atmosphere of the first part - the Nocturnes - was not all melancholy hopelessness, but of a suppression of feelings, of tragedy in the best sense of purification, whilst the harmonic hardness in the Scherzo only appeared as such. His playing proved convincingly that the violin is able to rise to the same dramatic intensity in the Cadenza which closes the third part - the Passacaglia - and is able to achieve the same precise culmination as the orchestra in this part of the Concerto. The shining fresco-type activity of the tone coloration with which he shaped the finale of the Concerto - the Burlesque - balanced the drama of the first three parts.

Father even developed his own concept of this finale which deviated from that of the composer to a certain degree: 'The only point in which the composer of the wonderful, sparkling music which is close to the spirit of the people disagrees, is in the term 'burlesque'. It does not seem to me to correspond either to the festive character or the Russian colouration of the music. The finale suggests to me the picture of a happy country party, sometimes even the bagpipes of travelling musicians. I would look for another name which conveys the content of the finale with its deeply Russian wild experience and its shining jubilant colouration.' "

Do you agree with your father about this?

"In my opinion, the terms 'country party' and 'burlesque' do not exclude each other. The humour is often exhuberant, indeed rough, in folk art.

I must confess that I didn't dare to approach Shostakovich's 1st Concerto for a long time, as I thought that I would be unable to offer anything new after father's interpretation. Only after a meeting with Dmitri Shostakovich at a music festival in Kischinjow and thanks to his cordial behaviour to me (he listened at the time to my performance of Prokofiev's 1st Violin Concerto and told me that he liked this interpretation), that I decided to play his Concerto."

The depth of his musical thinking, the strength of his conception, and sovereign ability to subordinate his almost unlimited artistic mastery to the presentation of the artistic nucleus were clearly apparent in David Oistrakh's interpretation of the Violin Concerto. This is also confirmed by the enthusiastic reviews following the Soviet and the American first performances of the Concerto as well as the subsequent performances in Moscow, London, Vienna, Paris and Tokyo. This acknowledgement of his interpretation of the Concerto by the composer was the important thing for father, and Shostakovich always called him 'the great artist'.

'As far as I am concerned,' Shostakovich wrote to father, 'I could fill thousands of tons of paper with compliments for you.'"

In the twelve years which lay between the composing of Shostakovich's 1st and 2nd Violin Concertos, many things changed in Oistrakh's life as well as in the Soviet art of performing. Your father's reputation as an outstanding musician of his day was even more strengthened, and he not only played the violin, but also conducted. In addition, a large group of young violinists appeared . . .

" . . . and in spite of this father was the first interpreter of the 2nd Concerto. After Shostakovich had finished the work on his new composition in 1967, he telephoned father, and asked him to visit him. As a rule, Shostakovich never talked about his unfinished composition, about plans which had not so far materialized. Even people close to him only found out about the new composition after Shostakovich had put it on paper. And he only did this when the creation of the concept had fully matured and had been worked out in the finest detail – all the preceding work took place in his head without any notes. I do not any longer know why, but in the case of the 2nd Concerto the secret was revealed earlier. Father knew that Shostakovich worked on it, maybe the composer told him himself – at that time they often met at the rehearsals for the vocal and instrumental cycle which the composer had written to verses by Alexander Blok.

The history of the composition of the 2nd Violin Concerto contains another little detail: Shostakovich wanted it performed on the occasion of father's sixtieth birthday but made a mistake by a year and completed it for father's fifty-ninth birthday. To make up for his mistake, he composed a violin sonata a year later.

When father came to Shostakovich, the composer sat down at the piano himself, and put the manuscript of the solo part of the Concerto on the violinist's desk. The music began. I have already said that I received this first performance of the 2nd Concerto on tape. The performance was excellent. It contained the character of the music, even the minutest details of the score. However, the most important thing was: one could already hear the spiritual and emotional thread running through the composition: to refine it was father's real and final task."

Oistrakh studied Shostakovich's 2nd Concerto in the summer of 1967 in Pärnu. The composer took note of Oistrakh's views and comments as far as details of the violin parts were concerned.

'Dear David Feodorovich,' Shostakovich wrote. 'Thanks for your letter. I am glad to hear that you already know the first and second parts by heart. I obviously accept your corrections . . .

Your letter made me feel quite excited. From the 2nd of October onwards, you will have so much to do because of me! The two Concertos and the 2nd for Cello and the 10th Symphony and Blok ... '

The Seven Romances based on poems by Alexander Blok were first performed in 1967 by Galina Wichnewskaja, David Oistrakh, Mstislav Rostropovich and Moissej Weinberg. David Oistrakh was quite affected by the music of this cycle with its instrumental accompaniment - each romance with a different cast.

'When we first played this cycle, there were several bad moments for me,' David Oistrakh later remembers. 'The violin doesn't take part in the first two numbers, I therefore had to sit on the platform and wait for my turn. I had terrible stage fright, my teeth were virtually chattering, my heart was already causing me some trouble when I had stage fright in those days. Also this time during the period of waiting, my heart started to hurt terribly and it got worse and worse. Of course I should have stood up and left the platform, but I couldn't afford to do this, since I knew that Shostakovich sat at home and listened to the radio (because of his illness he couldn't be present). I imagined with what excitement and tension he was listening and how worked up he became.

At last it was my turn. I played my part in the uniquely beautiful romance 'We Were Together', whilst my limbs were cramped by pain. Fortunately the cycle was tremendously successful and at the audience's request was repeated

*Dmitri Shostakovich. Photograph with dedication to David Oistrakh*

from start to finish. The second time round, my excitement evaporated, the heart trouble improved and everything went well.'

"Unfortunately Shostakovich broke a leg towards the end of the summer and was in hospital during the first performance of the 2nd Violin Concerto and the Blok cycle."

The first performance of the 2nd Concerto took place on September 13, in the little town of Bolschewo not far from Moscow. David Ois-

174

trakh and Kyril Kondrashin wanted to play the whole Concerto once again before performing it in the Great Hall of the Conservatory. In the first part they played Shostakovich's 10th Symphony under David Oistrakh, in the second part the 2nd Violin Concerto with Oistrakh under Kondrashin's baton.

"Father sent the recording of the Concerto in Bolschewo to the composer. Dmitri Shostakovich greatly valued his performances in both parts – as conductor and as soloist. I remember that father had several telephone conversations with Shostakovich to discuss with him the details of the interpretation of the Symphony and of the Violin Concerto."

The tape recordings of these conversations have survived. We hear Oistrakh's excited energetic voice, Shostakovich's somewhat muffled timbre and feel with each word a relaxed atmosphere of conversation, the mutual respect and high opinion they had for each other. When listening to this recording one almost stops breathing, particularly as both musicians have now left us:

"Shostakovich: David Feodorovich!
Oistrakh: Yes, my dear friend.
Shostakovich: I have just stopped for a little while. I am stopping after the 10th Symphony and then I shall listen to the Concerto.
Oistrach: Now, tell me . . .
Shostakovich: Tremendous. In my opinion it is tremendous.
Oistrakh: No, really?
Shostakovich: Simply tremendous. You know, the whole lot, but above all the 1st and 3rd movements and also the 2nd and 4th.
Oistrakh: And the rest, the tempi in the finale?
Shostakovich: The tempi are outstanding, simply outstanding.
Oistrakh: I also thought that the mood was there . . .
Shostakovich: Brilliant, and the whole thing extremely musical.
Oistrakh: How sorry I was that you weren't there.
Shostakovich: Well, I shall in a moment listen to the Concerto and then I will phone you again.
Oistrakh: Thank you my dear friend. I am most grateful to you. Thank you.

After listening to the Violin Concerto, Shostakovich phoned again:
Shostakovich: Very good. An excellent interpretation. Also by the orchestra in my opinion.
Oistrakh: They play well. Didn't you find the first movement boring?
Shostakovich: No, no.
Oistrakh: You know, it's because we were trying to keep the tempi as you wanted them.
Shostakovich: No, everything was good.
Oistrakh: Didn't the orchestra lag a bit behind a few times?
Shostakovich: No, never. Why do you think that?
Oistrakh: No, you know where the horns come in, I had the slight feeling . . .
Shostakovich: Well if one listens to it over-critically. I shall listen to it once again with the score. I have now only just heard it as it is. In my opinion, everything was very good.
Oistrakh: And how did you find the theme in the finale?
Shostakovich: The finale was also excellent.
Oistrakh: In my opinion it was brilliant.
Shostakovich: Brilliant.
Oistrakh: And the cadenza?
Shostakovich: It comes over very well.
Oistrakh: I also find that. I also feel that the 2nd movement is convincing and penetrating.
Shostakovich: Yes, the 2nd is wonderful.
Oistrakh: And the end of the 1st . . .
Shostakovich: Yes, yes.

175

Oistrakh: You are absolutely satisfied?

Shostakovich: I am absolutely satisfied and I am today very grateful to you, I am very grateful to you.

Oistrakh: No, don't mention it, I am grateful to you - for ever."

On the following day Oistrakh travelled to Gorki, where he conducted Shostakovich's 10th Symphony twice. On his return to Moscow he phoned the composer in order to discuss the recording of the first performance of the 2nd Violin Concerto in Bolschewo with the score in front of him:

"Shostakovich: Hello!

Oistrakh: Dmitri Dmitriyevich! Good day!

Shostakovich: Ah, David Feodorovich! Good day! Just a moment, I'll just get the score.

Oistrakh: I will also get the score. Immediately. [pause]

Shostakovich: All right, one after the other. Number 11, could one hear the piccolo flute clearly at the last performance?

Oistrakh: Very well.

Shostakovich: There is no doubt about this?

Oistrakh: No, I even asked some of the audience and they all said it could be heard quite clearly.

Shostakovich: 58 in the cadenza on page 87, the fifth bar, you accelerate the one sixteenth a little. [he sings]

Oistrakh: A little slower, yes?

Shostakovich: I would play that slowly.

Oistrakh: Is the tenuto right?

Shostakovich: Yes.

Oistrakh: Sostenuto. Poco sostenuto, yes?

Shostakovich: Yes, poco sostenuto, yes ... everything in the cadenza is alright. An excellent cadenza, very good. Now page 132. It all seems to race a bit here.

Oistrakh: Very fast, yes?

Shostakovich: It's a real chase ... Particularly on page 137.

Oistrakh: Yes, the finale comes over as very lively and for some reason seems to play fast as if of its own accord.

Shostakovich: It must be lively, but a little bit retarded. That's it.

Oistrakh: Page 138. I can hardly keep pace, and if it goes that fast it becomes rather confused.

Shostakovich: Yes, it must be played a little bit more retarded, controlled. But in general, what I hear on this recording is a glorious interpretation. Do you understand, I can only make the most stupid compliment possible: as if I had played it myself.

Oistrakh: Oh, but that is ...

Shostakovich: As if I had played it myself.

Oistrakh: That makes me very happy.

Shostakovich: And the ritenuti and accelerandi are not even marked.

Oistrakh: Do you know, Mitenka, this will surely have to be done for the printed edition.

Shostakovich: We shall mark everything.

Oistrakh: Exactly, all subtle nuances."

What was the future history of the performances of Shostakovich's 2nd Violin Concerto?

"Shostakovich was still in hospital. I visited him some time after the first performance of the 2nd Violin Concerto and told him about the great success of his composition and gave him father's kindest regards. Father was just about to start a tour of the USA where he was determined to perform Shostakovich's 2nd Concerto. The following day a letter came from the composer:

'Dear Dodik,
Igor visited me yesterday. I was

very happy to see him and hear about you. The whole Concerto was transmitted on our radio on November 19. It sounded very good. I listened to the whole Concerto, which sounded extremely good with your interpretation.

It was an immense joy for me. Please accept my most sincere thanks.

I am still in hospital for the time being. I am hoping to return home between December 15th and 20th.

I often listen to the recording of my Blok Romances and the 2nd Concerto and I think how lucky I am to have such an interpreter as yourself. I would like to see you as soon as possible and to hear you 'live', instead of on the radio or on the tape recorder. I wish you from the bottom of my heart much success on your tour. By the way, I don't doubt your success.

I kiss Tamara Iwanowna and you. Your very loving and grateful D. Shostakovich.' "

Soon afterwards in November 1967, Oistrakh played Shostakovich's 2nd Concerto in the USA. As in 1955, David Feodorovich proved himself an excellent pioneer for the works of the great Soviet composer.

" 'My dear Dmitri Dmitriyevich!' father wrote from America. 'I am very happy to tell you again that your 2nd Concerto has had an enormous and enthusiastic success and I hope that you heard on the radio how enthusiastically it was received by the audience. The orchestra played with great feeling and much understanding for the composition.

Ormandy was absolutely at his best . . .

There were many press reviews, the most serious and analytical review came from *The Times;* I am sending you this review. Your 1st Concerto which was played a few days later by Igor with Ormandy was also (as always) a success.

Tamara and I are flying to Canada in one hour. I now have to conduct your 10th Symphony in Cleveland, where it will be performed for the first time. In mid-January I shall play your 2nd Concerto in New York with Bernstein. I await these days with great impatience . . . '

These days when Shostakovich's music conquered the American Continent are still clear in my memory. The interest in the composer's new violin concerto was extraordinary. Father enjoyed this even more than his own success.

'I am very happy,' he wrote to Yehudi Menuhin, 'that Shostakovich's 2nd Concerto made a good impression on you. I am certain that you will soon be playing it.' The second interpreter of the 2nd Violin Concerto after father, and the first whom Shostakovich got to hear 'live', was myself. I studied the Concerto almost simultaneously with father when I spent my summer holiday in Repino near Leningrad in the bungalow of the holiday home of the Society of Composers, where Shostakovich also lived and worked. I listened to father's playing during the first performance of the Concerto not only with the attention of a listener but also with the passionate interest of the interpreter. I was waiting impatiently for father's letters from America.

In one of his letters father also mentioned his own attitude to the 2nd Concerto: 'Some musicians who like the 1st Concerto still consider it to be more interesting and important. It is difficult not to agree with this, but nevertheless I love the 2nd with all my heart and play it with pleasure. I assume that it will also give you pleasure.' "

Was Shostakovich present at your rehearsal of the 2nd Concerto?

"Yes, and I must confess that these rehearsals were more important than the later performances in the concert hall for me and for Roshdestvensky who conducted. Shostakovich, who in his remarks to the interpreter of his compositions was as always extremely tactful, was sitting in the hall and carried out a dynamic 'retouching' of the score. After the rehearsal he praised our interpretation and also expressed his satisfaction after the concert, when my wife and I had the pleasure of receiving him in our home."

Was this the first time that Shostakovich met you as an interpreter?

"Shostakovich presumably knew of my existence in 1935, when he and father were in Turkey together. 'Have you received my telegram with my congratulations on Garjushka's birthday?' father asked mother in one of his letters. 'Kiss the tiny one very hard from his daddy, tell him that today all our colleagues from the embassy and all artists emptied a glass for his health and Shostakovich called the toast.'

He got to know me as a violinist at the end of the 1940s during my first orchestra performance. I played Dmitri Kabalevsky's recently composed Violin Concerto.

As I stepped onto the platform and looked into the hall, I immediately saw father and next to him Shostakovich. You can imagine my excitement."

In 1956 Oistrakh wrote (after he had introduced Shostakovich's 1st Violin Concerto to the musical world) that he would be very happy if it were not the last time that the composer turned to the violin. At that time he wished for himself 'at least' one sonata for violin and piano.

"Shortly before father's sixtieth birthday Shostakovich composed a sonata which as already mentioned was the most beautiful present which he could have wished for.

I remember that Shostakovich sent father the score with a piano recording as temporary help. 'Dear Dodik,' Shostakovich wrote, 'I am sending you the score of the violin part and an improvised recording of the Violin Sonata full of excitement and fear. Yesterday M. S. Weinberg and B. A. Tchaikovsky played my Sonata on two pianos and I recorded the performance. M. S. played the piano part and B. A. the violin part.

I have found the courage to send you this recording as I expect that it may make it easier for you to get an impression of the opus.

Weinberg and Tchaikovsky are of course highly talented people, and they followed my remarks and instructions closely concerning the character of the tempi, etc.

However, Tchaikovsky extended the holds in the 3rd movement no. 65 bar 9, no. 66 bar 4 and no. 76 bar 4 a little too long.

If you find time and opportunity to listen to this recording then let it run with speed 9.

I send you my best wishes. I await your return impatiently. I dearly wish to hear your unique sound in my Sonata. I kiss you. Irina* sends you and Tamara Iwanowna her kind regards. The same from me with all my soul.

Yours, D. Shostakovich.'

'If you have time and opportunity'! Dmitri Dmitriyevich probably didn't know with what impatience father awaited the score of the Sonata and how moved he was when he listened to the improvised recording! Father played the Sonata for the first time with Gennadi Roshdestvensky and afterwards he performed it with Moissej Weinberg in the Society of

*Irina Antonovna Shostakovich – the wife of the composer.

Composers' club. Only afterwards, in May 1969, was the sonata publicly performed by the duo David Oistrakh – Sviatoslav Richter, a performance which became an event. The impression was so strong that I also felt the desire to study the Sonata. As with the 2nd Violin Concerto, I became its second interpreter. The piano part was played by my wife Natalia Serzalowa."

When Shostakovich was fifty years old in 1956, Oistrakh sent him a telegram which included among others the following sentence: 'I am proud of your soaring genius.' The feelings which David Oistrakh had for the composer are expressed very accurately by these words. They also contain something of the spirit of the city Petersburg – Leningrad, in which Shostakovich grew up and developed his abilities.

Oistrakh's last recording of a composition by Shostakovich took place in the presence of the composer in the autumn of 1972 in London during the festival week for Soviet music. David Oistrakh played his third interpretation of the 1st Violin Concerto with Maxim Shostakovich, the son of the composer, conducting in the EMI studio. 'It seems to me,' Oistrach wrote,

'that this recording succeeded in showing up essential traits of this composition which were not adequately developed in previous recordings. I am thinking particularly of the cadenza, which stems from a gradual dynamic intensification demanding an irreversible forward movement and a gigantic inexhaustible vigour which culminates in a brilliantly effective finale. I have at last succeeded in playing the cadenza in the way I imagined it should be played before I made my first recordings of the Concerto. For this reason, I regard the London recording as the most successful one'

"A critic later wrote in the journal *Gramophone*: 'It was a truly moving moment when those two great people, friends for many years, respectfully exchanged their opinions about debatable questions concerning balance and interpretation. You got the feeling of great warmth. This also contributed much to the recording. How depressing the thought is that this will never again be possible.' "

## Aram Chatschaturjan

One can consider the continuous contact between composers and interpreters of music as a good tradition in Soviet musical life. The artists' friendship between David Oistrakh and Aram Chatschaturjan is a convincing example of this.

" 'Aram Ilyich and I are almost the same age,' Oistrakh wrote, 'we are only separated by a few years. I had the chance of witnessing his first brilliant successes as a composer and I can remember exactly how impressed I was by his first compositions, among them the Violin Dance in B Flat Major, which counts as the first opus in the list of his compositions. Then followed the attractive song poem 'In honour of Aschugen'. These pieces are particularly dear to me. I have played them often. I still play them frequently and love them for their poetic mood and expressiveness, for the sparkling light which radiates from all of Chatschaturjan's compositions.'

Father was very susceptible to the directness of Chatschaturjan's talent, his convincing optimism, open emotions and the full-blooded materialization of the national characteristics of Armenian music.

*179*

*With Aram Chatschaturjan*

In addition to the already mentioned violin miniatures, father loved Chatschaturjan's Piano Concerto and his ballet *Gajaneh*. Father was in contact with the composer particularly at the time when Lew Oborin prepared the first performance of the Piano Concerto. Aram Ilyich knew that his violin compositions were in father's repertoire. However, the strong bond came about in a natural way, all the stronger when Chatschaturjan created his Violin Concerto.

The Violin Concerto is dated 1940, I was nine years old at the time. I am sure that certain important elements are missing from my memories of those days, but I remember exactly the summer day when Aram Ilyitsch came to us in Shodnja. One immediately noticed that he was completely filled with music, that he was only concerned with music and that he had to play it. He immediately made a dive for the piano and performed his just completed Violin Concerto. He played with such inspiration and expressiveness that father was virtually enchanted. Father's grandmother, who was relaxing in the next room and who was woken up by the sudden exploding volcanic storm of sound, came running into the living room rather terrified and convinced that something had happened, a fire or an earthquake." Grandmother wasn't all that wrong. After all, many critics compared Chatschaturjan's music with the powers of nature. An American reviewer wrote: Chatschaturjan's music was saturated with the radiating glow of the Caucasian sun. And what was your father's reaction to the Violin Concerto which he heard for the first time?

"Enthusiastic: 'A music full of individuality and honesty, melodic beauty, country colours and so intelligent that it virtually seemed to sparkle,' father emphasized. 'All these qualities, which still delight listeners, made an unforgettable impression on me at the time. I was immediately enchanted by the colouring of the wonderful music: the finale with its sweeping, dancing tearfulness, the second movement with its deep lyrical episodes, and the first movement with the incredible dynamic force of its first theme. Yes, altogether, the wealth of subtle details, orchestral solutions and effects, which one could first of all only guess at since the composer played his creation on the piano and explained to me how he intended to shape it in the score. Obviously a new significant composition had been created, for which a great future on the concert platform could be predicted. It was decided that my violin would accompany its birth.'

The first performance was fixed for the end of 1940. Father worked with great enthusiasm on the Concerto for the whole summer and autumn. Aram Ilyich quite readily agreed with father's corrections of the solo part and allowed him the greatest freedom as interpreter. Father, who at the time already enjoyed the composer's trust and respect checked both the violin part and the whole score at Chatschaturjan's request.

'Dear Dodik,' the composer wrote to father. 'I report: in five days I have written down the score for the first movement. Tomorrow I will start the third movement and intend to complete it in six days; then I shall start on the second, which is the smallest and easiest.

Dodik, I have an important request: enter all alterations in the score, throw out anything that is unnecessary and enter your corrections clearly. I very much hope that you won't turn this request down. Please don't think about it too much and don't worry: the violin

part which I borrow from you will be immediately returned after copying it ... ' "

David Oistrakh's creative participation wasn't limited to editing the violin part. A few years later he composed his own cadenza to the Concerto's first movement. This Concerto is nowadays played by many violinists. It was interesting to note the composer's reaction, who had a very high opinion of Oistrakh's cadenza. In 1958 he was together with David Oistrakh as a member of the jury of the 1st Tchaikovsky Competition, and was even further strengthened in his opinion, when he had to listen to his Concerto several times, always with a different cadenza. He wrote the following note to Oistrakh:

" 'Dear Dodik, That's how it is in life: you live next to each other, live in one and the same town, sometimes even in the same house, and one hardly sees one another, one doesn't even have the opportunity to say what one feels for the other and what he thinks about him ... I think that if you didn't like my Concerto, you wouldn't have composed such a wonderful cadenza for it. I prefer your cadenza to mine, your cadenza is a fantasy to my themes; it is in its form con-

vincing. With it you prepare the listener superbly well for the recapitulation, by allowing elements and rhythm of the first theme to resound.'

This is indeed an eloquent verdict for father's cadenza by the composer. I would only like to add that Aram Chatschaturjan frequently appeared as a conductor of his Concerto with father in Moscow, Leningrad, Jerewan, Kiev, Odessa, Charkow, Swerdlowsk, Tbilissi, Baku and also in foreign countries. Father also recorded the Concerto twice with Chatschaturjan as conductor (in London and Moscow). The composer's opinion of the cadenza, which father composed, was also hardened by practical experience. As far as father was concerned, he didn't just like Chatschaturjan's Concerto because of the beauty of his music and because of its impulsive form, but also because of his modern approach to this type of instrumental concerto, which was advanced beyond all traditions. He always stressed the importance of this Concerto as substantial enrichment of the violin literature."

Aram Chatschaturjan's demands on his interpreters are as well known as his temperament. Lew Oborin tells of the performance of Chatschaturjan's Piano Concerto in 1936 in the Sokolniki park, Moscow. This performance was meant to be the final rehearsal before its first performance in the autumn. Aram Ilyich could hardly wait to at last hear his composition performed. The orchestra was composed of different ensembles and although Lew Steinberg, an experienced and able conductor, was in charge, the performance was exceptionally poor. 'After it was all over,' Oborin relates, 'we only found the composer after a long search, in a dense thicket of the park, where he embraced a young birch tree and cried bitterly.'

"The actual first performance in the autumn was brilliant. Fortunately father didn't have a final rehearsal in Sokolniki, although I remember that he played the Concerto in the composer's presence sometime before the first official performance."

David Oistrakh played it repeatedly to friends, once in the summer of 1940 and also in Chatschaturjan's bungalow in the Home for Composers in Rusa near Moscow. Dmitri Borisovich Kabalevsky, who was present, later wrote about this evening:

'Oistrakh even apologized at the end that he had "not yet properly" studied the Concerto. This apology was of course quite unnecessary since he played it with sparkle and inspiration ... Oistrakh had an excellent accompanist, Sara Lewina, who also lived in Rusa during this summer. For all of us who didn't know that she had completed her piano course at the Odessa Conservatory, her brilliant piano playing and superb sense of colouring and rhythm came as a pleasant discovery.

We were all extremely impressed by the Concerto. We didn't separate for a long time afterwards and asked for a repetition of this or that episode.'

The first performance of the Violin Concerto turned into a celebration for the whole Soviet music world. In the hall you could see Miaskovsky, Prokofiev, Shostakovich and many other well-known composers and interpreters. David Oistrakh's playing was matchless.

"The composer was fully satisfied with father's interpretation and that of course influenced his opinion of father's playing in general:

'I regard you as an artist and violinist of epoch-making impor-

tance, that means that in your outstanding personality as an artist you reflect our Soviet era and that you stand at the top of the Soviet school of violin playing and interpretation. For this reason it doesn't only please me but it is flattering that my Concerto has stimulated your creative imagination and that you were prepared to improvise around my themes.' "

On that evening the orchestra was conducted by Alexander Gauk, who had also conducted the first performance of Chatschaturjan's Piano Concerto. He approached the score with great seriousness and inspired all musicians.

"Forgive me if I interrupt you, but I would like to recall a funny incident which father often mentioned and which he wrote in his memoirs of Gauk with whom he often played at the time. The incident took place in Leningrad at a hairdresser's.

'Tell me please, are you David Oistrakh?' the hairdresser asked.

'Yes.'

'And who is Igor Oistrakh?'

'My son.'

'And who is Gauk Oistrakh?'

Obviously the hairdresser had seen the posters which announced father's and Gauk's concerts and the hyphen between their names was a triviality which one could easily overlook."

Chatschaturjan's Violin Concerto passed on into the everyday musical repertoire with an almost incredible speed considering the 'academic' form of the composition. It was and is being played by almost all violinists. An exceptionally fresh interpretation of the Concerto was offered by George Enescu in Moscow in 1946 during his tour. Father had sent him the score a little earlier. Chatschaturjan's music was often played in Oistrakh's class where both Soviet and foreign students studied it with equal pleasure. David Oistrakh played Chatschaturjan's Concerto on his many tours, he recorded it three times and by this increased the already considerable popularity of the Soviet composer.

"The Concerto also helped father a great deal. 'I have to thank Chatschaturjan's Violin Concerto and therefore the composer for the fact that I got known in other countries and that I was warmly received in places where I had never been before. In many countries listeners also knew my other recordings but Chatschaturjan's Concerto played an important part in my existence as a violinist, a fact which I always think of with gratitude.'

Chatschaturjan's Concerto has also served me very well. As mentioned before, I played it during my first performance in the West. This was in 1953 in the Albert Hall in London. Soon afterwards I recorded the Concerto with the Philharmonic Orchestra under Goossens in London. This was my first recording for the famous Columbia. On that occasion I met Walter Legge, the outstanding musician and founder of the Philharmonic Orchestra, who at the same time was manager of Columbia and a brilliant sound editor."

May I add a nice detail from Walter Legge's memoirs concerning your father? After his wife heard for the first time Oistrakh's own old recording of the Chatschaturjan Concerto (there were no long-playing records at the time), one could notice an unmistakable sign of what mood she was in: if she was exceptionally happy, she hummed the finale of the Chatschaturjan Concerto at the speed with which it was played by Oistrakh. 'However,' Legge added, 'the high notes of the violin part are occasionally too high for her

voice . . . '

"Funny, when one thinks that Walter Legge's wife is Elisabeth Schwarzkopf."

The last words of this chapter should be Aram Chatschaturjan's congratulation to David Oistrakh on his fiftieth birthday:

'Dear David Feodorovich,

Soviet art is rich and great. We have an immense army of creative artists and amongst them not more than a few names who represent our cultural era. However, among the best there are the very best. I consider you as one of these very best, David Feodorovich.'

## Dmitri Kabalevsky

"I have already mentioned that my first orchestra performance as well as that of many of my colleagues was Kabalevsky's Violin Concerto. This Concerto altogether played an important role in my career as a violinist. I performed it very often when I was young. It was exactly this Concerto which led to my regular performances with orchestra and which got me used to cooperating with symphony orchestras.

I don't have to tell you how useful this was for me, particularly at the beginning, when I participated in competitions and when I went on my first guest tours."

Did your father also play Kabalevsky's Violin Concerto?

"He recorded it with the USSR State Symphony Orchestra with the composer conducting. Almost all Soviet violinists included this Concerto in their repertoire, some already in their youth, others in their mature age."

What was the difference in the performance of the Kabalevsky Concerto by a mature violinist compared with the performance of the same Concerto by a child?

"Father remarked 'In listening to the Concerto played by young violinists one normally notices many different faults; however, the directness, the youthful sincerity and the straightforwardness of emotions in Kabalevsky's work are sometimes presented so superbly well by students that one could almost become unwillingly jealous. The mature artist has to try just as hard to do justice to the challenge.'"

Did your father meet the composer during his work on the Violin Concerto?

"Oh no, their acquaintance, rather their friendship, went back much further. Kabalevsky created his Concerto in 1948 but father had already recorded two violin fragments for Grigori Roschal's film *The Petersburg Night,* which Kabalevsky later used as a basis for his 'improvisation' for the composition.

'I wanted to record the violin pieces as well as possible and to fully bring out their drama. At the same time, however, the recording technique wasn't exactly at its height, to be honest.

We met in the film theatre for several nights in succession. The night-long conversations about all sorts of subjects led to a friendship for life between Dmitri Borisovich and myself . . . '"

The musical taste and style of David Oistrakh and Kabalevsky was not always the same, but this did not affect their friendship in any way. Just to quote an example: the composer didn't share Oistrakh's admiration of Eugene Ysaye's music.

'I am returning Ysaye's Sonatas with thanks,' Kabalevsky wrote to Oistrakh. 'I have played them all honestly and painstakingly and I must confess that I was more surprised by the unlimited inventive spirit in the score and the unbelievable (that's how it appeared to me) instrumental solution than enjoying the usual pleasure for the music itself.'

These Sonatas as interpreted by Oistrakh produced an entirely different impression on Kabalevsky. In the same letter to Oistrakh, Kabalevsky wrote about the 3rd Sonata: 'I am no longer going to talk about the 3rd: with your interpretation you have convinced me that it is a 'fulfilled work', although I would have probably thought differently if I had played it on the piano before listening to your per-

*With Dmitri Kabalevsky*

formance ... ' Kabalevsky then draws this conclusion: 'It is quite possible that all these Sonatas have a meaning, particularly if perfectly performed on the violin; their 'soul' lies apparently exactly in their instrumentalization. This is the situation which we frequently experience with great interpreters, with Liszt as well as with Paganini.'

"We find the same logic and clarity in Kabalevsky's musical thinking. Father pointed to the popularity of his compositions and stressed as their main criteria the width of their melodic scope and balance in detail and, in general, the transparency of form and the delicacy of the compositional mastery. It was for this reason that father liked to listen to *Colas Breugnon* and Dmitri Kabalevsky's symphonies, his piano sonatas and also his Requiem. Like others, I myself knew that the composer admired father's art, of course not only for the reason that father performed his Concerto.

After father's death Kabalevsky wrote: 'David Oistrakh is one of the most wonderful figures in the artistic life of the twentieth century. He was the pride and glory of Soviet and all international music and he did it credit for almost half a century.

The combination of ingenious virtuosity with highest humanity, modesty and charm turned Oistrakh into a personality with whom it was a pleasure and joy to associate.

With his great recordings, the education of a multitude of students and with the many outstanding compositions which were dedicated to him and which he brought to life, David Oistrakh won immortality.' "

## Paul Hindemith

"Father gave a guest performance in 1961 in London with me. After the concert we returned to the hotel and briefly went to a restaurant. Paul Hindemith sat down at the next table. Using the opportunity we approached him; after the composer had made a few compliments concerning father's playing, father said incautiously: 'What a pity, maestro, that you haven't composed a concerto for two violins.' Hindemith immediately retorted: 'Then play my concerto "for one violin", Mr Oistrakh'."

David Oistrakh was one of those Soviet interpreters whom one has to thank that Hindemith, who already in the 1920s and 1930s had a firm place in the concert repertoire again became known in the years after the war in the Soviet Union. He performed Hindemith's Violin Sonata from opus 11 with Vladimir Jampolski at the end of 1956 and soon afterwards recorded it. However, he hadn't played Hindemith's Concerto. Did the meeting with the composer provide the trigger for him to study the Concerto?

"I would say it was the inducement, but by no means the cause. Father's repertoire already included many compositions by composers of the twentieth century. Whatever the reason, father studied Hindemith's Concerto shortly afterwards and the slight embarrassment which occurred during their first meeting was once more corrected by his wonderful interpretation.

I myself felt inspired by this meeting although I preferred another work by the composer. The conductor Gennadi Roshdestvensky and I were the first to perform Hindemith's Chamber music no. 4 for Violin and Large Chamber Orchestra in the Soviet Union."

Roshdestvensky told me about

*Paul Hindemith*

the memorable evening in 1962 when Hindemith's Concerto was played with him as conductor and in the presence of the composer, Shostakovich and Britten being also present. Your father played it with quite exceptional inspiration and the composer thanked him.

"At the same time, shortly after this concert performance, father recorded this Concerto, this time with Hindemith conducting. The recording which took place in the Decca studio was successful. Father's interpretation stimulated Hindemith to such an extent that he expressed the wish to play Mozart's Sinfonia Concertante with him on the other side of the record, which he used to play frequently in his youth – he was known as an excellent viola player. Although the great musician's interpretation of Mozart's Concertante proved extremely interesting, one could note the effect of the long break with his previous concert activity as an instrumentalist (Hindemith as before still appeared as a conductor). Father mentioned in a letter: 'I have recorded at Decca the Scottish Fantasy with J. Gorenstein for the other side of the record with the recording of Hindemith's Concerto with the composer conducting. Mama will tell you the sad story about the recording of Mozart's Sinfonia Concertante. This unfortunately didn't lead to anything ...'

Father carefully kept a small tape recording of fragments of the Sinfonia Concertante recording.

Later, in 1963, the plan was realized in London. This time he played the viola and I the violin."
I hope that this new 'incident' didn't cloud the good understanding between the violinist and the composer any more than the first one?

"Of course not. As in previous years on New Year's Eve 1963, father received the composer's greetings, just as in previous years. They consisted of drawings in Indian ink which the composer and a professional artist had drawn – still with a firm hand."

## Jean Sibelius

"When David Oistrakh first visited Finland in 1949, the receptionist at the Hotel Karelia in Helsinki handed him a telegram:

'Helsinki, 31 October 1949
I welcome you with all my heart on the occasion of your arrival in Finland. An admirer of your art, Jean Sibelius.'

I don't have to say how delighted father was. Sibelius, the most important and oldest Finnish composer was the author of one of his favourite violin concertos."
Oistrakh had played this concerto many times and recorded it three times with the great Radio Symphony Orchestra of the USSR in Moscow under Gennadi Roshdestvensky, with the Stockholm Festival Orchestra under Sixten Ehrling, and with the Philadelphia Orchestra under Eugene Ormandy.

"Father told us that he couldn't for a long time make up his mind about the speed of the first movement when he studied the Concerto. Tradition demanded slower playing than he himself felt was right. Finally father decided on a faster speed than the composer had fixed metronomically. How happy he was, when he found out at the meeting with Sibelius that the composer had deliberately slowed down the tempo, because he was afraid that violinists with their preference for a faster tempo would play the passage too quickly. Later after the composer's death, father often played it at music festivals which were named after Sibelius."
Did you also know Sibelius?

"Yes, I visited the composer in his home country on the occasion of my first tour to Finland in 1955. Sibelius received me most cordially in his villa Ainola. I was surprised that he wore evening dress no matter what the time of day, without appearing stiff or affected; he stood very upright, but was in no way overbearing or arrogant. Sibelius radiated the same feeling of controlled calm as the landscape into which his villa fitted organically. Involuntarily I commented 'What peace'. 'Sometimes it is disturbed by the sound of music,' the composer replied not without some humour. His words also contained a hint – people had told me that the composer liked to have something performed to him, and I had brought my violin along with me for this reason.

I chose Ysaye's 3rd Sonata and earned Sibelius' praise. 'You are a lucky man,' he said and remembered that he had had the occasion

*Jean Sibelius*

to hear the quartet: Fritz Kreisler, Jacques Thibaud, Eugene Ysaye (viola) and Pablo Casals.

The composer asked after father and Shostakovich's Violin Concerto, which he didn't know. When I handed the master of the house father's present (the first recording of Sibelius' Violin Concerto under Ehrling), he thanked us heartily. 'I shall listen to the record later when I am alone,' he said."
Presumably he already knew Oistrakh's interpretation, at least in general terms:

'To my great pleasure I recently heard my Violin Concerto in your brilliant interpretation on the radio. Allow me to express my fullhearted thanks for your individual and (in the highest degree) artistic interpretation, which I enjoyed very much. I am very glad that you included my Concerto in your repertoire. I send you my best wishes. Yours sincerely, J. Sibelius.'

"Sibelius surprisingly asked me: 'Do you play my Concerto?' I had to admit that I didn't play it, or at least not by that time. At the time I had a special feeling about the maestro's Concerto: I loved his music, but I didn't feel mature enough to interpret it.

'It seems to me that I am too young to play your Concerto,' I answered after I had recovered my composure.

'You don't have to wait until you are as old as I,' the composer joked. He was almost ninety at the time."

# Queen Elisabeth of Belgium

"Queen Elisabeth of Belgium still remembered father from the Brussels Competition in 1937. As a previous student of Eugene Ysaye and a chamber musician in ensembles in which Ysaye, the viola player L. Tertis and the violinist E. Dehardt participated during World War I, she accepted the sponsorship of the International Violinist's Competition which was named after her teacher and later after herself. Queen Elisabeth had a special liking for father, which lasted until her death.

After World War II, father again started his European tours; Queen Elisabeth attended many concerts and often wrote him letters from Brussels and Paris, Warsaw and Peking and also made him modest but moving presents. For example the *'platoki dlja poloshitj meshdu Podborodkom i skripkoi'* which she herself embroidered by hand (approximate meaning: Piece of cloth to put between chin and violin) since she knew how to write Russian. They often played music together."
Did the Queen remain a good violinist?

"Oh yes. I had the opportunity to convince myself of that when I played with the Queen in 1959. We played Bach's Double Concerto, she played her part faultlessly such was her great understanding for style. After we had finished the finale Queen Elisabeth confessed that one passage of the Concerto had proved very difficult for her. I suggested a different fingering to her. She tried the new fingering and said delightedly: 'Many thanks, the fingering with which I had played this passage was far too difficult for me. Ysaye had recommended it to me at the time.'

By the way, the Queen didn't just remain an excellent violinist, but also an outstanding human being. Age didn't seem to affect her in any respect, but I shall return to this later.

Father met Queen Elisabeth most

188

frequently in Brussels. This was quite natural if you consider that he regularly took part as a member of the jury in international competitions which were named after her.

'Dear David Oistrakh,' the Queen wrote at the end of the 1951 competition. 'Together with my best wishes for the journey I also send you something "tasty" in order to give you something to nibble at during the chess games in the airoplane.

Your incomparable playing remains for me as unforgettable as for everybody in Belgium. Irrespective of the joy of just listening to you, I was happy to see you again and to be able to play several times together with you.

I regret your departure; however, I am hoping to see you again soon and to listen to you.
Elisabeth.' "
David Oistrakh wrote about the Brussels Competition of 1955:
'The Belgian Queen pays the greatest attention to the competition, visits all rounds and observes with sympathetic interest the ups and downs of this very tense and extremely difficult competition.

She is not only a good musician who masters the violin like a professional but also an outstanding creative artist – her pictures and sculptures are exhibited in the National Museum in Brussels. Her patronage of the arts for this reason doesn't carry the character of an official patronage but finds its expression in an active participation in many fields of art. I would like to point out the cordiality and sympathy which she offers to all Soviet musicians who come to Brussels.'
In 1958, the Soviet government invited Queen Elisabeth as a guest of honour to the 1st International Tchaikovsky Competition in Moscow.

*Queen Elisabeth with Oistrakh in Prades*

'Your Majesty,' David Oistrakh wrote to her. 'To my great joy I have found out that K. J. Woroschilow, the chairman of the praesidium of the supreme Soviets of the USSR, has invited you to our country for the period of the 1st International Tchaikovsky Competition.

The Soviet musicians know only too well what a tremendous role your permanent activity and restless energy plays in the search, development and sponsoring of young talented artists.'

"Elisabeth accepted the invitation and came to the Soviet Union where she met many of her musician friends. She also came and visited our house and when sitting in the box of the Great Hall of the Conservatory she followed the playing of the competitors with the same excitement and sympathy as in Brussels.

I had the honour of being introduced to the Belgian Queen by father at the time of the Moscow Competition. One month later, when father was performing in Brussels, I received the following postcard from her:

'Dear Igor, your dear parents have visited me and your father has played like an angel. I was very happy that your father brought you along to meet me at the competition.'

Father again met Queen Elisabeth in 1961 – this time in Prades, where Pablo Casals had invited him to the music festival week which had been named after him. This gives me the opportunity to discuss the human charm of this remarkable woman. Father wrote in a letter soon after the finish of the musical festival week in Prades from Karlovy Vary: 'Elisabeth hardly ever left me, she came to my room at 9 o'clock in the morning when I was still in my pyjamas and unshaven, sat down on the edge of the bed and listened to me practis-ing. We lived in a hotel in the mountains seven kilometres from Prades. She was extraordinary – like a spring flower. Today she is eighty-five... I have sent her a telegram in Spain, where she is staying at the moment.' "

You have repeatedly quoted letters from Queen Elisabeth. It is not superfluous to mention that all her letters to your father were written in Russian.

"She learnt Russian from Dmitri Golde, who was close to her family and originated from Russia. He was an engineer professionally and a member of the Belgian Communist Party. During World War II Golde was a resistance fighter. Like Elisabeth, Golde met father for the first time at the 1937 Brussels Competition, listened to his playing and became his faithful admirer for ever. Their friendship was renewed in 1951 during the first competition after the war and lasted until father's death. Golde wrote a short but very affectionate contribution about father for the journal of the Belgian Society:

'One should not forget,' he stressed in this article, 'that Belgium was the cradle of Oistrakh's career and world fame. He would have undoubtedly anyway become a world celebrity, but his relationship with our country was particularly close thanks to the friendship with Belgium's First Lady.

The Queen kept her clear thinking even on her death bed up to her last breath and listened to music on a small record player until the moment when she closed her eyes for ever. Most of her record collection consisted of recordings by David Oistrakh.'

When father was Elisabeth's guest and played music with her, he used to play on a Stradivarius which belonged to her. The Queen left father this wonderful instrument. It was a relic which reminded him of his meetings with Elisabeth. After father's death, mother and I decided to give the violin to the State Glinka Museum for Music Culture in Moscow."

## Fritz Kreisler

Walter Legge, David Oistrakh's old friend, wrote in his memoirs that he heard Oistrakh for the first time in April 1937 in London. All five Soviet participants at the recently ended Ysaye Competition in Brussels performed at the USSR embassy. Immediately after the concert Legge sent a letter to the Soviet ambassador in which he expressed the desire to sponsor an Oistrakh recording. He wrote that the playing of the young violinist approached Kreisler's performances during his best years. However, Oistrakh's days were fully booked so that the recording session didn't take place. 'Twenty-five years later,' Legge continues, 'Oistrakh pulled my letter out of his pocket and said: "Can you remember this? To be compared to Kreisler, who through his records was my God from childhood on – this surpasses my most daring dreams." '

"Kreisler remained for ever, in father's opinion, the ideal of an artist and human being."
When did your father meet Kreisler personally?

"Also in 1937, when he first met Legge. Father's first performances in European capitals after his victory at the Brussels Competition led to a series of interesting acquaintances. The most important of these were, according to his own words, the meetings with Fritz Kreisler. His never-ageing art was the strongest of all impressions at the

time. 'How enchantingly the great old man plays!' father wrote in a letter full of admiration from Brussels."
The old man? In 1937 Kreisler was only sixty-two years old.

"Yes, but father was only twenty-eight. Furthermore, a purely pyschological factor also played an important part: Kreisler's gigantic figure appeared to project a previous epoch of the art of violin playing into the present.

'At the end of the 1920s, I listened to Fritz Kreisler's records for the first time. These recordings clarified for me many points of the art of violin playing and made me love the incomparable mastery of the great musician.'

I must say that I was also extremely impressed by Kreisler's records. I remember a time when I hummed for days the Serenade from Waldetz, which he had played with unique charm. I even tried to play the simple piece immediately after listening to the record."
David Oistrakh kept the program of the Kreisler concert of April 5, 1937 in Brussels as if it were a relic. First part: Bach's E Major Concerto, Viotti's 22nd Concerto; second part: Schumann's *Fantasia* and Paganini's D Major Concerto

(both pieces with Kreisler's arrangement).

" 'Kreisler's playing has made an unforgettable impression on me,' father said to the reporter of a Moscow paper. 'Already in the first minute, at the first sounds from his incomparable bow, I felt the extraordinary strength and magic of this outstanding musician.

The group of Soviet violinists was able to listen to Kreisler before the Concerto – we were invited to a rehearsal, which took place in the Palace of Art during the daylight hours of April 5th. Kreisler made an extremely pleasant impression, not only by his playing but also by his manners. During the rehearsal he kept looking at us young musicians as if he wanted to find out what impression his playing made on us.

After the rehearsal Kreisler spoke to us in an extremely friendly way. He asked us in detail about the position of Soviet music, inquired after Moscow and our performance at the competition. When he heard that Lisa Gilels had played the Paganini Concerto with orchestra at the third transition, he showed particular interest. He had recently composed the cadenza to his interpretation of the Paganini Con-

191

*Fritz Kreisler*

certo and wanted to play it with us at once. The cadenza had not yet been published and Kreisler didn't have the notes with him, he therefore decided to play it by heart. Again we were listening intensively. Kreisler played superbly. Afterwards we discussed his future plans with him.

'I would love to visit Moscow,' Kreisler said, 'but this is rather difficult for me, I am already an old man.' We heard Kreisler again in the evening. The concert hall was overcrowded. I have never been witness to such a fantastic success of a violinist."

Did your father admire all aspects of Kreisler's artistic activity equally?

"Father considered Kreisler's 'transcriptions' (in reality these are really his own compositions) as exceptionally outstanding pieces. He played some of them himself. He regarded Kreisler's violin playing as unattainable.

'If one were to ask me, which of the European musicians made the greatest impression on me, I would immediately name Kreisler,' father wrote. 'Kreisler appears to me as a giant. Kreisler is the culmination of the art of violin playing . . . to listen to Kreisler is a great pleasure. He cannot be compared with any of the most outstanding violinists of our time. He has his own Kreislerian style which makes him stand out even among the best musicians.' "

Kreisler's wish to travel to the Soviet Union could not be materialized, but he carefully followed the achievements of the Soviet violinists. In spite of his old age, he visited Oistrakh's concert in New York in 1955, gave him a standing ovation and congratulated him afterwards in the artist's dressing-room.

"Father visited the by now very old violinist during his second tour of the USA in 1960/61. Kreisler was moved by this attention, especially when he found out that a concert in honour of his eighty-fifth birthday had been arranged in the Moscow Conservatory. Oistrakh's students on that occasion played almost all of Kreisler's violin compositions. This extremely cordial conversation lasted for hours. Unfortunately it turned out to be the last.

To my great regret, I myself never met Kreisler. The great violinist died on the day when I came to the USA for the first time. A violinist whose creations formed a whole epoch of musical culture.

Fritz Kreisler himself pointed to David Oistrakh as one of the most outstanding violinists. In 1960 he mentioned Zino Francescatti, Jascha Heifetz, Nathan Milstein and Isaac Stern as the most outstanding violinists of the time and in particular emphasized:

'Oistrakh has an ability which many others lack. He doesn't play too fast. This is rare today. We live in a time of money and power, of strength and above all of speed.' "

## Joseph Szigeti

In 1948 Joseph Szigeti wrote the accompanying text to a recording of Chatschaturjan's Violin Concerto, published in the USA:

'I consider myself lucky that it will soon be possible to hear David Oistrakh's exemplary playing in this country, thanks to this record. After I had listened to him in 1937 at the International Ysaye Competition in Brussels (as member of the jury which awarded him the 1st Prize), I always regretted his absence from the American violinist's stage. The release of these records partly close this gap. Joseph Szigeti, February 17, 1948.'

"When father came to New York in 1955, the president of the company Columbia Artists, who had arranged his first American tour, handed him a welcoming note from Szigeti. Added to it was a sheet of paper, a copy of the above quoted text, which father obviously didn't know of."

Oistrakh already knew Szigeti's violin playing as a young man. Since then he had undertaken several tours of the Soviet Union. Oistrakh heard him in Odessa as well as in Moscow. Oistrakh later wrote in a comparison of the con-cert styles of Poljakin, Milstein and Szigeti:

'Poljakin's playing attracted me with its extraordinary precision and beauty of sound. His playing was characterized by great temperament and grace of detail and spark-ling virtuosity. I attended Joseph Szigeti's concert with tremendous interest. Szigeti did not possess the ease of Miron Poljakin and Nathan Milstein. One noticed quite clearly that he had to overcome difficulties. What was fascinating about him was his strong artistic willpower, the peculiarity of his style and the originality of the interpretation. I later frequently listened to his per-formances and records and dis-covered new traits in his art.'

Jakow Sak told me with how much attention David Feodorovich lis-tened to two of Szigeti's concerts which took place in Odessa in 1962. They sat next to each other and one could see the enthusiasm on Ois-trakh's face, which was caused by the performance of works by Bach, Corelli, Mozart, and Tartini-Kreisler. One year later Jakow Sak again sat next to Oistrakh when Szigeti played with Egon Petri. After Oistrakh had heard Beethoven's Kreutzersonate, he briefly commented: 'That's art!'

*Joseph Szigeti*

Szigeti's success in the Soviet Union was indeed tremendous.

"Yes, father admired his art. Shortly after his return from the Brussels Competition, he welcomed Szigeti in Moscow in 1937. They frequently met in different coun-tries after the war and took part jointly as members of the jury in competitions in Brussels as well as in Moscow. Szigeti visited the Soviet capital in 1962, 1966 and 1970, each time with the same pleasure."

*193*

It was almost a quarter of a century later in 1962 that Szigeti came again to our country. He was amazed by the great change which had taken place in the cultural life of the Soviet Union in the meantime.

'In the 1920s', he wrote, 'it was difficult to find a grand piano and one had to play in unheated dark rooms. You now have wonderful concert halls, excellent grand pianos and a new group of outstanding musicians, who were trained during these years. In this I can see the living passage of history passing in front of my eyes.'

"Musicians who observed Szigeti in the first days of the Tchaikovsky Competition noticed and related how moved he was when he entered the Great Hall of the Conservatory. He was obviously thinking of his triumphs, which he celebrated here before the war. I still remember that Szigeti fell ill during his stay in Moscow and that mother sent him fresh vegetables and different dishes to his hotel, dishes which she herself had prepared. The violinist was very moved by that.

On Szigeti's invitation, my parents visited his house by the ocean at Redondo Beach, one hour from Los Angeles. In Switzerland, however, where Szigeti later moved, no further meeting occurred.

In 1954 Szigeti visited my rehearsal in Montreux. It was the first time that I met him. After he had heard how I played the Beethoven Concerto he gave me (still a very young violinist at the time) some very useful advice with the modesty and charm which was characteristic of him."

Did your father know Szigeti's books *A Violinist's Notebook* and *Beethoven's Violin Compositions*?

"The volume which in the Russian edition also contained the memoirs *Between the Strings* was read by father with the greatest attention and he advised his students to immediately study this book carefully. A nerve inflammation in the fingers interrupted Szigeti's concert activity quite early. His books were his artistic legacy to the young violinists.

In a letter dated 1972, Joseph Szigeti, or Joschka as he usually signed his name, wrote to father: 'I very much hope that you are not overstressing yourself. Every time when my doctor advises me to take everything calmly (not to overstress myself) I think about the road you have chosen by devoting yourself to the creation of a new generation of violinists.' "

*Szigeti and Oistrakh during the Tchaikovsky Competition*

# George Enescu

'It is the sacred mission of music to extinguish hatred, to calm passion and to unite hearts in a brotherly bond, just as the antique world

194

meant with its Orpheus myth.' These words of George Enescu, spoken during the last days of World War II contain the artistic and human creed of the great Rumanian musician, composer, conductor, violinist and pianist.
When did Oistrakh meet him?

"In 1945 during his first tour of Europe after the war, which also took him to Rumania."
Did your father already know Enescu's compositions and his reputation before this tour?

"I am not sure about Enescu's compositions; however, father knew several recordings of Enescu the violinist before they met. I can remember exactly that father once listened to his recording of a Mozart violin concerto on the radio."
Enescu not only enjoyed great artistic authority in his home country but also love and respect as the result of his fruitful activity in the public sector. He was over sixty in 1945, but still in excellent artistic form, gave many concerts as a pianist, violinist, quartet musician and conductor. As musician and co-founder of the Society for the Rumanian–Soviet Friendship, he actively supported the music of Soviet composers. He was happy to meet each of our artists – Daniil Schafran, the Guillaume Quartet, Juri Briushkov and other musicians who visited Rumania at the time. Did your father on that occasion listen to Enescu's performances?

"One day after his arrival in Bucharest, father visited a solo concert given by the violinist. The program also included a sonata by Franck and compositions by Bach. The sensitive interpretation of the Franck sonata and the understanding of the idea of the composition go back to the circumstance that Enescu, who had studied in France, had lived there for a long time and had been in contact with the best French musicians.

In spite of the sceptical statement that Bach solo sonatas and partitas were unsuitable for the general Rumanian public, Enescu specifically included them in his program.

'If I succeed in finding at least one listener in the province, who likes the partita by Bach, I can regard my objective as achieved,' he said."
Many years later Enescu shortly before his death recorded six sonatas and partitas of this much loved and revered composer. The very peculiar interpretation found many admirers and many enemies. What was your father's attitude to this, since it is well known that he played Bach in a very strict manner?

"Father thought that Enescu's Bach was related to that of Casals: the same persistent search for original text, the same introduction of differential variants in the performance, the same attempt to reimpose the character of the dance to certain slower passages, particularly to the 'Allemands'.

'Enesu's Bach is much more valuable,' father wrote, 'than the "correct" Bach of some violinists in whose interpretation individual traits are lost.'

Father already had strong impressions from Enescu's performances in 1945 in Bucharest:

'Never, in not one single passage and in no nuance of the playing of this incomparable artist was the impression created that he was trying to demonstrate to the listener his qualities as a violinist. No, his interpretation was saturated with deep wisdom which bore witness to the highest ethical and musical ideas and to a long search of the road to artistic truth, a search which led to a reversal of what was achieved and to an overcoming of old traditions. But the most important thing was that Enescu virtually radiated his tremendous joy at submerging fully in the art. The grateful audience also had the same feeling.'"

It always appeared to me that the statements of one artist about another clearly reflect his own view of the world. In listening to your last quotation I can see David Oistrakh himself. He played so much exactly for the reason that he enjoyed making music and because he had the gift of giving pleasure to others through his music. Presumably two artists who were innerly and so closely related – by which I mean their ethical relationship to art – would attract each other?

"As artists as well as human beings. I know that father immediately 'fell in love' with Enescu and always spoke enthusiastically of him. There was also a repercussion which naturally didn't escape him. The Rumanian violinist heard on the radio the transmission of the first concert of Soviet artists in Bucharest and received father most cordially after his own violin evening, when father went into the dressing-room to congratulate his Rumanian colleagues.

'Everybody insists that this is

Guarneri del Gesu,' he joked, whilst showing father his wonderful violin."

Did the artistic contact between the musicians only start later?

"No, it started immediately. In Bucharest, Enescu conducted Tchaikovsky's Violin Concerto with father's and Lew Oborin's interpretation. They again played together a year later when Enescu performed in Moscow. This time Enescu appeared as conductor, violinist and pianist. During one evening in the Tchaikovsky Hall, he played as violinist with Lew Oborin in one of the B Flat Major Mozart Sonatas, and the Franck Violin Sonata, then as pianist with father in Greig's C Minor Sonata. In the symphony program the two played the Bach Concerto for Two Violins (conducted by Kondrashin), and then the Chatschaturjan Concerto with Orlow conducting. Enescu was conducting at two concerts, Tchaikovsky's 4th Symphony and 1st Piano Concerto (soloist: Emil Gilels).

The following incident occurred concerning this Bach Concerto performance: 'During the rehearsal, we politely offered each other the 1st violin part and it turned out that each of us had always played the

*George Enescu*

2nd violin part. A somewhat self-conscious Enescu now for the first time in his life played the 1st violin part with complete ease and mastery.'

During Enescu's stay in Moscow the management of the Conservatory arranged a meeting with him. Father had prepared the fugue of the American composer Dubenskij for nine solo violins. Each had its independent part. One day before the meeting with the guest, one of the interpreters fell ill. I had to stand in for her, which wasn't easy

196

since it meant I had to learn by heart a complicated polyphonic part of the fugue in one single night. In exchange for this, I had the great opportunity not only of seeing the great master, but also to play to him. At that time, I was still a student at the Central School of Music.

On another evening father visited Enescu in his hotel room. All the composer's travel companions were engaged on this evening and father met Enescu alone. He sat in a chair and in dim light played Bach's Sonata in G Minor.

Father also thought very highly of Enescu as a composer, just as Pablo Casals did when he called him one of the most important composers of the twentieth century. Father found the musical drama *Oedipus*, which he heard in 1958 at the Enescu Festival in Bucharest, particularly impressive, he also liked the 3rd Violin Sonata, which appealed to him because of its improvised form, the freshness of its harmony and its melodic and rhythmic wealth."

In 1945 David Oistrakh gave the composer the score of Chatschaturjan's Violin Concerto as a present. In 1946 Enescu first played the Concerto in Bucharest and then in Moscow. He interpreted it temperamentally, precisely and in a very individual style, as if the Armenian music, which formed the basis for the Concerto, passed through the filter of Rumanian folk instrumentation.

"Father, who loved Chatschaturjan's Concerto very much and played it very often, had a high regard for Enescu's interpretation. The Moscow meetings between the two musicians were unfortunately their last. Three years after George Enescu's death (1958) father took part (as a member of the jury) in an international violin competition named after Enescu and praised the performances of the young Rumanian violinists, in particular the playing of Stephan Ruha, whom he knew from a recent Tchaikovsky Competition in Moscow. Later father wrote about George Enescu: 'The meetings and conversations with the ingenious Rumanian artist, who had a remarkably many-sided musical talent, much intelligence and warmth – as one finds in truly great people – will always remain a dear memory to me.' "

## Jacques Thibaud

"Before father had met Jacques Thibaud personally, the patriarch of the French violin school, who already at the turn of the century was adored by the Parisians as the prince of music, he befriended two of his pupils who took part in the Wieniawski Competition in Warsaw in 1935. They were the Polish violinist Grażyna Bacewicz, later a well-known composer, and the French violinist Ginette Neveu, who later won that competition."

Grażyna Bacewicz, who often met David Oistrakh, dedicated her book *Special Criteria* to him, with the laconic but brilliant essay 'King David'.

We have already just quoted a passage from this essay when we discussed father's teaching principles. We mentioned Ginette Neveu in our conversations about father's participation at the Warsaw Competition. She died tragically in an aircraft crash in 1949. Her teacher suffered the same fate four years later. The plane with which she was flying on a tour to Japan crashed near Barcelona."

Yes, the life of an artist ... Many people imagine that there is only applause in such a life as well as

197

flowers, stage lights and fame.

"We interpreters also know the other side: the daily hellish work, sweat, excitement, stage fright and the great moral responsibility."
When David Oistrakh and Jacques Thibaud met, each surely had the opportunity to play to the other. What happened at their first meeting?

"Thibaud played, father listened. That was in Moscow in 1936 during one of the French violinist's tours. Thibaud made a particularly strong impression on father, particularly when he played Mozart's 4th Concerto, the *Ciacona* by Vitali, the Sonata by Franck and the *Rondo Capriccioso* by Saint-Saëns. He later wrote:

'The first sounds already conquered one with their extraordinary elegance, their dashing and individual style in which outstanding virtuosity was coupled with the finest polish of details. The violin sang in his hands and enchanted one with its range of colour and shades. Thibaud's concerts were a great experience for me as a musician. They transmitted to me a clear idea of the style of performance of the French School of Violinists.'

The two violinists also met each other socially, although their initial acquaintance was somewhat superficial. Their position in the world of artists was at the time still very different.

However, already a year later, immediately after father's victory in Brussels, Thibaud, who was a member of the jury at the Eugene Ysaye Competition said: 'From today Oistrakh will achieve world fame. One will want to hear him in all countries.'

The friendships between the two also started at the time. However, it was temporarily interrupted by World War II. They met again later in 1951 at the competition in Brussels, this time both were members of the jury.

The first meeting after the war was in 1950 at the international festival 'Spring in Prague'. 'When I heard his interpretation of the Beethoven Concerto,' father said later, 'I forgot that I was listening to an artist who was already seventy years old (the ultimate age limit for a violinist), that is how I was affected by the youthful vigour of his inspired playing.' "
What impressed your father most about this man Thibaud?

"Thibaud presented an example of an artist in whom life and creative activity were so closely interwoven that they formed one unit. This is the only way to explain why, everytime father told us about his meetings and conversations with Thibaud, he would change to discuss Thibaud's merits as a violinist and whenever he remembered his own performance with orchestra under Thibaud, he involuntarily started to talk about Thibaud's high human qualities.

'Thibaud was not just an inspired artist. He was a man of crystal clear honesty, lively intelligence and charm, a real Frenchman . . .

The personal meetings with Thibaud, the contact with this wonderful musician and man left a permanent impression. His openness to the world, his objective judgement and constant well-meaning attitude and kindness and the unshakeable belief that art must serve the cause of peace and the contact between simple people – all this will live in memory of those who knew Thibaud.' "
You mentioned joint performances of David Oistrakh and Jacques Thibaud?

"Yes. Father played twice under Thibaud's baton, in Brussels in 1951 and Paris in 1953. In the first concert they performed concertos

*Jacques Thibaud*

by Bach and Beethoven (in the same evening Oistrakh also played Chatschaturjan's Concerto under F. André), in the second concert they performed Mozart's 5th Concerto. Father talked enthusiastically about the pleasure which he got from playing under this conductor who was so sensitive towards soloists and who anticipated their intentions in advance.

The fact alone that this great, famous artist who had already passed the age of seventy undertook the task of accompanying father is undoubtedly evidence of the great respect and sympathy which he had for my father.

In 1953, when Thibaud stepped on his rostrum, he said to father: 'The overcrowded Palais de Chaillot, with its 3,000 seats which haven't proved sufficient to take all who want to hear you, this is the best proof of how well the Parisians remember your playing in the French capital in the time before the war.'

Father talked about this on his return from Paris. Since his meeting with Jacques Thibaud took place during an international competition named after him and since they had met the last time at the Queen Elisabeth Competition in Brussels, in which the Soviet violinist Leonid Kogan (1951) and Nelli Schkolnikowa (1953) had won, father took these friendly words also as praise for the whole Soviet violin school." Thibaud had furthermore asked Oistrakh two years before the Paris competition for the participation of young Soviet violinists. In the case of Leonid Kogan, Thibaud could still remember very clearly the highly gifted young man who was introduced to him by Abram Jampolski in Moscow in 1936. He must have remembered this when he voted to give him the first prize at the Queen Elisabeth Competition (just as almost fifteen years earlier he had voted to give Oistrakh the top prize).

"Father never tired of admiring the pleasure which Jacques Thibaud experienced when he played the violin and faced an audience. When father talked of the style of the head of the French violin school, he above all emphasized Thibaud's cordiality, his optimism and the originality of his interpretations.

'His interpretation of the classics was never forced into a stiff dry and academic frame. His performance of French music was incomparable. He performed such compositions as the 3rd Concerto, the *Rondo Capriccioso* and the *Havanaise* by Saint-Saëns, Lalo's *Spanish Symphony*, the *Poème* by Chausson, the sonatas by Gabriel Fauré and César Franck as well as many others in an entirely new way. The interpretation of these compositions

*199*

became examples for the young generation of violinists.'

Of course father, who himself was a fanatical worker, had respect for Jacques Thibaud's energy. 'Won't such a long journey be too tiring for you?' father asked him in Paris before his tour to Japan. 'Oh, not at all,' Thibaud answered. 'There are only thirty-six small flying hours.' However, fate was unrelenting towards the artist."

I would like to conclude our conversation about the friendship between the two violinists with a letter from Louis Joxe, the French ambassador in the Soviet Union, to David Oistrakh.

'12 September, 1953
Maestro,
I have the honour of thanking you for your letter of the 6th September in which you expressed your feelings on Jacques Thibaud's death.

I was deeply moved by your letter. I had the privilege of knowing this great artist and always admired his talent and valued his simplicity and kindness. I therefore share your sorrow with particular sympathy.

I know how much Jacques Thibaud admired your talent and how happy he was to play with you and to ac-cept your young fellow-countrymen at his home.

Maestro, please accept my greatest respect. Yours sincerely,
L. Joxe.'

## Jascha Heifetz

Music enthusiasts as well as professional musicians called Jascha Heifetz the 'King of the Violin'. Your father was also called this. I assume that you can tell me something about the relationship between the two 'kings'.

"I do this with pleasure. Even more so as I also had the luck to meet Heifetz personally. Father met him in 1934 when he toured the Soviet Union. I can remember that father told us that chance had played a part in helping him to hear Heifetz in Moscow. One day before his concert, father had to leave on a tour of the Soviet Union. He regretted it tremendously: to miss Heifetz's performance! However, by chance, father was late and probably for the first time in his life missed the train. Because of this, he was able to participate in the rehearsal in the morning and in the solo concert in the evening which Heifetz was to perform in. His impression was extremely strong: the perfect and immaculate way he played, which virtually radiated a hypnotic effect, fascinated each lis-tener."

And where did your father hear Jascha Heifetz playing later on?

"Mother recently remembered that my parents on tour in the German Federal Republic decided to use their only free days to listen to Heifetz. It didn't worry them that they had to travel to Zurich. Mother said how the masterfully-played Kreutzersonate had affected her on that evening."

By the way, Heifetz also heard Oistrakh playing in Zurich in 1956. Oistrakh gave a guest performance with the Leningrad Philharmonic Orchestra on tour in Western Europe and played Mozart's 5th Violin Concerto under Kurt San-derling. On this evening Otto Klemperer (who happened to be in the hall) along with Heifetz turned up at the artist's dressing-room to congratulate the Soviet violinist.

"Father heard Heifetz several times: in London he played the Brahms Concerto, in Paris the Tchaikovsky Concerto and the

*Poème* by Chausson. The two never played together, but often for each other. I know from father that the meetings were always friendly and easy. Such a meeting also took place in London, when both were performing in England. Chance brought them together in the same hotel. They spent the whole evening in long conversation, exchanging memories of joint musical friends and each played the other's violin. How much I would have liked - guided by a kind fairy - to be present in the London hotel room on that evening."

You mentioned you own acquaintance with Heifetz.

"I gave my début in America in 1962. After a concert in New York (Alfred Wallenstein, who often played with Heifetz, was conducting), a lady whom I didn't recognize turned to me and said that she liked my playing.

'My brother is also a violinist,' she mentioned casually. As a matter of courtesy I inquired where he was working, or words to that effect.

'His name is Heifetz,' she replied and added that she would call her brother in Los Angeles and tell him to listen to my concert.

'You are surely going to travel to California?' she asked.

'Yes,' I answered rather subdued.

My tour of America lasted about two months but I never forgot the conversation with Heifetz's sister. I thought more and more about it the closer my performance in Los Angeles (which finished my tour) came. With this thought in mind, I began to rehearse even more intensively and I became more and more nervous.

Finally the day of my concert arrived. Strangely enough I calmed down. I knew that Heifetz lived in Beverly Hills and very rarely visited concerts and I finally convinced myself that my nervosity had no foundation at all. I found it particularly easy to play that evening or, to be more accurate, in the first part of the concert.

During the interval an unrecognized gentleman came to the dressing room and introduced himself as the brother of my violin teacher at the Central School of Music, Valerie Iwanowna Merenblum; his name was Pyotr Ivanovich and he was also a well-known violinist.

'Bravo, you are playing magnificently,' he said. 'Jascha is sitting next to me, he also likes your playing.'

It was almost like a repetition of the scene in New York.

'Which Jascha?' I asked.

'Heifetz, of course,' was the answer which made me 'fall from the skies'. I could only be glad that my Guarneri was at this moment resting well protected in its case. I am sure I would have dropped it in shock.

I don't know how I played in the second part. However, when I returned to my dressing room after the first encore, I recognized none other than Heifetz amongst the guests there.

'Mr Heifetz, I was hoping so much that you wouldn't come,' I had said it before I realized what I was saying. He wasn't hurt by this at all - he understood the shyness of the young violinist only too well. The audience was still applauding and seeing my embarrassment he said: 'Go, the audience is asking for you. I will wait here until the concert is over.'

He waited for two or three more encores. This is how our acquaintance started.

The next time I came to Los Angeles, I was so careless in a letter to Heifetz in which I asked him for a signed photograph that I gave him the telephone number of my hotel.

In the evening I was supposed to play Prokofiev's 1st Concerto and the *Rondo Capriccioso* by Saint-Saëns under Mehta. In spite of my expressed wish not to be disturbed, the telephone rang in the afternoon. I reached our for the receiver and after one second had lost any idea of sleep.

'Mr Oistrakh,' I heard Heifetz's voice. 'I got your letter. I will bring you my photograph at the concert this evening.'

We talked for along time after the concert. He spoke in Russian as at our first meeting. He liked my violin but he thought that my bow was too light. He strongly recommended that I should get a heavier bow, which I did after some time. The next morning Heifetz phoned me to say goodbye.

'I am disappearing to Mexico,' he said and thanked me once again for the previous night's concert and gave me some very useful advice."
If I have understood correctly, you never heard Heifetz playing?

"To my greatest regret, I never heard him playing in a concert. I only know his playing from records which I have collected.

What impressed me very much was a visit to the Heifetz class in the University of California, to which he invited me in 1971. Heifetz practised with a Japanese violinist and a young Frenchman. They worked on Tchaikovsky's Concerto, on Brahms' 2nd Sonata and on a *Hungarian Dance*."
You were used to the way your father worked with his pupils and were now confronted by totally

*Jascha Heifetz*

different teaching principles in Heifetz's class?

"After only a single visit to Heifetz' class it would hardly be fair for me to pass judgement on his teaching principles. Like father, Heifetz played a lot to his class, which probably had a strong effect on his students. Unlike father, who polished all details of interpretation with his students, Heifetz, ob-

viously in an attempt to stimulate the artistic individuality of his students, didn't explain in great detail how to master the tasks.

The following details is for instance significant: Heifetz interrrupted one student's playing to make a brief correction and then immediately afterwards asked him to continue his playing. He deliberately prevented the violinist and the accompanist on the piano from agreeing at which bar they should start, since he obviously suspected that the two would harmonize better by this method and that their feeling for chamber music would become more refined by this approach."

Are there any souvenirs of your father's meetings with Heifetz in his house?

"Not many. One photograph with a very kind dedication and his letter to my mother after father's death:

'Beverly Hills, 2 November 1974
Madame Oistrakh,
Please accept my sympathy and condolences in your sorrow and our loss.
Jascha Heifetz.' "

## Leonid Kogan

After having discussed some of your father's colleagues who were older than he, men such as Jampolski, Zeitlin, Mostras and Poljakin, it would be interesting to hear something about his relationship with his younger colleague, Leonid Kogan. The triumph of the young Kogan at the Brussels Competition in 1951 appeared to continue the success series of the five Soviet violinists at Brussels in 1937.

"Leonid Kogan grew up under father's eye, just like many other Soviet violinists. In the four decades in which father taught at the Conservatory many mature musicians began their concert life. Although Kogan went to Professor Jampolski's class, he regularly listened to father's playing at examinations, class evenings and other performances.

He heard Kogan for the first time in 1938 at a concert evening given by Jampolski's students. Kogan was then fourteen years old and obviously not yet a student. He was studying at the Central School of Music, but he was allowed to take part in the performances of adults. Leonia, as he was generally called

on that evening, played pieces by Tchaikovsky: the *Melancholic Serenade* and the *Scherzo-Walz*. Father described his impression: 'Kogan played very precisely, with astonishing mastery and maturity. I was amazed by his sound and the breath of the movement.'

Father later had frequent opportunites to convince himself of the correctness of his statement.

As far as I am concerned, I will never forget the effect that Kogan's playing had on me when I first heard him in 1949. He performed Paganini's 24 Capriccios – in the Small Hall of the Moscow Conservatory, this alone was an achievement. The concert has remained in my memory, and will for ever, as an unique experience.

Leonid Kogan once described how he heard father for the first time. He was still a young man at the time: 'I was seven years old when I met David Oistrakh as a violinist. David Feodorovich gave concerts in my home town of Dnepropetrowsk. If I remember correctly, it was in 1932. He played with the pianist Wsewolod Topilin in the hall of our music school. I can say that this concert gave the strongest impression that I ever got from a violin performance or from

*203*

any other musical performance. David Feodorovich fascinated me immediately. I heard the performance of the 'master class' which this young man presented (at the time he appeared to me to be very grown up, I now understand that David Feodorovich was very young).

It was an absolutely perfect, inspired performance, equally fluid as well as crystal clear – I suspect that one can now hardly ever hear harmonic music-making of such fluidity, such incredible technical brilliance or perfection as David Feodorovich was able to present.'

In his youth Leonid Kogan didn't miss one of father's concerts. Like many of his contemporaries he was an Oistrakh supporter and in 1935 followed the result of the Warsaw competition; he heard details about father's phenomenal success in Brussels from Abram Jampolski: 'Of course I felt the enormous fascination which radiated from his great talent. I tried to discover the secrets of his art . . .'

We have already mentioned Jakow Sak's opinion that the 1935 and 1937 competitions didn't perhaps just allow Oistrakh's star to rise in the musical heavens but rather only strengthened his position – that of a mature violinist. Just like Sak, Kogan was also convinced and he told me that several times: Oistrakh didn't just get the first prize in Brussels, he established his reputation as an artist and violinist of world class.

Kogan points out that father had already mastered an immense repertoire at the time: 'He could have played six to eight competition programs and that would not have needed much preparation. It's not like today, when we young students prepare ourselves a whole year before our competition and after it above all ask the question: What should we play in addition to the competition's program? For many young musicians this is a difficult question apparently. In those days the question never arose.'

In spite of the considerable age difference (sixteen years), father treated the young Kogan without any superiority, just like a colleague and equal."

Kogan returned to Moscow in 1943 from Pensa, where he had been evacuated with the Central School of Music, and he again started his studies at the Conservatory. In his first term, he frequently visited Professor Oistrakh. Many of David Oistrakh's friends gathered in the Savoy Hotel (David Oistrakh's home at the time) in the evening, made music and listened to music.

" 'It was so interesting to talk to him and to be with him,' Kogan remembers, 'that I always forgot what time it was. It seemed to me as if minutes had passed when in reality hours had gone by . . . I was always amazed by how much he played, no, not practised, but played. He liked to play for his friends at home, and how he played! . . . Many friends came and he radiated so much warmth to them. Each of them was a welcome guest.'

Leonid Kogan told me that father once, after coming back from a walk when it was — 25°C outside, immediately reached for the violin. With fingers red and swollen by the frost he played the melody from a Beethoven chorus and Handel-Thompson's Octave Variations from the Passacaglia."

Fourteen years after the triumph of the five Soviet violinists at the Eugene Ysaye Competition in Brussels, there was once more a competition in Brussels for the first time since the end of the war. Then, in 1951, it was named after Queen Elisabeth. The jury included David Oistrakh, the victor of the

1937 competition. Among the participants were the Soviet violinists Leonid Kogan, Michail Waiman, Olga Kaworsnewa.

"Father already wrote in his letters from Brussels about the successes of the Soviet competitors: 'You of course know that our position is good, our youngsters play very well, they are at the centre of the audience's attention – above all, of course, Leonia, then Mischa. This pair have no serious rivals . . . Leonia and Mischa will probably get the first two prizes.'

Father later told us that Kogan was so far ahead that his victory was already certain before the end of the competition. The audience as well as the jury were enchanted by the artistic mastery of the Soviet violinist and his brilliant virtuosity. In the third round he played the Paganini Concerto with the exceptionally difficult cadenza by Sauret. Few violinists dare to perform this in a concert, and certainly not at a competition."

Oistrakh wasn't wrong: Leonid Kogan won the 1st Prize, Michail Waiman the 2nd. Leonid Kogan talked with particular warmth about the last day of the Brussels competition. When the results were announced and he approached

*With Leonid Kogan*

David Oistrakh, he noticed tears in his eyes which he had difficulty in suppressing. Oistrakh embraced Leonia (as he affectionately called Kogan) tenderly, confessing that this day had been twice as exciting for him: remembering only too well how much nervous energy he had used up in the same competition in

1937. The year 1951 remained especially important to Leonid Kogan. When he talks of this time, he always thinks of Oistrakh: 'He devoted his undivided attention to us competitors. He did everything to enable each of us to give his best and to represent our country's honour. All members of the jury who represented other countries respected David Feodorovich; I noticed this also later during all five Tchaikovsky Competitions.' Oistrakh and Kogan taught for many years at the Moscow Conservatory, each of them supervised a large class. Leonid Kogan told me that he was always impressed by Oistrakh's teaching methods:

'It was remarkable on which moments in the student's performance he placed emphasis. His main objective was to penetrate into the musical creation. It appeared to me that he taught his students more than pure violinistic details, which he by the way demonstrated to the class outstandingly well, since he mastered the instrument superbly well even under the most unfavourable conditions. He aroused inspiration in his students and gave them a feeling for form, for a sense of maturity and integrity.'

Oistrakh and Kogan sat next to each other during the five International Tchaikovsky Competitions. Kogan made the following observations of the chairman David Oistrakh: 'First of all, he tried to discover really new talent and enjoyed the emergence of a new artistic individuality. This is his immense merit as a member of the jury of various international competitions.'

"When Leonid Kogan's son had grown up, father listened carefully to Pawel's first performances in the Conservatory. In 1966, shortly before the 100th aniversary of the Moscow Conservatory, father, myself, Kogan and his son rehearsed Vivaldi's Concerto for Four Violins with Orchestra. By the way, that was the only time when father and Kogan played together. Father remained true to his ways: just as he had treated Leonid Kogan in his youth, he now treated his son Pawel, as an absolute equal.

Leonid Kogan doesn't just remember this concert, but father's sense of humour in particular. 'Do you know,' father commented on Pawel's playing, 'he knows his part better than the three of us, since we couldn't find much time for rehearsal. He, however, devoted himself to the matter with the necessary seriousness.' "

Kogan always speaks of David Oistrakh with great warmth:

'All of us, and of course I myself, were always conscious that we had a remarkable man in our midst. An exceptionally kind, intelligent man, who induced us all to approach our work with even more responsibility. He was, if one can say it this way,

I loved David Feodorovich very much and he returned the same feeling. He handled me, right from the beginning of my career as a violinist, with the greatest good will, commented warmly about me and gave me much valuable, wonderful, professional advice, which helped me a great deal and for which I shall always remain grateful. I was always suprised by the *esprit de corps* among his colleagues. David Feodorovich, this remarkable ingenious artist, will in the future often be discussed by musicologists and music historians. In studying his personality, we ourselves learn much that is useful and new.'

"I would only like to add that I am also on friendly terms with Leonid Kogan. I feel the greatest respect for him and admire his art. I was very happy to have been invited to the International Queen Elisabeth Competition in Brussels in 1976, as a member of the jury, side by side with Kogan, just as my father was many years ago."

## Isaac Stern

Isaac Stern wrote on a photograph which he gave to David Feodorovich: 'For David Oistrakh, the great artist who does the violin honour with his playing'. Their friendship lasted for almost quarter of a century. They met in 1951. In one of the letters from the Brussels Competition, in which your father took part as a member of the jury, he wrote to your mother and to you:

'We recently drove to Antwerp to listen to Stern. He played Bach's A Minor, Mozart's G Major and Brahms' Concerto superbly well. He is in Brussels at the moment to listen to the competition and is staying on just to listen to my concert. On the 30th I am playing a solo concert in Lüttich and on the 31st in Brussels.'

"After his return from Brussels, father said: 'I have seen and listened to a new "star" from the violinists' heavens. I regard his style as highly individualistic and I am happy that I went to Antwerp to attend his concert. The name of this violinist is Stern, Isaac Stern . . .'

Father and Stern became friends on that occasion. The American violinist described his first meeting with David Oistrakh: 'We almost at once discovered our mutual passion for music and our urge for mutual understanding and friendship, for true comradeship, even closeness, as if we had been friends for many years. This closeness remained between us until his death. He received my last message one day before his death in Amsterdam.'

In 1955 Stern heard father's second concert at Carnegie Hall in New York. Walter Legge describes his impression: 'When Oistrakh had finished, tears appeared in the eyes of Stern, who was sitting in the box.'

The idea of a joint performance between the violinists David Oistrakh and Isaac Stern this time occurred simultaneously to four musicians: father, Stern, Ormandy and Legge. But its realization was not made any easier by the fact that father's program for the USA tour was so full that there wasn't a single gap. In spite of this, the desired artistic contact took place between the two violinists, not in the concert hall but in the Columbia recording studio in Philadelphia. Father and Stern recorded a Vivaldi Violin Concerto for Two Violins with the Philadelphia Orchestra under Ormandy."

A letter which Eugene Ormandy recently wrote to mother contains details of this recording session. There was a little dispute with Stern, just as with Oistrakh's performances with Enescu and Menuhin, this time about the second violin part.

"Yes, exactly, it was a question of the second violin. I remember father told us that, while he was still playing the Tchaikovsky Concerto with Ormandy, Stern went into the studio next door to fetch his part for the Vivaldi Violin

*Meeting with Isaac Stern*

207

Concerto, which he didn't find so simple."

Who did play the first and second violin? Which of the two violinists won? Did your father tell you anything about this?

"He talked rather more about the uniquely friendly atmosphere at the recording session. I read the following note by Stern about the recording session in Philadelphia in the program of a concert in father's honour, which took place in the Royal Albert Hall in 1975 with my participation:

'We played the Vivaldi Concerto for Two Violins. Afterwards we listened to it, discussed it, rehearsed it once again and recorded it again in only thirty-five minutes. Later, at the change of the year 1955/56, we were again to play four further double concertos. We tossed a coin to decide who should play the first violin in the first concerto and then who should take over from him. The following circumstance is also remarkable: years later, when I listened to the recording, I found it difficult to determine which of us played which part.' "

Ormandy's memories deviate on this point somewhat from those of Isaac Stern. Ormandy claims, in one of his letters, that a truly

*David Oistrakh, Isaac Stern, Eugene Ormandy during a recording in Philadelphia in which both violinists interchanged first and second violin*

'Solomonic' verdict was made after long considerations as to how to distribute the solo parts: four or eight bars of the part for the first violin would be played by Oistrakh, Stern would play an equal number of bars of the second part and the following four or eight bars would be played in reverse order.

"Irrespective of the 'absolute democracy' of this decision, this recording session was turned into a rather funny meeting. Each 'changing of roles' – to move one's eyes from one violin part to another, was not easy. In the beginning it was accompanied by jokes both from the two soloists as well as by the members of the orchestra. Humour, that was the only 'medicine' which could have any healing effect on this incredibly difficult day."

It is interesting that David Oistrakh's reaction was exactly the same as Isaac Stern's, when he listened to the joint recording:

' "Today, I spent the whole time in the Conservatory, and when I came home to have my evening tea, I put on the record of our Vivaldi Concerto. I hadn't heard the record for a long time and no longer knew which of us played the first violin . . . It was a great pleasure (a wonderful recording!), but it was impossible for me to make up my mind as to which of us was on top or below,' father wrote to Stern." Stern came to the Soviet Union in May 1956. With the exception of Yehudi Menuhin's short visit to our country immediately after the end of the war, Stern's visit was the only longer visit of an American violinist to the Soviet Union.

"I attended Stern's rehearsal in the Great Hall of the Conservatory with father one day before his performance in Moscow. It was late in the evening, the hall was empty and the lights switched off, except for a few lamps on the platform. This atmosphere intensified the already great impression which Stern's playing created. Amongst other pieces which he played were the Adagio and Fugue from the 1st Sonata by Bach. A romantic, free, as well as convincing interpretation. I met Stern a few days later in Leningrad. At his request I played Bach's G Minor Sonata and Ysaye's 3rd Sonata in his room in the Europa Hotel.

On that occasion Stern told me that when performing the Bach solo compositions, he tried to transmit even the minutest detail of interpretory concepts and to make them clear to the listener in the last row of the audience. His last concert in Moscow convinced me how much Stern succeeded. By the way, he didn't just appeal to each concert goer because of his Bach interpretations.

Father was particularly attracted by Stern's extraordinary modesty and his immense artistic demands, which he made on himself. There were many things in Stern's masterly violin playing which he regarded as very remarkable, but which cannot easily be put into words. Anyway, father was very impressed by the extraordinary accuracy of his playing combined with the very modest use of vibrato.

This trait was remarkable, considering that no other violinist played in this way at the beginning of the 1950s. I believe that Stern adopted this principle from Casals.

Father was fascinated by Stern's great talent, his musical talent as well as his purely instrumental talent, the 'endlessness' of his bow, the deep penetration into the most varied musical styles (from Bach and Vivaldi to Bloch and Copland), the virility and wisdom of his interpretation: 'Isaac, my dear, your recording of the Berg Concerto and Bartók's Rhapsody is outstanding; listening to it was a pleasure for me. I congratulate you and thank you for this great pleasure.'

Stern found the following words to describe father's art: 'An unexpected explosion of virile power and a tenderness of the finest nuances, the steady beautiful sound which all parts of the bow create, never overdone and never exaggerated. And always an astonishingly clear intonation characterized by harmonic accuracy.' "
Issac Stern's art possesses a magnetic power, which can hardly be expressed in words; it cannot escape any concert visitor - radiation of his rich creative nature and his great human charm. Stern appeared to me as a man, just as he expressed his individuality in his music and made his listeners happy - very similar to David Oistrakh. In what respect? That is the question. In his optimistic mentality or his great personal modesty?

A good friend of mine, who is in

no way professionally interested in music, commented on the photograph of David Oistrakh and Isaac Stern at the rehearsal of Vivaldi's Double Concerto: 'Surely these two are spiritually related, they have the same smile.'

## Jefrem Zimbalist

David Oistrakh was already a friend of Jefrem Zimbalist when he invited him to take part as a member of the jury at the 1st International Tchaikovsky Competition in 1958. When did they first meet each other? Perhaps during David Oistrakh's first tour of America in 1955?

"No, on that occasion they met in Philadelphia for the second time, twenty years after their first meeting. They met for the first time in 1935 in Moscow, when Zimbalist was performing in the USSR.

It wasn't easy for Zimbalist at the time, since he had to play in Moscow and Leningrad shortly after Jascha Heifetz, who celebrated triumphs in both cities. In spite of this he succeeded in being recognized without effort. Auer's students – among them Heifetz and Zimbalist in particular – were indeed very different. Father described the border line between their artistic method accurately when he wrote:

'Heifetz conquered the public, he conquered them with the power of his art. Zimbalist enchanted the audience by appealing to the deepest and most secret depths of heart and soul.'

Father remembered a few points from the Zimbalist concert particularly well: Paganini's D Major Concerto with the extremely virtuoso cadenza by Sauret, which hardly anyone dared to play at the time, Beethoven's Violin Concerto and several violin miniatures.

Father was most impressed by Zimbalist's melodic playing, by his power of expression and the grace with which he performed even the most difficult passages. Father also talked about the excellent Bach interpretations."

David Oistrakh often regretted that it wasn't possible for him to attend a Zimbalist concert during his tour of the USAG. I know this from him in person. Are there any further views about Zimbalist?

"Father always emphasized that one was always affected by the simplicity of Zimbalist's art. It didn't astound one, but enchanted one.

'Zimbalist's playing radiated extraordinary kindness. It seemed to flow from his bow and communicate the purity of the artist's heart to the listener. There was no unnecessary detail, nothing that could be called violinistic unbalance.

Everything comes so easily and naturally that one believes that one has only to reach out for the violin to play just like him, but then it turns out that behind this ease and 'simplicity' stands an almost unlimited virtuoso mastery.

I have never, neither before nor after, experienced such violin playing in which each element of luck was excluded: too much pressure from the bow, a muffled note, a rhythmic imperfection.' "

You will perhaps remember Pawel Kogan's words, which I quoted when we discussed the creative path of the young David Oistrakh in his first years in Moscow? Kogan described your father with almost exactly the same words.

"Perhaps the inner relationship between father and Zimbalist was

210

based exactly on this point. Father valued Zimbalist's modesty and he always enjoyed his company – they met no fewer than four times at the Moscow competitions. On the occasion of Zimbalist's seventy-fifth birthday, father published a very cordial note about him in the journal *Sovetskaya Musyka (Soviet Music)*. Zimbalist also felt greatly for father: 'I heard a few days ago that you are coming in winter, that will be a feast for me. I often think of you and I am longing for you.

I thank you from the depths of my heart for your wonderful, kind letter and the note in the journal which has moved me deeply. I feel that you describe me with far too glowing colours. I don't deserve such praise from such a great artist and musician. Your friendship is very dear to me and I often think about you with love and respect.

Thank you, dear David! Your letter and contribution have induced me to continue working and to try and prove of use to the younger generation.'

Participation as a member of the jury at the International Tchaikovsky Competition meant a great deal to Zimbalist. This was not only because he was interested in competitions, but because he

*With Jefrem Zimbalist*

was an experienced teacher and year-long director of the Curtis Institute in Philadelphia. The competition, the stimulating contact with Soviet musicians reminded him of his own youth as an artist, of his country of origin, which he hadn't forgotten, although he had already lived in the USA for more than half a century.

Father understood this only too well and didn't write about Zimbalist purely by chance, that '. . . this may have been the reason why he liked the storm of applause with

standing ovation with which he was greeted by the audience, which filled the Great Hall of the Conservatory.'"

## Pablo Casals

"The meetings with Pablo Casals are some of the strongest musical impressions father had in his life. The great cellist was on the threshold of his eighty-fifth year when father met him following his

*211*

invitation to come to Prades in 1961."

Casals had left his home country as a sign of protest against the Franco régime in Spain immediately after the fall of the Republic (1939) and he refused any form of public concert activity. His oath of silence was an act of great ethical strength.

"One can only understand the whole effect of this decision if one convinces oneself of the ideal form the master was in, in spite of the burden of his age. I met Casals in the summer of 1964, that is three years after father. I played with Casals and the pianist Chorszowski Brahms' B Major Trio and Schubert's E Flat Major Trio. In 1965, I was again lucky enough to play with Pablo Casals: this time the notes of the E Flat Major Trio by Beethoven were on the desk, the piano part was taken by Natalja Serzalowa.

I found it moving as well as remarkable that during our joint rehearsals Casals frequently asked me if I wasn't tired. By the way, even the medical experts were amazed at his unique toughness, as he himself once told us.

Father also admired this strength. He wrote and talked about it several times. Of the eleven con-

certs which took place in the structure of the music festival in 1961, Casals took part in nine! In 1964 he played in six out of nine evenings. 'He kept all of his valuable artistic qualities to the full,' father wrote, 'it is a real miracle.'

In 1960, one year before father travelled to Prades, Sviatoslav Knuschewizki had lived as a guest with Casals in Acapulco (Mexico). He reported fully about the warm reception which he had received. I still remember that father was very flattered by Casals' invitation to take part in the concerts of the music festival in Prades. The best musicians from all parts of the world used to go there to Casals from 1950 onwards. Casals remembered his concerts in Russia at the beginning of the twentieth century, his meetings with the composers Rimsky-Korsakof, Cui, Glazunof, Rachmaninov and the outstanding cellist Wierzbilowicz. Casals expressed the wish to come to the Soviet Union as a conductor, 'as long [as he said] as it isn't too late'. He had a high opinion of the achievements of the Soviet music school. Father thought this was the reason why Casals treated him personally with such attention.

'When Menuhin and I arrived,

Casals was playing the finale of Brahms' E Minor Sonata with Mietczyslaw Chorszowski - the beautiful lyrical sound immediately impressed us. Then followed the warm reception by Casals, the first welcome. I immediately expressed my regret at not having had the luck to listen to the whole Sonata. "Then we'll play it specially for you", he replied.' "

What was the atmosphere like at the music festival week in Prades? You participated in it didn't you?

"It was determined by two factors: the uniquely beautiful landscape of Southern France in the foothills of the Pyrenees and by Casals himself. A man who was unusually democratically minded and open hearted, who was virtually in love with his Mont Canigou, and the local scenery, which reminded him so much of Spain. The judge of the village was passing by and once saw Casals enraptured by the view of the mountains lit by the rising sun. The lawyer trotted down the same path every day of his life to his place of duty, but with the exception of the path, he had never noticed anything. When he saw the maestro, who looked into the 'blue', he asked him with great astonishment: 'What are you looking at?'

Casals replied: 'At the Conigou, of course.' "

I also heard from your father that the master cellist never let a day pass without taking a walk on the slopes of the Canigou to breath the aroma of the mountain pastures. This reminds me of another artist: just like Casals, no longer the youngest, although not quite so old, also living in southern France (if not also in the eastern parts of the Pyrenees, but in the Bouches-du-Rhône departement), just as much in love with nature and mountains and one peak in particular, the Mont Saint Victoire, which he painted over and over again: Paul Cézanne.

"To be honest, I wasn't thinking of Cézanne, but the idea of togetherness and the blending of the artist with nature always forced itself on one when observing Casals. Father was quite right when, returning from Prades in 1961, he told us about Casals as a person, emphasizing his modesty, simplicity and charm.

Of course, any form of pomposity and official atmosphere was completely missing in Prades. The listeners - and many of them came from all over the world - were allowed to attend the rehearsals, irrespective of whether they took place in Casals' residence, in the small village of Molitain-les-Bains or in the acoustically perfect romantic church Saint Pierre in Prades itself, where the chamber-music festival took place. Father wrote:

'The organizers of the festival are having a rather tense relationship with the curate of the Eglise Saint Pierre, and it occasionally leads to arguments. Since there is unlimited access to the rehearsals many people are coming. According to the view of the head of the church, the 'summer look' of the audience disturbed the 'holy place', but . . . the considerable profits, however, forced the curate to make concessions in the end.'

Casals insisted that there should be no applause during the rehearsal and at the concerts. The audience simply welcomed and said goodbye to the artists by standing up in silence."

Your father knew Pablo Casals' musical style from his records, what did he think about the 'live' cello playing? What impressed him most about this?

"Immediately after his first visit to Prades, father wrote: 'Casals is an extraordinary personality, he plays with youthful verve, the intonation is incredible, the mastery unique, the power of expression in his performance moves one to tears. One has the feeling that the composition is X-rayed to its final depths. He hears and understands his partners to the last detail and doesn't ignore the slightest nuance and shading. Yet he still remains the leader.' "

David Oistrakh later worded his impressions in a more concrete form. In an article about the Spanish musician he illuminated the great humanity, the extraordinary combination of virility and emotion, the passion and ability of self control, freedom in phrasing, the easy flowing style of sound and the hypnotic effect on the audience.

"Having played for many years in trios with Oborin and Knuschewizki, father must have obviously been attracted by Casals' preference for chamber music. Earlier on, Casals had played for many years in an ensemble with Alfred Cortot and Jacques Thibaud. He now played with musicians from different countries who came to the festival in Prades: Menuhin, Szigeti, Stern, Grumiaux, Primrose, Istomin, Serkin, Paumgartner and many, many others.

*213*

*Oistrakh, Queen Elisabeth and Pablo Casals in Prades*

Father also played with Casals, and that was his most exciting recollection of Prades. In 1961, he played with Casals and the pianist Julius Katchen, with whom father had already played in his own concerts sonatas by Mozart, Beethoven and Brahms, Schubert's B Flat Major Trio (opus 99) and Beethoven's E Flat Major Trio (opus 70, number 2). At the time, Prades was the only place where one could hear Casals' cello.

'Casals didn't say much at the rehearsals,' father wrote, 'his ideas were clear and precise. Furthermore I knew many of his records and we had enough time to study both compositions thoroughly.'

Father's knowledge of the chamber-music repertoire proved of enormous help to him in Prades. He told us that Casals played the cello part of the Beethoven Violin Triple Concerto on the platform in order to get ready for the performance.

'I immediately joined in with him. We thus played almost the whole of the first movement of the Concerto and afterwards a few passages of the second movement and already approached the coda of the third movement which contained the cello passage of almost unsurmountable difficulty. In this moment we were asked to come onto the platform. Casals got up and put the 'prong' of his instrument on the floor and played the incredibly difficult movement with phenomenal ease.' "

It is well known that Casals' interpretations are characterized by great inner freedom. Could this perhaps have made it difficult to play with him?

"Indeed, there was nothing in Casals' playing that was fixed for all time. His interpretations are not only removed from all common standards but they are also very flexible and changeable, both as a whole as well as in detail. Instrumentalists know only too well how difficult it sometimes is in an ensemble to achieve unity in the strings. As far as Casals is concerned, he continuously changed the legatos as well as the bowing which obviously demanded exceptional elasticity from his partners.

When I prepared myself for my first meeting with Casals, I carefully studied the recordings of the Schubert Trio and the Brahms Trio. I tried very hard to penetrate into the typical characteristics of his interpretation and I thought that I had achieved something in this direction. However, I was already discouraged during the first joint rehearsal with Casals. The master not only played differently from his records but he even now varied the performance of some passages.

Nevertheless, it was 'effortless' to make music with Casals, because – I quote father: 'All intentions are extremely logical and follow the great inner laws of interpretation. The nuances are very concrete and have relief. The will, the initiative in leading the ensemble is based on

Casals' ability as a conductor and one subordinates oneself to him willingly.'

Father and I kept several letters which we had received from Casals:

'Prades, 17 August 1964
Dear Mr Igor Oistrakh! I would like to tell you again how happy I was to see you in Prades, to listen to your wonderful concerts and to play with you. It was indeed a pleasure which I shall always remember. Please give your father my best wishes and kindest regards. The concerts with him still remain in my memory.
With thanks and in the hope of seeing you again soon.
With best wishes, also from my wife,
Pablo Casals'

The second letter was addressed to father and myself:

'Saint Juan, 2 January 1967
Dear friends, I am most grateful for your congratulations on my birthday and for your friendly wishes. The memory of the wonderful musical moments with you in Prades will always continue to remain in my memory and I sincerely hope that I shall see you again in the nearest future. In admiration, love and with the best wishes for your whole family.
Your Pablo Casals.'

# Sviatoslav Richter

The sonata duo David Oistrakh and Sviatsolav Richter made its début in 1968. At whose suggestion did this happen?

"One could say that both musicians were moving towards each other for some time. Father said that Prokofiev once expressed the wish to hear them both together. He was thinking particularly of his Violin Sonata in F Minor, which they later frequently played together."

But after Prokofiev's death in 1953, years passed before their first joint concert.

"You have to consider that father was an extremly faithful and steady person as far as his sympathies – the purely human ones as well as the professional ones – were concerned. As long as he played regularly with his old partners, Sviatoslav Knuschewizki and Lew Oborin, he couldn't afford to play with any other cellists or pianists." Did he never do this?

"No more than once or twice: in Prades with Pablo Casals and Julius Katchen and with Milŏs Sadlo and Dmitri Shostakovich, whose trio they performed at the 'Spring in Prague'."
Were Oborin and Knuschewitzki so jealous?

"It would be more correct to say that father was very scrupulous and high minded. Unfaithfulness was organically foreign to him, although this strong word would never have occurred to his partners. But looked at critically, we musicians are all somewhat sensitive."
Was Richter in the picture as far as this was concerned?

"It appears to me that he was impressed by the firm artistic contact which linked the trio Oistrakh – Oberin – Knuschewizki. However, after father remained alone, Richter turned to him with the request to be allowed to play with him. It was a request not a demand. Richter felt a particular respect for father; during their almost thirty-year acquaintance he never called him anything else but

David Feodorovich."

When and under what circumstances did they first meet?

"I don't know the exact date, presumably first in Odessa, where both were living at the time. Richter is only seven years younger than father. However, in youth this is a considerable age difference. Mother often said: When she and father were studying at the Conservatory, Richter was still hopping about on one leg under the windows of their house. Mother attended the class of Sviatoslav Richter's father, the pianist and organist Theophil Richter. Father was also well acquainted with Richter's teacher Genrich Neuhaus; the professor told him about his favourite student, and in addition father heard Richter's playing long before the pianist became famous."

One can probably add to this that Richter, as far as I know, like Oistrakh, stayed in Moscow during the dangerous war years. His regular concert activity started at that time in the capital.

"I don't know if they were in contact with each other during the first war years, I wasn't living in Moscow at the time. I only know from father that he was enthusiastic about Richter's first performance in Moscow in 1943. He played Sergey Prokofiev's 7th Sonata. Father was no less impressed when Richter played in the Union's competition in 1945. But perhaps I should first tell you how I met the pianist. I spent the summer of 1944 with friends at their Datscha near Moscow. A rather big party gathered one Sunday. The lady of the house showed true Russian hospitality. In the evening somebody asked a person who was unknown to me to play something on the piano. Slawa, as they called the pianist, didn't need much asking. He sat down at the instrument with obvious pleasure and began to play. The guests' tiredness immediately disappeared. The pianist also didn't show any sign of being exhausted, although we had spent the whole day in the fresh air and been on long walks. The improvised concert lasted about two hours. The pianist's name was Richter, the impression which his playing created was magnificent."

You mentioned the first performance of Profofiev's 7th Sonata.

"Richter studied it in four (!) days and performed it brilliantly in 1943. Father was one of the enthusiasts who, even after the lights had been switched off and most listeners had left, stayed in the October Hall or the Trades Union building. They succeeded in getting the lights switched on again and the Sonata was played for the second time."

And the competition in 1945? Did you, together with your father, listen to Sviatoslav Richter, who was then thirty years old?

"Yes, and I shall probably never forget his performance of the B Flat Minor Concerto by Tchaikovsky and the 8th Sonata by Prokofiev. The interpretation of these compositions also made father feel enthusiastic. He had only shortly before played the first performance of Sergey Prokofiev's 2nd Violin Sonata. The impression of the direct contact with the composer was still fresh in his memory. Richter's performance convinced him absolutely.

The following incident was connected with the performance of the 8th Sonata in the competition: the lights in the hall went out as Richter played. He continued to play the Sonata by candle light. However, as he reached the emphatic ostinato in the finale, even the candles on his piano went out. He completed the Sonata in complete darkness."

216

Can you tell me something about the atmosphere at the rehearsals of David Oistrakh and Sviatoslav Richter?

"The first rehearsal as well as some of the following ones took place at our house. They first of all rehearsed Schubert's Duo in A Major. I turned the pages for Richter. He was untiring, requested new repetitions over and over again – almost longed for them and was very impatient about the slightest faults in his own playing, which probably only he himself was able to hear. Father, who was used at the trio rehearsals with Oborin and Knuschewizki to point out to Lew Nikolayevich on occasions, that it was necessary to repeat a passage, now seemed to have been put in his position: 'What was wrong this time?'"

I remember with what interest I went to the first Moscow concert of the duo Oistrakh – Richter. Each of the two musicians was far too well known for people not to expect differences in their artistic individuality.

"Who can prove that the opposite of such differences, that is a similarity – provided that it even exists, particularly with the artists of this master class – that such a similarity is a pre-condition for the value of a chamber ensemble? I for my part would not claim that the musical 'handwriting' of Oistrakh, Oborin and Knuschewizki or – since we talking about a trio – of Thibaud, Cortot and Casals were related to each other. It would be more correct to say: as truly great artists they knew how to find this unity in the process of playing chamber music."

Everybody who heard Oistrakh and Richter playing together for the first time were amazed by the tonal balance of their playing.

"Father, who always paid great attention to the dynamic balance of violin and piano often called Sviatoslav Richter's playing exemplary, since the pianist proved he possessed the superbly developed sense for playing chamber music."

His forte in a chamber-music orchestra never reached the strength of the forte which he used as a soloist.

"It wasn't just father who made this observation, but I did also. This intensified partner feeling was partly the result of Richter's old habit of playing with other musicians: first with the pianist Anatoli Wedernikow and the singer Nina Dorliak, with the cellists Mstislav Rostropovich and Daniil Schafran, with the Borodin Quartet and later with Dietrich Fisher-Dieskau. But it would be wrong to only talk about the dynamic balance of the sonata duo Oistrakh and Richter. It was really a question of balance of much greater importance. A critic who reviewed their concert at the Lyon musical festival week in July 1967 stated: 'Here we find an unrestricted dominating freedom of soloists, who were both willing to serve at the same time, we were enchanted by the smoothness of the balance they achieved.'"

How and when Richter and Oistrakh found the time for their joint performances is almost impossible to understand. A typical detail: on August 22, 1971 Oistrakh replied to Ljuba Kormout's proposal to play together with Richter on August 20, of the following year: 'Of course I would like to play with Richter on the 20.8. (if we meet each other before then!).' In spite of all difficulties, the first program, which included Schubert's Duo in a A Major, Brahms' 3rd Sonata and César Frank's Sonata, was followed by a second and third program. Oistrakh and Richter played sonatas by Beethoven (nos. 1, 3, 6, 10), by Brahms (no. 2), the 1st Sonatas by

217

Bartók and Prokofiev, they performed in concert tours in Tours, Lyon, Paris, London, Salzburg, New York, Philadelphia, Leningrad and Moscow. Their performance of Dmitri Shostakovich's Violin Sonata formed a special chapter in their artistic cooperation. He was a composer whom they both admired equally and whose compositions they interpreted superbly. One should just point out Oistrakh's interpretation of Shostakovich's 1st Violin Concerto or the Cycle of his Preludes and the Fugues in Richter's interpretation.

Surely, quite irrespective of their unity concerning certain stylistic aspects and in addition to the already mentioned dynamic balance, there were other important principles, whose harmonic accord formed the pre-condition for the success of the Oistrakh – Richter ensemble?

"Of course. Above all the desire which both of them equally inspired, to live up to the composer's ideas. The spiritual bond between the two partners rested to an importance degree on the conviction that exact obedience of the composer's wish - whether in tempo, in the dynamic, in agogics or in the general concept - is the best

*Sviatoslav Richter, Dmitri Shostakovich, David Oistrakh*

method of interpretation."

Was Oistrakh able to convince himself during his joint tours with Richter of the enormous demands the pianist has to make on his own person and with what care and conscientiousness he rehearses?

"Father was amazed by Svia-toslav Richter's incredible energy for work. This application was particularly noticeable during their first joint performance, which took place in the music festival weeks under Richter's patronage in Tours (France). I think that the directness of the performance of these two great artists in the concert hall, a re-built corn barn in the middle of beautiful landscape, accompanied

*218*

by bird song and occasionally by the cackle of chickens, must have left a permanent impression on the audience.

Father was no less impressed by the iron application, by the pianist's strictly regulated daily activities, which differed a lot from the generous freedom which ruled on that occasion. Richter played solo, with father and with Dietrich Fischer-Dieskau; he played literally from morning till evening."

Did your father meet Dietrich Fischer-Dieskau on that occasion?

"I think so. The violinist and the singer immediately felt attracted to one another, they even planned joint concerts and discussed possible programs. Their wish remained unfulfilled.

After father's death, Dietrich Fischer-Dieskau sent mother a very kind letter which we have already quoted."

In the concert which Sviatoslav Richter and Oleg Kagan gave one year after David Oistrakh's death, they performed Beethoven's 2nd, 4th and 5th Sonatas in memory of

*Sviatoslav Richter and Oistrakh during the Music Festival weeks in Tours*

the great violinist. The program was introduced by Mozart's Unfinished A Major Sonata, the sounds of which stopped abruptly and symbolically on that evening.

# Paul
# Badura-Skoda

A sonta evening of David Oistrakh and the Austrian pianist Paul Badura-Skoda took place in the Great Hall of the Moscow Conservatory in 1973. The name of this pianist was already well known to Soviet musicians after his last performances in our country, also from his lectures in Moscow and from the Russian translation of his recently published book *Mozart Interpretations* which he had written jointly with his wife, the musicologist Eva Badura-Skoda. However, people from Moscow had never heard the duo David Oistrakh and Paul Badura-Skoda before.

"The two artists had already given concerts in Vienna and had also made joint recordings."

I can remember that one morn-

## 219

ing we met Badura-Skoda, who had given a concert the evening before, in the artist's dressing-room of the Tchaikovsky Concert Hall in Moscow.

We had planned to record a conversation for the journal *Sovetskaya Musyka* which one of my colleagues was supposed to carry out. The first question sounded something like this: You often play with different partners, how is it possible for you, a great expert in the interpretation of different styles of music, Mozart for instance, to reach musical harmony with an artist who has a less clear concept of this composer?

'This is a very complicated question,' the pianist answered. 'In general one could answer it like this: the more important the artistic individuality of the partner, the more pronounced his personality, the easier it is to reach agreement.' He then immediately quoted as an example his playing with David Oistrakh.

"Father saw such a partner in Badura-Skoda, who had a pronounced individuality and was a personality as well. They knew each other for a long time.

'When I met David Oistrakh in 1959 or 1960 at Doblinger,

Vienna's Greatest music shop, he said with a friendly smile: "I have just bought a book about your Mozart interpretation." This fact was even more moving for me since I hardly expected that a world-famous great violinist like David Oistrakh would take the trouble to read a book which was mainly concerned with the problems of piano playing.'

However, their first début took place only in 1971 at the Salzburg Mozart Festival. The triumphs of the sonata ensemble which father had formed with Sviatoslav Richter were still in everybody's memory and yet he was already setting out with a new very difficult 'task': to play Mozart with a pianist and Mozart authority."

Let's return to Badura-Skoda's words about playing with Oistrakh. What did he feel about David Oistrakh's Mozart interpretation, this artist who had written in an article: 'Knowing the style is just as much a pre-condition for an artistically satisfying performance as the mastery of technical problems.'

"He was altogether very satisfied: 'There was a very happy agreement on the Mozart style from the beginning, that unique mixture of happiness and seriousness, humour

and melancholy, gentle childishness and manly vigour.'

As far as details were concerned, he noted a steady growing perfection in father's Mozart interpretations: 'If at the beginning there were still a few peculiarities typical of the older romantic school (great sound, predominance of legato playing, stronger tempo variations and an occasional *Rutscher* on a string), this became clearer, slimmer and less slack as time went by.' "

As the great expert on Mozart's ornamentation and as a scrupulous explorer of the arpeggios, gruppettos and trills in Mozart's compositions, Badura-Skoda emphasized with what care and love David Oistrakh tried to find the right way to play the ornamentations. He stressed in particular: in his opinion there was nothing which was determined once and forever: 'Often several possibilities were tried before we decided on the most "beautiful" one.'

Good taste, a quality which Mozart himself regarded as being of first importance never let Oistrakh down: 'The sounds were always crystal clear and the much feared fine articulation of Mozart came over in his bowing as if by itself.'

220

*With Paul Badura-Skoda*

"Well, taste or no taste, quite irrespective of this, father was always interested in the problems of Mozart interpretation. Badura-Skoda's book which he had bought in Vienna a long time before its publication in the Soviet Union gave him a lot of information in this respect, just as much as the numerous Mozart concerts in Salzburg and the Requiem with Bruno Walter conducting.

Father and the Austrian pianist soon became friends. Badura-Skoda visited us at home and long conversations developed in Moscow and in Vienna. Paul told us about his teacher Edwin Fischer, who was an example for him of everything that is 'true' in music. Father, for his part, tried to satisfy the pianist's curiosity and to tell him about his meetings with Prokofiev, Shostakovich and his long friendship with Oborin and Knuschewizki. They understood each other very well, both when they were playing music and also during conversation and this understanding meant a great deal to both of them. Of course humour wasn't missing; they told each other those typical musician's anecdotes in which truth and fiction are interwoven.

The following anecdote goes back to Badura-Skoda: 'During our last concert in Vienna in 1974, I asked David to play an A instead of an A sharp (it concerned a phrase in the Schubert Duo in A Major, DV 574, in the Trio of the Scherzo).

'Up till now, I have always played an A sharp, but to please you I will play an A,' David Ois-trakh said with a kind smile. And this is how it was played (surely not just because he liked me). If my argument wouldn't have convinced him as a musician, no friendship in the world would have induced him to give up his conviction.

David told me two interesting anecdotes in connection with this question which show that even genii are not infallible:

'When I asked Prokofiev at a problematical point in his Violin Concerto: 'Should it be a G or a G sharp?" he went to the piano, tried it with a G, then with a G sharp, again with a G, and so on. In the end he said: 'Ask my secretary, he knows it!' – Shostakovich was quite different: when I asked him the same question, he looked carefully at the piece and said with great certainty after thinking about it for a moment: 'G!'. Two years later when he had forgotten the incident I asked him the same question, he said (with the same certainty): 'G sharp!'

During Badura-Skoda's stay in Moscow, father used to take him by car from our house to the Rossija Hotel. Father used to say that he enjoyed driving through the city at night. Paul was very moved by the older colleague's care. One day, father invited him to the Small Hall of the Conservatory to an evening of the students in his class. After the concert, which as usual didn't finish until after 11 pm, father discovered to his dismay that Paul couldn't be found. He waited, looked around and even looked into our eighth classroom ... However, Paul was already in his hotel. He had never thought that father would still think of him after this evening full of excitement with his students. When he heard father's worried voice on the telephone, he was even more moved."

Igor Davidovich, you have just mentioned Edwin Fischer. It seems to me that Badura-Skoda's liking for your father, whom he called David, was based among other things on the fact that when they got to know each other better he discovered traits (both of an artistic and personal nature) in him which reminded him of his teacher, Fischer.

## Eugene Mravinsky

"In a peaceful moment, father decided to recall all the conductors he could think of with whom he had played. He rather naïvely thought he would be able to produce a list of names in a few minutes. He was then distracted by something else and his notebook was left on the table. During the course of the week he took it again and again to complete the list, which had already grown quite long covering four pages. It appeared that only the names of Berlioz, Wagner and Mahler were missing!

As far as Soviet conductors are concerned, with whom father was in artistic contact for many years, I would like to mention Eugene Mravinsky as one of the first.

Mravinsky was five years older than father, but his first triumph, the brilliant first performance of Shostakovich's 5th Symphony, was celebrated like David Oistrakh's in 1937. The two met earlier: at the beginning of the 1930s when father played in a matinée performance in Leningrad under a young unknown conductor. At the time Mravinsky was mainly a conductor of ballets.

He conducted performances in which the young Galina Ulanova danced.

'It was even then characteristic of him that he should demand tidiness of his orchestra, a rounding up of form and a perfection of detail. In other words the qualities which are now admired by the whole music world,' father remembered." Did David Oistrakh hear the first performance of Shostakovich's 5th Symphony?

"No, he heard the performance conducted by Mravinsky in Moscow. Father often talked of this evening: '1938, the first performance of Shostakovich's 5th Symphony in Moscow. The orchestra of the capital's philharmonic was conducted by J. Mravinsky. He lowered the baton and the Great Hall of the Conservatory burst out with an ovation. Everybody stood up, ran to the platform and the shouts of enthusiasm rose to a single roar.' "

Presumably your father was impressed by the courage of the conductor, who at the beginning of his career had dared to perform Shostakovich's 5th Symphony. Mravinsky himself confessed when thinking back to the past: 'I can still not understand how I dared to accept such a proposal without any particular wavering or hesitation. Had it been made today, I would have considered it for a long time, doubted it and in the end I most probably wouldn't have had the courage to accept.'

"When father listened to Mravinsky on that occasion, he obviously had to think of his own 'courage' in relation to the Prokofiev Concerto which he performed at the finals at the Odessa Conservatory. Yet he was at the time fifteen years younger than Mravinsky for the first performance of Shostakovich's 5th Symphony." Eugene Mravinsky won the first prize for conductors in the Union's Competition in 1938 and became 1st conductor and artistic manager of the Symphony Orchestra of the Leningrad Philharmonic Orchestra. He directed one of the great symphonic orchestras of the world with great success for over three and a half decades. During this time, Oistrakh and Mravinsky met repeatedly, both in the Soviet Union and also in other countries. Were there any particular highlights?

"Their joint performance at the first 'Spring in Prague' was sensational. The Tchaikovsky Concerto, performed in the newly liberated capital of Czechoslovakia in 1945, was regarded as a hymn of peace.

I also met Mravinsky in 1949. Father, Kurt Sanderling and I were rehearsing Bach's Double Concerto in Leningrad. Mravinsky came to a rehearsal and listened carefully.

I was soon to perform a concert with Mravinsky. I remember with what extraordinary care he prepared himself for the performance of a composition which was as simple for a conductor as Kabalewski's Concerto. But the final result was so marvelous!" Oistrakh and Mravinsky's most important joint artistic achievement, if one can put it this way, was the first performance of Dmitri Shostakovich's Violin Concerto in 1955, a composer who came equally close to the musical feelings of both musicians.

"As an admirer of Dmitri Shostakovich's music, father had a high opinion of Mravinsky's interpretations of his symphonies. Mravinsky was the first interpreter of many of these symphonies. Father called his interpretations examples of deep expression. It was obviously a great pleasure for father to play with Mravinsky's Orchestra at the first performance of Shostakovich's Violin Concerto."

Shortly afterwards Oistrakh went on a long tour of the USA, where he played and recorded the Concerto with Dmitri Mitropoulos. However, the Concerto was again performed by Oistrakh and Mravinsky in the following year, 1956, and in several West-European countries. All who listened were agreed in their opinion. One critic expressed himself in this way: 'Berlin was enthusiastic about the Orchestra of the Leningrad Philharmonic, and the Shostakovich Concerto with David Oistrakh formed the highlight of the evening.'

Father took part in a guest tour of the USA with the Leningrad Orchestra in 1962. He of course played in concerts which Gennadi Roshdestvensky conducted, but the daily contact with the orchestra and Mravinsky's presence at the rehearsals taught him a great deal as a future conductor."

I would like to select a thought from the numerous enthusiastic views expressed about Mravinsky, which has been frequently uttered, that an orchestra consisting of a hundred musicians and its conductor make an impression on the audience as a whole, as an indivisible unit. David Feodorovich

223

appeared to have understood this particularly well when he himself stepped on the rostrum and began to realize how difficult it sometimes is for the conductor to establish ideal contact with the orchestra.

" 'A truly artistic atmosphere of "teamwork" is only possible if its conductor possesses colossal discipline, extraordinary will-power and a high cultural level,' father wrote. 'Mravinsky is such a man. He comes to the rehearsals so "fulfilled" and knows exactly towards which objective he wants

*Oistrakh and Mravinsky*

to guide the "team", that he always succeeds in "collecting", uniting and inspiring the orchestra musicians. Everybody knows how strongly this affects the audience if they have even only once listened to an orchestra under Mravinsky. I remember concerts in America in front of audiences "spoilt" by the excellent orchestras in their own country. The enormous halls in New York, Chicago and other cities were always overcrowded. A real triumph which is really worth a great deal!' "

There were many things which united Oistrakh and Mravinsky. In David Oistrakh's last years, Mravinsky was particularly eager to establish contact with the violinist and regretted that they only met on rare occasions. In spite of his permanent tours which got him in contact with today's best conductors, David Oistrakh always kept his feeling of great artistic respect for Mravinsky.

"Gennadi Roshdestvensky often talked to me about his impressions of Mravinsky's method of working confirming my own observations.

'During our joint tours when I had to listen to the same compositions within a relatively short period of time,' Roshdestvensky

later wrote, 'I always admired Mravinsky's ability to maintain the feeling of freshness in oft-repeated compositions. Each concert was a first performance and everything had to be re-rehearsed before each concert. How difficult this sometimes is!'

In reading these words I thought: each concert – a first performance! These words really came from father's heart, they reflected his own attitude to work!"

Exactly, I just wanted to add that the inner artistic relationship between the two musicians had a fruitful effect on their cooperation. With this inner relationship, I of course don't just mean the methods of work, or their attitude to concert activity, but rather the real essence of their artistic individuality – which is much more important. Genrich Neuhaus wrote immediately after Mravinsky's victory at the Union's competition in 1937:

'The most outstanding quality of Mravinsky's talent is the harmony of different qualities which make a great conductor. These qualities are: a strong temperament, clear organizational willpower, great love of the subject, excellent knowledge of the score, tremendous technical perfection, an exemplary taste and high culture. A combination of these qualities is rare and therefore a precious event among us practising conductors.'

Replace conductor's practice with violinist's practice and the mingling of harmony, temperament, willpower, taste and culture (all of course combined with absolute technical perfection) gives the portrait of David Oistrakh.

# Kyril Kondrashin

'Oistrakh has in many respects contributed to my development as a musician.' This is how Kyril Kondrashin began his report about David Oistrakh when I asked him to talk about his friendship with your father. Kondrashin was one of those Soviet conductors with whom Oistrakh was in particularly close contact. Can you recall meetings and conversations between your father and Kyril Kondrashin?

"The violinist and the conductor met when I was hardly seven years old. My more conscious impressions come from the period after the war. I can well remember the kind affection which father had for Kondrashin as a musician and as a man.

'What was most impressive in his art?' father wrote and answered this question himself: 'The sincerity of the musical feeling, the fluency and grace which were essential for the performance of the Mendelssohn Concerto.' "

The Mendelssohn Concerto was the first composition which Oistrakh played with Kondrashin conducting.

" 'I heard Oistrakh for the first time during my days as a student,' Kondrashin wrote. 'I was studying at the Moscow Conservatory and didn't miss the opportunity of attending one of his performances. When I moved to Leningrad in 1937, Oistrakh was already a victorious, famous violinist in Brussels. I therefore regarded it as an even greater honour when I received his invitation to undertake the accompaniment of the Mendelssohn Concerto at one of the Leningrad Concert evenings in 1938. After a certain time, there was also a joint performance with David Feodorovich in Moscow. I shall be grateful to him for the rest of my life for his trust in me.'

Many years later Kondrashin responded with the same trust when father made his first attempt as a conductor - but we will talk about this later. At this point it would not be unnecessary to mention that Kondrashin had a rather delicate accompaniment to fulfill at the début with my father.

Kyril Petrovich was of the same opinion: 'Whether I conducted well or badly at the time? I was so excited that I wasn't able to judge my performance objectively. However, David Feodorovich immediately conquered my heart with his obliging kindness: he assisted me in the very best way in the finals of the Mendelssohn Concerto which is extremely difficult for the conductor.'

Father told me about his numerous performances with Kondrashin in Leningrad, where the conductor worked at the small opera houses. Kondrashin also regularly stood at the rostrum of the Philharmonic. Father talked about the emotional shape of his interpretations, the virtuous precision of detail and the ability to let the orchestra follow his artistic concept. I could myself discover that this was correct when I began to perform concerts and met Kyril

Petrovich. On his part Kondrashin observed Oistrakh's continuous process of artistic perfection: 'I could often enough convince myself of the tremendous artistic demands which David Feodorovich made on himself. He was never satisfied with what he had achieved. Interpretations which he performed today didn't satisfy him tomorrow for this or that reason. He played Mendelssohn's Concerto quite differently after the war than at the time of our first acquaintance. The same is true of the Brahms and Beethoven concertos which he played with a much livelier tempo in 1946 than in the last years of his life.

It is not just by chance that Kondrashin mentioned the year 1946. He conducted the cycle 'The Development of the Violin Concerto' for four evenings, and father performed it in Moscow in the concert season 1946/47 (the whole cycle took up five evenings). They met particularly frequently at that time, talked about music and father acquainted Kondrashin with the violin concertos by Elgar and Walton.

They also made recordings together. I have already told you how, with the desire to show me the difficulties of playing the violin and performing a concert in front of 'eyes', father took me to a night recording with Kondrashin conducting. Their studio work had already begun in the days when recordings were still made on soft wax records. When I began to perform concerts these days were fortunately over, but father told me how difficult it was to maintain the inner connection since the wax disc only ran for four or five minutes. If the musicians or sound editor had some criticism during the recording, one had to stop, whether one liked it or not, until a new quantity of wax had been warmed up. Father recorded in this way with Kondrashin Lalo's Spanish Symphony amongst other compositions. If you listen to the record – the recording was superbly successful – you don't even guess at the difficulties the artists had to overcome at the time."

Kondrashin accompanied the competitors of the third round during the 1st International Tchaikovsky Competition in 1958 in which two future winners performed: Oistrakh's student Valeri Klimow and the north American pianist Van Cliburn. During the competition Kondrashin's mastery as accompanist was particularly striking. On this occasion he proved his high musical culture as a conductor, the fine feeling for style and the most important thing: the ability to not only catch the artistic intention of the interpreter, but to guess it in advance, which he acquired during his long activity in the opera house working with the singers. On the occasion of Kondrashin's sixtieth birthday David Feodorovich remembered the 1st Tchaikovsky Competition with the following words: 'Kondrashin's participation in the competition raised the artistic level of the performances of the competitors to no small extent. Van Cliburn, the winner of the 1st Prize had to thank Kyril Petrovich for his triumph to some extent.'

"Shortly afterwards Kondrashin played with Cliburn in the USA. He was the first Soviet conductor to perform in the USA. The success of his concerts is therefore all the more remarkable. Kondrashin, who has directed the Symphony Orchestra of the Moscow State Philharmonic since 1961, performed quite frequently overseas alone as well as with his orchestra. Father and I also performed frequently with the Moscow

Philharmonic Orchestra in the USA."

Kyril Kondrashin said in his memoirs that during those long guest tours, which after all lasted for several months, the qualities of David Oistrakh's character were quite apparent:

'We travelled to Canada from the USA, where we had to give a concert in the small town of Burlington only 50 miles from the border. When we started off, five hours before the start of the concert, we assumed it would only take us two hours to get there. However a customs official caused difficulties at the border because of some formalities and we had to remain in our bus for five hours for their clarification. The concert was to start at 9 pm but we only left the border post at 9.30 so that we only arrived at our goal at 11 pm. People were expecting us nevertheless. The hall was full, the audience had been informed throughout, where we were and when they could expect our arrival. There was coffee and sandwiches for all the musicians. The concert started after 11 pm. I asked the manager of the hall whether we should shorten the program. "Only if you are very tired, we would love to hear everything!" he answered, somewhat surprised.'

Kondrashin then reports that the whole program was of course played: an overture, Shostakovich's 9th Symphony, Brahms' Violin Concerto and *La Valse* by Ravel. The friendly mood of the audience was wonderful: the orchestra played as if there was no stress and as if it was totally refreshed. David Oistrakh played the same way: fresh and with tremendous dash. Only the overwhelming majority of the orchestra was relatively young, whilst David Feodorovich had passed his sixtieth year.

"I could add a funny story which is connected with Kyril Petrovich, although I myself wasn't a witness. He told me the story himself. During the last ten to fifteen years of his life, father complained about being overweight but he certainly didn't despise food. After a concert in which father had played under Kondrashin in New York, Kyril Petrovich asked: 'Dodik, would you like to have something to eat?' 'Under no circumstances,' father replied. 'Don't you dare tempt me.' However, the composer later went to a nearby delicatessen with his wife Nina. He immediately recognized a well-known back: with the pleasure of the true connoisseur David Feodorovich was just in the act of filling a large basket with delicacies. 'Everything here looks so appetizing,' he said with a rather embarrassed smile. 'Do you know, Kyril, I couldn't resist the temptation.' 'There was no doubt,' Kondrashin concluded, 'that Dodik had known the way to this shop for some time.' "

In addition to the regular performances with Kondrashin conducting, something else brought them

*With Kyril Kondrashin*

closer tother: when Oistrakh conducted the Symphony Orchestra of the Moscow State Philharmonic which was managed by Kyril Petrovich. We have already touched on this.

"'Kondrashin played an important part in my development as a conductor and was very helpful with advice,' father wrote. 'My friendship with the Orchestra of the Moscow Philharmonic was even more strengthened and I got to know Kondrashin's great talents as a teacher.'

Father played with the best orchestras of the Soviet Union, conducted the most famous orchestras of the world, but the closest contact as a conductor linked him after all with the Moscow Philharmonic Orchestra.

In addition to working with the 'large' orchestra in its full instrumentation, father also worked with the 'small' one – by that I mean the soloist ensemble of the Moscow Philharmonic, whose direction is in the hands of the leader and violinist Valentin Shuk. Father played both as soloist and conductor with this group of music enthusiasts; playing on many records with them, among them his last in his home country, a recording which remained unfinished: a folder which covered all of Corelli's Concerti Grossi. I completed father's work on this.

'I was frequently present at Oistrakh's rehearsals as conductor,' Kyril Petrovich reports. 'I had always been of the opinion that playing under his baton was exceptionally useful for the orchestra, particularly for the strings. His comments to the strings were remarkably tactful and unobtrusive. He rarely interfered in details but when he said something, his words were precise and in spite of being laconic changed the sound of the orchestra substantially. This was only natural: there was nobody among us with such an insatiable desire to analyse the process of his own performance and to perfect it perpetually.'"

One can often observe that two musicians who frequently meet on the concert platform and who find common points in their joint interpretations remain strangers to each other in human respects. It is much rarer that the character and human qualities correspond as well as the artistic desires. There exist in such cases not only the premises for cooperation but also for true friendship. Oistrakh and Kondrashin were examples of such a relationship.

" 'David Feodorovich never spared himself, he couldn't imagine life without work and he despised idleness and passive recreation,' Kondrashin said. 'In this respect I admired him, perhaps because of my own similar inclination. Nor can I stand about doing nothing all day.'

Father played with Kondrashin for the last time in autumn 1974 in Kiev. It was a performance of the Brahms Violin Concerto to which we have already referred in our conversation about father's final years. Next to Mahler, it was Brahms whose compositions were most frequently heard in Kondrashin's program and who was also one of father's favourite composers. I fully agree with your thought about the inner relationship between the two artists, but I would also like to mention that the two greatly admired the works of Dmitri Shostakovich. Kondrashin allowed the composer's 4th Symphony, which had been forgotten for a long time, to be 'resurrected', conducted the first performance of his 13th Symphony and also the first performance of the Execution of Stepan Rasin. He was the first conductor to perform the whole symphonic cycle of Shostakovich and recorded it."

When David Oistrakh died unexpectedly in Amsterdam, Kondrashin was in Monte Carlo.

"'I was of course quite unable to stand at the rostrum and continue the rehearsal,' he wrote to mother. 'We tried to send you a telegram in Amsterdam. But the post office workers went on strike just at this moment so that my telegram was returned undelivered . . .

You may remember that I recently said in the Tchaikovsky Hall that you are obliged to survive David because he couldn't live without you . . . How terrible to imagine that everything happened so quickly: I now blame myself terribly for these words. May God prevent one from being such a prophet!

Dear Tamara! . . . I would only like to say to you that you should pool all your strength and preserve everything as completely as possible, everything that is connected with Dodik's life and work.

Go through his archives, I am sure it will be important for many books which will be written about him. May this help you now to fill your life, which you devoted to him, with a new work and new meaning. This is your holy duty because this is also done for him.' "

# Evgeny Svetlanov

'It is said, there are no miracles in the world. That may be right, yet in spite of this, miracles occur. The greatest of all miracles is man himself. We frequently get used to things and people, who are actually miracles and who live amongst us – I would now like to speak about such a man.'

This is how the Soviet conductor Evgeny Svetlanov began an article about David Oistrakh. Svetlanov, just like Gennadi Roshdestvensky, who was the same age as himself, belonged to a generation of musicians that appeared before the public in the 1950s. They can thus be called Oistrakh's younger contemporaries. What was their relationship with David Oistrakh, personally and artistically?

"The age difference in the 1950s in addition to the difference in their positions in the world of music were quite openly apparent between father and the conductor Roshdestvensky, who was making his début, and Svetlanov. Naturally a lot depended on father in this situation and on his attitude to young gifted musicians. When I talk to both of the today and recall events which go back twenty years, father's sympathetic interest in each of these conductors, by the way just as in all musicians, becomes more and more apparent.

Evgeny Svetlanov completed his course at the Moscow Conservatory where he attended the conductors' class of Professor Alexander Gauk. Father had been on friendly terms with Gauk for decades, and he had already played Beethoven's Concerto under Svetlanov in 1958. That was in spring, in the autumn of the same year father offered the outstanding pupil of Gauk's who was already recognized in his early years, the opportunity of conducting another violin concerto. Svetlanov, a many-talented person (pianist, composer and conductor) was known as a brilliant pianist at the time. Particularly memorable was his performance of Rachmaninov's 3rd Piano Concerto. He had already composed a rhapsody for orchestra and several symphonies. Evgeny Svetlanov was conductor at the Bolshoi Theatre since 1955."

You just mentioned that David Oistrakh made a proposal to Svetlanov that he should conduct one of his concerts but you kept the most important part secret: it was a question of your father's jubilee concert.

" 'When David Feodorovich celebrated his fiftieth birthday,' Svetlanov remembers, 'two concerts with orchestra were given in the much loved Great Hall of the Moscow Conservatory. He played one of these concerts with my teacher Alexander Gauk ... he offered me the chance to conduct the other one, I, who was only just a beginner as a conductor. I was so excited that I just didn't dare believe the reality of the proposal. The concert took place in spite of this and we never separated from that time until Oistrakh's death.'

In autumn 1958, two of father's concerts were connected with his fiftieth birthday, although he turned down any celebrations. The atmosphere at these concerts was extremely pleasant and the success gave father new impetus."

I shall never forget the Great Hall

*Evgeny Svetlanov*

of the Conservatory during the preparations for this jubilee performance; it was not just by chance that Svetlanov regarded it as 'our much loved hall'. We were here able to experience so many musical peak performances. During the day, when normal rehearsals took place, the hall appeared particularly bright and festive. The sun's rays, which fell through the upper windows, let the paintings of the great composers in their oval frames stand out brightly in the semi-darkness. They

appeared to listen to the playing in the empty hall as serene and just judges. This is probably the reason why everybody who steps on the platform of the Great Hall of the Conservatory at the same time has a feeling of breathtaking oppression as well as winged inspiration.

Oistrakh rehearsed both programs in succession. Teacher and student alternated on the rostrum. During the rehearsals David Oistrakh walked down into the stalls where his violin case lay on a chair. Oistrakh was immediately surrounded by orchestra musicians, many of whom he had known for years; vivid conversations began which were frank and full of humour. It was always a pity to have to interrupt the comradely conversation to continue the rehearsal. However Oistrakh's playing immediately fascinated the orchestra and work proceeded gaily and in a stimulated manner. On the evening of both of the concerts, the whole of Moscow's music world appeared. These concerts in the Great Hall were exclusive artistic treats. Svetlanov conducted Mozart's Violin Concerto (no. 5) as well as the concertos by Sibelius and Shostakovich.

I have told you all this in detail deliberately because I know that you, Igor Davidovich were not in Moscow at the time.

" 'I consider myself lucky. My joint performances with David Oistrakh will remain in my memory for ever,' Svetlanov wrote. What was it that linked father with Svetlanov, in addition to the great admiration Svetlanov had for the artistic career of the great violinist, which the conductor described as 'a restless and permanent climbing of the musical Everest'? If I ask myself this question, it appears to me that Svetlanov, with his own musical inclinations must have been very close to the harmony in father's art. Close to the fulfilment and intensity of his artistic activity and the unending urge for musical self-expression, the search for new forms of making music better in an ensemble or as a conductor."

A further important element in the unity of Oistrakh's and Svetlanov's views is even more remarkable since it concerns both violin playing as well as conducting: the problem of the relationship between the violin solo part and the orchestral accompaniment.

'Playing with David Feodorovich always turned into a creative act,' Svetlanov wrote. 'He never regarded the orchestra as an "ac- companying element" ... David Feodorovich knew only too well that the orchestra was an equal partner in instrumental perform- ances. He always stressed this.'

"If you consider that father played with Svetlanov such com- positions as the Beethoven, Brahms, Shostakovich and Hindemith con- certos, you can understand Svetlanov's words. Considering this in their deeper connection, these words in principle meant the freedom of making music with such a master of chamber music as father was.

'Although making music with him proved to be an extremely responsible activity,' Svetlanov stressed, 'I never felt any sort of shyness or embarrassment.'

In this connection one has to mention that Svetlanov's masterful and 'plastic' way of conducting turned working with him into a pleasure. With this I quote father's own words and I also speak from my own experience. By the way, my own first performance with Svetlanov conducting took place in the Moscow Bolshoi Theatre in 1960. Father and I were at the time playing the Spanish dance *Navarra* by Sarasate in a festival concert. I later often played with Evgeny Feodorovich particularly after 1965 when he became chief conductor and artistic manager of the State Symphony Orchestra of the USSR."

David Oistrakh played with the State Symphony Orchestra under Svetlanov in foreign countries as well as in Russia, particularly England. The first meeting in a foreign country with the conductor had already taken place: in autumn 1965 on a guest tour with the Orchestra of the Moscow Philhar- monic in the USA. Oistrakh played Bach's A Minor Concerto with Svetlanov in the Carnegie Hall in New York and the following even- ing he performed Brahms' Concerto for Violin, Cello and Orchestra with Mstislav Rostropovich.

"Father and I were on a joint tour of America. We both played in the Carnegie Hall, not together but after each other. I played the Mendelssohn Concerto under Svetlanov. Afterwards, father and I continued our guest tour of the USA. He later told me of another evening with Svetlanov when they played Beethoven's Violin Concerto in Minneapolis. The guest tours in England which you mentioned earlier took place three years later. Father played Shostakovich's 2nd Concerto under Svetlanov in the

231

Albert Hall and the Brahms Concerto in the Royal Festival Hall."

The memorable joint performance of Oistrakh, Richter, Rostropovich and Svetlanov, about which people in Moscow were to talk for a long time, took place on the 29th and 30th of December 1970. The Beethoven Concerto for Violin, Cello, Viola, Piano and Orchestra was played twice. The Great Hall of the Conservatory once again witnessed a music festival, itself comparable to a precious 'instrument', which like an outstanding violin not only bedazzled one by its external beauty and splendour, but above all by its outstanding acoustics.

"Father preferred to play in the Great Hall of the Conservatory when he was in Moscow. There are not many halls, not even in other countries, which satisfied him to the same extent. Concerning my father's traits, which Svetlanov noted, I would like to point out that he was always extending his repertoire and on the look out for new scores by Soviet composers.

'There are not many artists who do not put their personal success before everything, who run the risk of getting less public acclaim but offer their audience a new composition which may not be over-popular (but is no less valuable). We often have to thank these artists for new discoveries, for the experience of enjoying something outstanding and previously unknown.'

These lines, written by Svetlanov, appear to have been written especially about father. Both enriched their repertoire by their persistence in introducing new compositions."

What then did Svetlanov think of your father as a conductor? Was his relationship slightly coloured by professional rivalry? Such a nuance, if it could have existed, would have affected their relationship in spite of their understanding as conductors, I mean the problem concerning their position in the orchestra: the orchestra musicians never felt a rein, a forcing of their artistic will under the batons of Svetlanov and Oistrakh.

"We have already discussed how Svetlanov expressed himself so positively about the search for new forms of musical self-expression, a trait which was so characteristic of my father. He considered father's career as a conductor in the same way: without the slightest indication of rivalry. Quite on the contrary, he welcomed his courage as an artist. Svetlanov stressed how quickly father mastered the new profession and how he managed to transfer his stylistic flexibility, which characterized him as a violinist. He also wrote about the careful preparation for each new performance and about the taste with which the program was worked out. He understood only too well what demands the permanent changing, the switch from the violin to the baton, must have put on father, even more so when one considers that father frequently acted as conductor in the first part of a concert and performed as a violinist in the second part. He stated that father succeeded without any doubt in conquering this switching over of one artistic activity to another.

In 1973, when father was very ill for such a long time, fate brought them together in a hospital near Moscow: 'We were housed in different sections. We phoned one another each evening,' Svetlanov reported. 'I told him that he must return to music, he must play, conduct and teach again. I only asked him to restrict the scale of his activity.'

At that time in 1973, Svetlanov showed particularly clearly that he

*David Oistrakh shows what he had learned from Svetlanov (amongst others: Director of the German State Opera, Berlin)*

had a heart. He saw that my father was not only fighting against his illness but also against the nagging doubt, whether he would ever be allowed to stand on the concert platform again. He knew how much faith in the future meant for a sick person and he didn't restrict himself to telephone conversations. When he was still in hospital Evgeny Svetlanov wrote an article dedicated to father, which was published at the beginning of 1974 in the periodical *Nedelja* (*The Week*). During our conversation we quoted this article several times. I maintain that it had as much of a healing effect on father as his medicines.

'David Feodorovich phoned me the next day, thanked me for the article and said: "Dear Evgeny Feodorovich, I am very moved. Only one thing worries me: you write about all this in the present …" I hastened to reply: "How could it be any different? You still have to give mankind much joy with your music. That is how it's definitely going to be!" '

David Oistrakh recovered, played again and performed in concert, but never again had the opportunity of appearing together with Svetlanov. Their last performance on the concert platform took place in June 1971. Just as thirteen years earlier, when they first performed together, they played Beethoven's Violin Concerto.

"They expected to give four joint concerts in Paris in December 1974.

'However, it never came about,' Svetlanov wrote, 'he had already left us … The Orchestra de Paris, the best orchestra in France, devoted these concerts to his memory. Georges Soria, the French writer and music expert wrote the following lines: "After the brilliant performance of the Brahms Concerto, David Oistrakh died in Amsterdam like a soldier in battle. In a battle for the great high and mighty music, which he served to his last breath." ' "

That is exactly how it was. Oistrakh's weapons were violin and baton. One recognized Oistrakh's violin from its unique sound. It was even loved there, where it was only rarely heard. There are acts of heroism in war but not only in war.

233

Oistrakh's life was a heroic deed, an outstanding example to be imitated by all of us.

Svetlanov devoted his poem for violin and orchestra to 'The bright memory of David Oistrakh'. The music grabs you with its strong lyrical optimism; the great virtuoso cadenza of the poem seems to symbolize the violin, the queen of instruments.

# Gennadi Roshdestvensky

"Gennadi Roshdestvensky is the same age as I. We both went to the Central School of Music where we studied piano and we later studied at the Moscow Conservatory at the same time. We were friends from our school days and played a great deal of chamber music together. A personal bond developed out of this and with the years a real artists' friendship. Roshdestvensky justified the hope of a great future as a pianist from the time he was a student of Lew Oborin. Our sonata evenings in Moscow and Leningrad brought us even closer together. He often visited us at home and in this way got to know my father who knew his parents very well: the conductor Nikolai Anossow under whose baton he had frequently played and the singer Natalia Roshdestvenskaya, whose name Gennadi Nikolayevich bears.

'I was very much attracted by David Feodorovich's personality at my very first meeting with him,' Roshdestvensky explains. 'He greeted me with great cordiality even when I had only just begun to conduct. Later on, I was always embarrassed to play with him in concerts, since I was so conscious of the great responsibility of such performances. It was amazing that he managed to shape our relationship in such a way that it seemed we were standing on the same level, irrespective of the age differences and the different artistic "calibre". You never got the feeling that he considered himself superior. Such a trait was completely strange to him.' "

Gennadi Roshdestvensky had at the same time known David Oistrakh's violin playing for a long time before he listened to the violinist in person, which emphasized the difference between them even more strongly.

" 'I heard the name Oistrakh on the radio during the war, 1942/43, when I was living in Gorki as a result of the evacuation. I remember the Glazunof Concerto which he often played at the time, also the Tchaikovsky Concerto and various violin pieces. These childhood vague memories live with me even today. In my imagination I associate them with a winter evening, a town in deep snow and the black funnel of the loud speaker which resembled the open bud of a flower. As a human being Oistrakh seemed to hover in unachievable heights. The sound coming from the radio was almost superterrestrial to me.'

Roshdestvensky frequently played with father in Moscow and Leningrad, in Western Europe and in the USA. They soon got used to performing on the concert platform together. What father admired about Roshdestvensky's talent was the rare combination between the specific abilities of the conductor and the qualities of the musician. They resembled each other in their superior mastery of style and form. In addition, and I know this from my own performances with Roshdestvensky, he always gave pleasure with his fine adjustment as an accompanist. The soloist and conductor understood one another without words. Almost all classic and several modern violin concertos were performed by them together. At father's request, Roshdestvensky orchestrated Locatelli's piece 'The Labyrinth', which frequently had to be repeated in father's orchestra concerts. Fortunately a major part of their joint programs has been recorded."

But the artistic friendship between your father and Roshdestvensky wasn't just limited to their meetings on the concert platform or in the recording studio?

"Of course not. I remember the time when Gennadi Roshdestvensky, who at the time hadn't travelled a great deal in the world, frequently came to our house to listen to music and to the latest records which father brought back with him by the dozen from each of his foreign tours. Roshdestvensky presumably didn't become the passionate record collector, as we know him now, without father's influence."

Gennadi Roshdestvensky reports that he heard Honegger's music (the 5th Symphony under Charles Münch) for the first time in Oistrakh's flat and was not only impressed by the music itself but also because David Oistrakh was able to tell him about the French composer and his meetings and joint performances with Münch.

"Roshdestvensky once expressed what he thought of father as a violinist with the following words: 'As a violinist Oistrakh stood on a gigantic unreachable peak. I have never lost the feeling of the greatest respect and admiration for him.' Roshdestvensky was in addition impressed by father's permanent desire to extend his repertoire. The concertos by Elgar and Walton which father performed in the cycle 'History of the Violin Concerto' in the 1946/47 season were regarded by Roshdestvensky as the 'Discovery of America'. There were good reasons for Roshdestvensky to stress this: 'Already at our first meeting Oistrakh's personality grew far above the idea of an outstanding instrumentalist and it was combined in my mind with the all-embracing concept of a musician.'

Of their joint performances one should above all mention the jubilee concert in 1968 in honour of father's sixtieth birthday. There is also a recording of this performance.

I also find father's performance of Hindemith's Concerto with Roshdestvensky conducting memorable, together with four interludes from Benjamin Britten's opera *Peter Grimes* and Shostakovich's 10th Symphony performed in the presence of all three composers.

'When David Feodorovich began to conduct, he occasionally asked my advice concerning the technique of conducting. I enjoyed this very much and considered it flattering,' Roshdestvensky tells us. I don't think that anything about their relationship changed because of this. Earlier as well as later, music was the key factor which determined the character of their contact.

This also applies to their joint performances as violinist and pianist. However, Roshdestvensky never appeared with father in public as a pianist.

'To my pleasure I have played

the piano for several years with David Feodorovich; sometimes purely by chance he got the first best notes of music out of his cupboard. Almost all Mozart sonatas were performed. We met particularly frequently at a time when David Feodorovich gradually started to play the violin again after his illness. On that occasion we played Bartók's 2nd Sonata. I was always happy when such evenings occurred.' "

Oistrakh once proposed to Roshdestvensky to perform for the public. That was in 1968 when he obtained from Shostakovich his just completed violin sonata. He later performed it with Sviatoslav Richter, he first of all played it from sight with Roshdestvensky. Gemnadi Roshdestvensky had the same phenomenal ability as David Oistrakh: he could play from sight without any preparation. I can confirm this from my own experience. Before our first joint performance of the 2nd Violin Concerto by Shostakovich, Roshdestvensky played the whole concerto for me on the piano without interruption."

Roshdestvensky himself describes the way he played Shostakovich's Violin Sonata for the first time

*Concert with Gennadi Roshdestvensky*

from sight with David Oistrakh: 'It was a great event for me, although I was under immense stress since I had to play the difficult piano part from sight. After we had finished David Feodorovich phoned Dmitri Dmitriyevich and said that he would like to perform the sonata with me; however, I got out of it as I would never have been able to perform the passage in the third movement, where the piano part is composed in three lines, to perfec-

tion. David Feodorovich tried to persuade me: 'You will surely still practise ... I have also talked to Shostakovich: It is terribly difficult, couldn't we do something about it? No, there is nothing we can do about it, just practise,' he said. Later I asked Richter about this passage and he himself admitted that he had to practise it for a fairly long time.'

What was Roshdestvensky's opinion about Oistrakh as a conductor?

"You know his opinion was and is extremely favourable, as Gennadi Nikolayevich used to say.

He sometimes attended father's

rehearsals as a conductor and observed the great attention with which father followed the strings and how keen he was to ensure that they played naturally.

'I often observed how the orchestra musicians reacted to Oistrakh as a conductor and I was always happy about their willingness, enthusiasm and warmth which they showed him. This was always the case. It was the respect which they had for him as a musician.'

Father met Roshdestvensky for the last time in Stockholm just one month before his death, but not at a joint concert. Roshdestvensky, who conducted the Stockholm Philharmonic Orchestra, attended father's concert with the Swedish Radio Orchestra. The program included *Eine kleine Nachtmusik* by Mozart and Prokofiev's 1st Concerto, later in the second part he conducted *Harold en Italie* with a Swedish viola player. Roshdestvensky, who knew that father had only just been ill, was surprised by the high degree of difficulty of the program chosen for that evening." And he drew the obviously and most important conclusion about the dynamic perfection of Oistrakh's art as a conductor: 'At the beginning of his career as a conductor,' he wrote, 'some weaknesses in his manual technique did not go unnoticed by the orchestra musicians. They would not have forgiven anybody else for such weaknesses. However, I often enough had opportunity to convince myself that Oistrakh overcame these technical insufficiencies. I remember his first performance in Moscow and his last performance (which I attended) in Stockholm. The difference was amazing.'

The news of David Oistrakh's death reached Roshdestvensky in Cleveland. At the suggestion of the orchestra musicians they opened the concert with the Air from the 3rd Bach Suite (without conductor) instead of the overture to *Prince Igor*. The performance of this movement of the suite was dedicated to the memory of the great violinist.

"In those days I gave my first concert in honour of my father, which was followed by many others: in Saratow I conducted Tchaikovsky's 6th Symphony.

This symphony was played in November 1974 under Roshdestvensky's baton, who replaced David Oistrakh at the rostrum of the London Orchestra.

'I learnt a great deal when I played with Oistrakh,' Roshdestvensky wrote, 'above all the holy fulfilment of one's duty towards one's art, which is something simple and natural like an organic part of one's own existence.' "

## Otto Klemperer

"Father only played once with Klemperer conducting, but they met several times. Father welcomed the German maestro on a tour of Leningrad and Moscow together with other well-known Soviet musicians. Klemperer visited our country several times.

They met after the war on the following occasion: father was playing Tchaikovsky's Violin Concerto in Budapest. At the end of the first part most of the audience broke out into a loud applause, breaking the sacred tradition of the Symphony Hall, according to which there must be silence during the intervals between the movements of larger orchestral pieces. The applause had already began to fade away but a huge man, who sat in one of the first rows, continued to applaud. 'You fools,' one could hear this powerful voice in the whole hall, 'you don't know when to applaud.' It was Otto Klemperer."

Did you, Igor Davidovich, also know Klemperer?

"In 1954 I was to play Aram Chatschaturjan's Concerto in Lucerne. Most surprisingly Otto Klemperer appeared at a morning rehearsal which André Cluytens was conducting. As a result he heard me play before I had had the opportunity to hear him. A few days later, he gave me the honour of attending my solo concert in Zurich. I remember that on that occasion a string from my violin broke. When I visited Klemperer many years later in London to congratulate him on a brilliant performance of a symphony program, I was surprised that he remembered both my concert in Switzerland as well as the broken string.

I experienced Klemperer as a conductor several times. Under his baton, I heard in Vienna and in London Bach's B Minor Mass, Beethoven's 4th, 5th and 7th Symphonies, the German Requiem by Brahms and several symphonies by Mozart. These impressions are unforgettable. Particularly moving were his interpretations of the Beethoven symphonies. I had the impression that the music of one giant was being interpreted by another giant. Klemperer's Beethoven interpretation had a certain influence on my own approach and interpretation of his compositions. Even more important for me was a letter from the great conductor, who very kindly commented on my recordings of the Beethoven Violin Sonatas.

Father and I also once listened to Klemperer conducting an opera, unfortunately only once; it was in the London performance of Beethoven's *Fidelio*, a tremendous event for both father and myself. After the performance we went behind the stage of the Covent Garden to thank Klemperer. I always tried to express my admiration to the conductor. I remember that in Vienna in 1968 when I congratulated him, I had to listen to this from him: 'Why do you congratulate me? I haven't achieved anything special.'"

There is a comment of Roshdestvensky about Klemperer:

'This man achieved extraordinary results. He creates music by means which have nothing to do with the usual idea of the technique of conducting literally in front of one's eyes. A tremendous flow of willpower, which puts the orchestra and audience almost in an hypnotic trance combined with extreme simplicity and complete renunciation of so-called artistic mannerisms – this is what determined the creative countenance of this artist.'

"When father listened to *Fidelio* with me, his reaction was comparable with that of Roshdestvensky. On top of this, father had only recently started to conduct and he was very interested to find out what the professional secrets of the great Klemperer were."

When David Oistrakh celebrated the Brahms Cycle in Vienna, Klemperer was already eighty-three years old. In spite of this the aged musician attended Oistrakh's rehearsals. At the time the Austrian and German papers published a short dialogue between the two: 'I

listened to my performance of the violin concerto, he expressed the wish to play the Beethoven Concerto with me, which was, of course, very flattering for me, but also made me very excited and nervous. 'Which cadenza do you play?' the maestro asked me. 'The one by Kreisler,' I replied, and since I noticed a shade of disapproval on Klemperer's face, I enquired which cadenza he preferred. 'The one by Joachim!'

At the time, I had the luck to be allowed to talk with Klemperer a great deal, mainly about music and reproducing art. I listened to the recordings of his own compositions, which he said were solely made for the purpose of understanding how music was composed.

In 1970 I was able to meet Klemperer's invitation in London and perform the Beethoven Concerto with him conducting. According to the conductor's request, I had, in the meantime, studied the cadenza by Joachim."

You introduced Gennadi Roshdestvensky to Klemperer on that occasion?

"Yes. Roshdestvensky prepared in Covent Garden the first performance of the opera *Boris Godunov* by Mussorgsky with Boris Christov

*With Otto Klemperer in Paris*

am very happy to welcome you as my colleague,' Klemperer said when they met in the Imperial Hotel.
'I didn't know,' Oistrakh replied, 'that you now play the violin.'

"Klemperer indeed had a high opinion of father's ability as a conductor, as shown among other things by a telegram which he sent father on his sixtieth birthday, that is soon after the concerts in Vienna.

'London, 24 September 1968
To the great conductor and the

wonderful violinist I give my best wishes on his sixtieth birthday. From his old colleague. Otto Klemperer.' "

You also took part in the cycle of your father's Brahms program, Igor Davidovich.

"Yes, at the time I played under father's baton the Brahms Violin Concerto and, together with Michail Homizer, the Double Concerto. After Klemperer had in the title role. I took Gennadi with me when I visited Klemperer in his apartment in the Hyde Park Hotel for a preliminary discussion before the orchestra rehearsal."

When Gennadi Roshdestvensky told me about this day which was very memorable for him, he stressed particularly that Klemperer by no means regarded Beethoven's compositions as 'sacred pieces'.

"When I asked the maestro during the discussion at the Hyde Park Hotel whether he would let me play the passage in the Beethoven Concerto a little faster, he simply replied: 'Play it the way you feel it.' After finishing the first rehearsal in the hotel, Klemperer praised me, but simply advised me to play the introductory octaves in a somewhat more virile way.

The sole orchestra rehearsal took place on the following day. I played a little in the artists' dressing room before I was called to the platform. However, the maestro went directly into the hall, went onto the conductor's rostrum and lifted the baton. Beethoven's tremendous music sounded. The orchestra manager came to me very worried to fetch me somewhat late. Indeed, I had to play the introductory octaves 'in a virile way' in order to make my entrance felt during the performance."

Did your father also play with Klemperer?

"Yes, in Paris, at an outstanding recording of the Brahms Violin Concerto. It is of high artistic value. The creative individualities of the two outstanding musicians were combined in a remarkable way."

In the conversations with Peter Heyworth, which were published in London in 1973, Klemperer said that World War II had interrupted his regular performances in Europe. Since he hadn't received an invitation for a long time, it was already too tiring for him to take on Gilels' and Oistrakh's offer that he should visit Russia, which was made a long time later on.

"Gennadi Roshdestvensky emphasizes the grandeur of his personality in his report about Klemperer. 'Klemperer,' he wrote, 'came out as victor in his duel with Fascism - forced to emigrate from Hitler's Germany, he remained true to the ideals of Beethoven's *Fidelio*, the ideal of the whole of humanity.' Klemperer also conquered himself when he returned to the conductor's rostrum for the second time, although his serious illness allowed no doubt that he would have to give up conducting."

# Eugene Ormandy

"Ormandy was a conductor, who in his spirit stood the closest to father. Having been an outstanding violinist in the past, Ormandy knew only too well how much effort the career of a touring artist demanded. He repeatedly said to father: Don't perform in such an intensive way, violin and baton are too much of a strain when used at the same time."

Did Ormandy follow his own advice? Just remember the day when he stood for ten to twelve hours without interruption on the rostrum to perform the Mendelssohn and Tchaikovsky Concertos with Oistrakh and then afterwards recorded Vivaldi's Double Concerto with Oistrakh and Stern.

When did your father meet

240

Ormandy?

"During his first American tour in 1955. The impression which the Philadelphia Symphony Orchestra under Ormandy made on Oistrakh was unforgettable."

Ormandy and his orchestra musicians felt the most cordial sympathy for Oistrakh. I remember that the Philadelphia musicians noticed David Feodorovich at one of their Moscow concerts and broke out into an ovation from the platform of the Great Hall of the Conservatory. One rarely experiences such an event.

" 'Dear Tamara and David,' Ormandy wrote at the end of 1955. 'I hope that you don't mind me calling you by your first name, but we love you as if we have already known you all our lives.

We feel extremely enriched after meeting you in America and after your performance with the Philadelphia Orchestra. You must know that you conquered our hearts just as you have those of the members of the orchestra.'

Eugene later told father repeatedly that he would like to play with him at least once every year. He attended all of my father's solo performances in America, sometimes also the rehearsals. I remember that we, father and I, came into the concert hall in Philadelphia one morning to rehearse Prokofiev's Sonata for Two Violins and we noticed Ormandy and Mehta in the stalls.

You mentioned earlier the guest tours of the Philadelphia Orchestra to Moscow. However, the first

*Oistrakh greets Eugene Ormandy*

American Symphony Orchestra that came to the Soviet Union, as you will no doubt remember, was the Boston Orchestra under Charles Münch.

Serge Kussewitzki had dreamt of this tour, he who had conducted the Boston Orchestra for over a quarter of a century.

On this occasion Ormandy wrote to father: 'You of course know how

241

sad I was that we couldn't come to Russia this year. How much I would have liked to come with our orchestra. But I am very happy about the great success of the Boston Orchestra.'

The friendship between father and Ormandy lasted for almost twenty years, I would even say the friendship between our families and homes. Father and mother, my wife and I were repeatedly most cordially received by the hospitable Gretel Ormandy in Philadelphia. One could notice how the Ormandys were drawn towards father and that the conversations and contact with him gave them great pleasure."

But the most enjoyable thing for both musicians was probably when they met on the concert platform?

"Oh, yes, father valued Ormandy's musical originality and his incomparable cooperation with the orchestra. I once heard a concert with father in Philadelphia in which Eugene conducted Tchaikovsky's 4th Symphony. It was an outstanding interpretation, and this was all the more remarkable since it is very difficult for foreign conductors to get the feeling of Tchaikovsky's score. For this reason it is even more difficult for

them to surprise us with new interpretations of this Symphony which is performed so often. I often heard father say that if there ever was ideal contact between a conductor and an orchestra that was the case with the Philadelphia, and I found this brilliantly true.

In addition to the Mendelssohn and Tchaikovsky Concertos, father played the Bach Concerto (in E Major) and the Sibelius Concerto with Ormandy. Eugene is a unique accompanist - I can bear witness to this, since I played Shostakovich's 1st Concerto under his baton in London. I believe that the artistic friendship between father and Ormandy was the pre-condition for the warmth and cordiality in their relationship."

Ormandy wrote in a letter to Tamara Oistrakh a few months after David Feodorovich's death:
'Our deep, sincere friendship started soon after the first rehearsal when he played with the Philharmonic Orchestra. Our respect for his art and knowledge not just about the violin but about music and interpretation grew with each concert. It is difficult to analyse David Oistrakh's genius, which was composed of so many aspects of the great man and the great musician.'

242

# Tamara Oistrakh: Instead of an Epilogue

"David's death came to me completely unexpected, although I had lived in permanent fear and worry for many years. And yet the death came suddenly - at the time in Amsterdam in November 1975 he felt well as he had never before felt in the preceding years. But could there be anything to weaken the pain over the loss of a man with whom one has spent a whole life? Almost fifty years, of which we travelled for twenty years together throughout the whole world!

I became completely listless when David left me. I wasn't strong enough to cope with his absence. When awake and asleep his image followed me. The home which attracted both of us so much lost all attraction for me. By their irritating presence the objects around me made me feel even more strongly that they were longer lasting than human beings. The silence weighed on me unbearably, although it became my only form of existence. I didn't dare to listen to music. I could only tolerate the presence of strangers with great effort. They tried to distract me, but all I could think about was David and to talk about him. I still had to discover the lost sense of purpose in my life.

Friends, who maintained contact with me in spite of my withdrawal, tried to persuade me: You must write about David, talk about him, transmit a picture of him to people so that they may get to know him better. Was their wish sincere, or did they, purely out of concern for me, try to search for a method of protecting me from a senseless existence? I suspect it was the first. Whatever it was, because of my nature I felt unable to work on an independent book about David; yes, even to participate in the production of *Conversations with Igor Oistrakh*, which was prepared by Viktor Jusefovich and which was originally to be called *Conversations with Tamara and Igor Oistrakh*. I attended their meetings completely empty and silent.

But life goes on. Material about David had to be found for the book so I was compelled to get our family archives into order. It sometimes appeared to me that I was drowning in an endless ocean of letters, press reports and photographs.

But then the day arrived when the just-completed book lay in front of me. It was difficult and yet easy for me to read it. David's whole life and in consequence our own passed in front of me. Much of it became clearer and more conscious than before. In the turmoil of tours I could not find the time to catch my breath, and sometimes the clarity of impression and even David's triumph, which followed one another closely, became a habit, even a hindrance to understanding the ultimate - what he meant to music lovers in the whole world. However, in reading the *Conversa-*

243

*tions*, it was up to me to shorten the time or to extend it. Submersing myself in the past I found myself thinking that it was the present for me. The return to reality frightened me, I hardly put the book down when I picked it up again and began to read it until the last page had been turned. And then I felt the desire to write a few concluding lines.

Many more books will probably be written about Oistrakh. His character will be in many ways more sharply crystallized, the authors will be less prejudiced – contemporaries are after all a little subjective. Nevertheless, I can see the advantage this book has in its documentary value not only for the reason that it has been planned as a dialogue and that my son is the author's conversation partner. This book is characterized by something more fundamental. Based on numerous documents, the author finds the correct tone for the evaluation of David Oistrakh's personality, his character, his convictions, his attitude to his surroundings and to his art. David's most fundamental and remarkable trait was his ability to maintain the youthfulness of his spirit until the end of his life and this makes the figure of this musician appear particularly true to life.

David died at the height of his fame, without having lost the slightest trace of his unforgettable mastery. When I nowadays meet somebody who has retired 'at the right time' and who lives a balanced and boring existence, I remember the endless discussion with David concerning his intensive rhythm of life and I understand better and better: pension and retirement would have had a much worse effect on him than all the physical and nervous strain. The book by Viktor Jusefovich let me re-think and re-live many things; it woke me out of my listlessness. It is surely all the more dear to me for this reason.

*David Oistrakh memorial by Lew Kerbel*

NATIVE AMERICAN PEOPLE

# THE
# PAWNEE

by Elizabeth Hahn

Illustrated by Katherine Ace

ROURKE PUBLICATIONS, INC.

VERO BEACH, FLORIDA 32964

# CONTENTS

**Library of Congress Cataloging-in-Publication Data**

Hahn, Elizabeth, 1942-
    The Pawnee / by Elizabeth Hahn.
      p.   cm. —(Native American people)
    Includes index.
    Summary: Examines the history, traditional lifestyle, and current situation of the Pawnee Indians.
    1. Pawnee Indians—Juvenile literature. [1. Pawnee Indians. 2. Indians of North America—Great Plains.] I. Title. II. Series.
    E99.P3H36 1992        978'.004975—dc20        91-19517
    ISBN 0-86625-391-2                                      CIP
                                                                        AC

# INTRODUCTION

The name Pawnee comes from the word *pa-rik-i*, which means "horn." It is a fitting name for the tribe. Pawnee warriors wore their hair so heavily coated with paint and grease that it stood straight up like a horn on their heads.

The Pawnee were once a great and numerous people. The tribe was actually made up of four smaller and separate, but closely related, tribes: Chaui, Kitkehahki, Pitahauerat, and Skidi. Around the year 1300, an estimated 15,000 Pawnee migrated from parts of what are now Texas and Kansas and eventually settled in an area that was to become Nebraska. It is believed that drought, which devastated crops and reduced available game for hunting, had forced the Pawnee to move north into the Great Plains.

When the Pawnee moved, the northern lands were open and wild territory. The tribe settled first in what today is northern Oklahoma, and along the Arkansas River in southern Kansas. There they lived well because the land was fertile and game was plentiful. Later they were also able to get additional supplies and weapons from French traders in the area.

Over the next 400 years, the Pawnee grew until they numbered about 35,000 at the height of their civilization. Their increased numbers required more space for tribe members to live, farm, and hunt, so the tribe pushed farther north into Nebraska. As crops flourished in the area's rich soil, the Pawnee continued to thrive. Because the Great Plains were sparsely populated, the Pawnee became powerful and prosperous. They spent the spring and summer months planting and harvesting their crops. During the fall and winter, they hunted abundant game such as deer, antelope, rabbit, birds, and the king of Plains animals, the buffalo.

Unlike many other Native Americans, the Pawnee made great efforts to get along with the white people who came through and later settled the area. One of the first white people they met was the Spanish explorer, Coronado, who was looking for *Quivera*, "a land rich in gold." The 1541 meeting was a friendly encounter, as were the later meetings with French traders. Throughout the 1700s, the Pawnee often granted the settlers "right of way," the right to go across their land. And Pawnee warriors were famous for helping white soldiers fight the Native American tribes who were Pawnee enemies.

The peaceful coexistence with the whites lasted until the white settlers were no longer satisfied with just a "right of way" across Pawnee land. As more and more settlers arrived on the Great Plains, they began to eye the rich Pawnee land all for themselves — and they took it. Their greed led to the downfall of the Pawnee, and today there are only 3,000 members left of this once great Native American tribe.

*Pawnee village at Loup Fork, NE, 1870.*

# Way of Life

**P**AWNEE life was governed by the cultivation of crops such as corn, beans, pumpkins, and squash, and by the herding habits of the buffalo. Most of the year, the Pawnee lived in villages of earth-covered houses built alongside the rivers where they tended their crops. Twice a year, they would leave the villages and carry their tipis (tee-PEES) out to the grasslands of the plains to hunt buffalo. Tipis—or tepees, as they are commonly known—are portable, tent-like houses.

Corn was very important to the life of the Pawnee—so important that they gave it a special name, *atira*, which means "mother." Planting season began in April after the ground had thawed. The women of the tribe left their houses early in the morning to go out into the fields with their children and dogs. The women worked the soil with hoes made of buffalo bone and rakes made of deer or antelope antlers. They shaped the soil into little mounds in which they planted the seeds. Each year at harvest, the women carefully saved seeds from the best ears of corn. These would be planted the following spring.

The Pawnee had amazingly sophisticated techniques for growing different varieties of corn. Many of the types of corn first grown by the Pawnee are still used by farmers today.

To insure a good crop, seeds that had been dried and saved over the winter were soaked overnight in a "special medicine" before they were planted. The "special medicine" was a secret fertilizer, the recipe for which was passed from mother to daughter through generations. Four or five of these specially treated kernels were planted in each little mound of soil. At the same time, the women planted beans around the corn. The growing cornstalks made natural poles for the climbing vines of the bean plants.

5

As soon as the first green shoots appeared, the men of the tribe built tall wooden platforms beside the cornfields. It was the women's job to climb up on top of these platforms, and to shout and wave their arms to scare away any birds that came to eat the new corn seedlings. The women were real, live scarecrows! They protected the corn in this watchful manner for about a month. Then they piled more dirt around the new plants, and left with the men and children for the summer buffalo hunt on the plains. There, most of the tribe lived in their tepees and hunted until fall harvest time.

At harvest time, almost all of the corn taken in was dried because it had to last through the long winter and spring. It was stored in giant *parfleches* (PAR-flesh) —buffalo skin pouches. Large pits were dug in the ground to protect the parfleches. The Pawnee covered the tops of these storage pits with branches and grass, leaving only a small hole so that they could take out corn when they needed it. These storage pits were an early form of the silos that the white settlers later built above ground to store their corn and wheat.

Throughout the winter, the Pawnee took out portions of the dried corn and boiled it to make it soft enough to eat. Other times they ground the kernels into cornmeal for bread that they baked on hot stones. Corn was the Pawnee's main food.

# The Buffalo Hunt

Twice a year, whole Pawnee villages moved out onto the plains to hunt buffalo. The first time was about one month after the crops were planted. The second time was after the crops were harvested in the fall.

Before the 1500s, when the Pawnee got their first horses from Coronado, these hunting expeditions were all made on foot with only dogs to help carry equipment. The dogs either carried packs or pulled a *travois* (trav-WAH), a kind of sled or wagon made from two long poles. One end of each pole was attached to the dog's shoulders; the other end dragged along the ground. Strips of rawhide were tied across the poles to form a frame for carrying supplies and buffalo meat after a successful hunt. It was the women's job to manage the dogs with their travois.

The horse revolutionized transportation. When the Pawnee acquired horses of their own, the treks out in search of buffalo became much easier. Horses became one of the Pawnee's most valuable possessions. Since horses did all of the work of the dog—and more—the Pawnee called them Spirit Dogs.

In the actual hunt, buffalo were caught and killed in several different ways. Sometimes the hunters would steal up close on the downwind side of the herd so that the animals could not pick up their scent. One hunter would signal, and suddenly all the men would whoop and shout, and jump up and down, and wave flaming torches to scare the buffalo. The animals would race off in a panic and trample one another as they tried to escape. Other times, the hunters planned it so that the animals stampeded right over a blind cliff, called a buffalo jump, killing themselves. Either way, the Pawnee had a successful hunt without firing a single arrow.

At other times, individual Pawnee hunted by the riversides where the buffalo came to drink. The animals were easy targets as they stood at the water's edge or among the cottonwood trees along the shore. Buffalo loved to stand and scratch their backs on the low-hanging cottonwood branches.

# Buffalo: Source of Food, Clothing, and Tools

Pawnee men may have hunted the buffalo, but it was the women who turned almost every part of the buffalo into food, clothing, and many other items necessary to everyday life. Immediately after the kill, the women began the butchering. The animal's still-warm liver was considered a special treat and was eaten right on the spot. Some meat was cut up for roasts, but most of it was cut into paper-thin strips and hung on racks to dry in the sun. This dried meat, called jerky, was good to eat even months after the hunt. The women also pounded some of the dried meat into small pieces that they mixed with berries and fat to make *pemmican*, a nourishing food that could be carried easily by warriors on raids or by the tribe members as they moved about.

Buffalo skins taken in the late fall and winter were the furriest, so they were used to make warm buffalo robes, or blankets. Skins taken in the spring and summer were scraped clean and made into rawhide. Rawhide had many uses. Some was made into parfleches, hunting shields, or drums. Others were sewn together to make covers for tepees. It took from 7 to 27 hides to cover a tepee. Thread to sew the hides together was made from the tendons of buffalo legs.

Rawhide that was to be used for clothing was softened by rubbing it with a mixture of buffalo brains and fat. Then the women cut and sewed the pieces into leggings, shirts, and dresses.

Some rawhide was stretched and left to dry to form a kind of canvas for paintings. Pawnee artists covered these canvases with colorful designs or with "picture writing" to record their stories and adventures. The artist first drew the picture with a piece of charred firewood and then colored it with a brush made of buffalo hair and bone. The colors themselves were mixed in buffalo horn bowls.

The Pawnee also made a kind of rope from strips of stretched rawhide. The wet rawhide rope was used to fasten stone heads to war clubs and arrow points to the wooden shafts. Left to dry, the rawhide shrank to make an extremely tight bond.

The hair of the buffalo had many uses. In addition to being made into brushes, it was woven into rope or rolled into balls for games. Unwoven, it was used to stuff cradleboards, pillows, and moccasins, to keep feet warm and dry.

Buffalo horns and bones were made into tools, spoons, and drinking cups. And the animals large shoulder blades became hoes for the women to use in the corn fields. Even the manure, known as buffalo chips, provided fuel for Pawnee campfires.

*Interior of a Pawnee earth lodge. The fire is in the center. To the west stands the altar and sacred drum. Furniture is arranged around the circular wall.*

# Pawnee Houses

The Pawnee used two kinds of houses: tepees (or tipis) and earth lodges.

Tepees were well suited to the nomadic life of the hunting Pawnee. These portable houses were sturdy enough to withstand the strong winds that swept across the plains, and light enough for the women to transport them easily. Collapsed, the tepee formed its own kind of travois. Two of the tepee's main poles were tied to the shoulders of a horse or dog, and the other poles were left to drag along the ground. The buffalo-skin tepee covering could be loaded on top of this travois. When the tribe found a place to camp, the women could easily detach the travois from the horse and set up the tepee. In the hot summer months, the bottom part of the tepee covering could be rolled up a few feet off the ground to let the breezes cool the inside of the tepee. And in the winter, the coverings could be pegged to the ground and extra buffalo skin linings added to the coverings for insulation against the cold. Women tended a fire in the center of the tepee to keep the earth floor warm and to cook.

Earth lodges, the Pawnee's permanent homes, were made of logs that were covered with earth and grass. These structures were round, to copy the dome of the sky. Each lodge was about 40 feet in diameter and 15 feet tall at its highest point, the smoke hole, located in the center of the roof. The entrance to the lodge was a covered passageway, about 12 feet high, 7 feet wide, and 8 feet long.

Pawnee men built the round houses by placing very sturdy upright logs, side by side, in a large circle. Then, they put rafters over the tops of the log poles to support a roof. Willow branches were placed across the rafters, and dirt and grass were piled on top of the branches to make the roof. The smoke hole, about 2 feet wide, was left in the center of the roof. Finally, a layer of dirt was packed on the roof and sides of the lodge to complete the structure.

The space inside the lodge was planned very carefully, and it did not vary from one lodge to another. The fireplace or hearth was always in the center. On the west side of the lodge was a sacred place called *wiharu*, or "the place for wonderful things." Wiharu was also the name that the Pawnee gave to the garden of one of their gods. It was a wonderful and bountiful garden where corn continually ripened and where buffalo were plentiful.

The Pawnee placed a buffalo skull, symbolizing the importance of the buffalo, in the lodge's wiharu. The buffalo skull was placed so as to face the rising sun. A sacred bundle, a packet of special objects, was hung from the rafters above the buffalo skull.

Beds or sleeping platforms were built around the north and south sides of the lodge. The beds were made of buffalo robes and pillows stuffed with buffalo hair. The beds of honor were those nearest the wiharu, on either side of it. The oldest children slept there. Next along the circle came the beds of the aunts and uncles, then the parents and the younger children, and then, nearest the entrance, the grandparents. Sometimes more than 10 closely related families lived in one lodge. Then, too, favorite dogs and horses were often allowed to stay inside the lodge. A typical Pawnee village was made up of 10 or 12 lodges.

Later, pioneers discovered that these earth lodges were well suited to Plains life. White settlers built similar sod houses all over the prairie in the late-19th and early-20th centuries. The thick sod was excellent insulation against both the cold and windy winters and the hot, humid summers.

*Pawnee earth lodges at the fork of the Creek and Loup Rivers near Genoa, NE.*     *(Photo courtesy of Nebraska State Historical Society)*

*Members of the tribe gather around the campfire.*

*A group of young Pawnee women.*

12

# Family Life

Children usually lived with their mothers, but not always with their fathers because a Pawnee man could have more than one wife. A child's father, therefore, might be living with a different wife in another lodge. No matter where fathers lived, they took great care to provide for all of their children.

Pawnee children treated their parents with great respect, and they also had a close relationship with their grandparents since they all lived together in the same lodge. Grandmothers were like second mothers as they tended to a child's daily needs. Grandfathers' jobs, however, were less strenuous. They played games with their grandchildren, sometimes teaching them lessons through tricks. One popular trick was to pull a grandson out of bed early in the morning, carry him outside, and drop him in the snow. This practice was meant to toughen up young boys.

Until they reached marrying age, which was about 15, young girls lived at home to learn their mother's work. Boys, on the other hand, sometimes left their mother's lodge when they were about 10 years old to live with one of their uncles. The uncles taught their nephews how to ride, hunt, fight, and make tools and weapons. Marrying age for young men was about 18.

13

# Clothing

During the summer, men and boys usually wore only a loin cloth and moccasins. To keep warm in the winter, they added long leather pants and a buffalo robe to their outfits. Women and young girls wore buffalo-skin dresses and moccasins in the summer. In the winter, they also added buffalo robes and leggings similar to the men's long leather pants.

Both Pawnee men and women pierced their ears, and they loved to wear lots of earrings. No one ever wore a hat except when it was part of a costume for a ceremonial occasion.

Unlike some of the other Plains tribes, the Pawnee did not tattoo themselves, though they did paint their bodies for ceremonial and protective purposes. Men often plucked out their eyebrows and facial whiskers. When they first saw the beards of white men, the Pawnee thought them strange and ugly.

*Pawnee business council.*

# Community Organization

Pawnee villages had a code of behavior derived from an understanding that survival depended on every member working together for the benefit of the whole community. Sharing was the foundation of daily life, whether it involved the harvest or the bounty from a hunt. Villages were governed by chiefs, while priests led the religious ceremonies. Society was democratic in that an ordinary Pawnee man could rise through the different levels of society and be voted chief.

Even though a man might be voted chief by his people, his power and authority were directly related to the possession of his family's sacred bundle, or *chuhraraperu*, which means "rains-wrapped-up." Rain was extremely important to the Pawnee for daily living and for raising their crops. The gift of rain symbolized many blessings from the gods.

The sacred bundles were believed to have been originally passed down to Pawnee men by the gods. The contents of the bundles varied slightly, but each had to have a pipe and tobacco, paints, certain parts of birds, and some corn. All of the items, believed to have sacred powers, were carefully stored in a special parfleche. Because the gods played an important role in Pawnee life, their gifts were treated with great reverence.

# Religion

With no mountains on the Great Plains to obstruct their vision, the Pawnee had an endless and unbroken view of the night sky. From their observations, they painted very complex and sophisticated star charts. In fact, Pawnee religion was deeply rooted in the existence of these heavenly bodies.

The Pawnee's main god was Tirawa, who, they believed, had created the Earth and all other heavenly bodies. Tirawa governed the movements of the stars and the planets and he governed all time and life on Earth. The Pawnee year began in the early spring when Tirawa first spoke through the thunders—spring rain storms. His power continued through all the seasons. He guided the Pawnee in the preparation of their fields, which the Pawnee viewed as Tirawa's land, and his power was present in the development of seed-corn, and in planting and finally harvesting the crops. And his power was present in their buffalo hunts. The Pawnee paid tribute to Tirawa in a number of ceremonies, each of which was linked to a seasonal event.

Many of Tirawa's bright stars and planets were also worshipped as gods. Next in power to Tirawa and his wife, who was called "the Vault of the Heavens," was their child, Tcuperikata, the Evening Star. Tcuperikata had the privilege of giving birth to the first human being on Earth, a girl. Moreover, Evening Star was the one who communicated Tirawa's wishes to the Pawnee people on Earth through her four assistants, Wind, Cloud, Lightning, and Thunder. It was her garden, the sacred place called Wiharu, that contained fields of continually ripening corn and many buffalo. All life on Earth sprang from this garden.

Second in power to Tcuperikata was her husband, Morning Star, the father of the first human being on Earth. The Pawnee believed that this girl baby, the first human being, was carried down to Earth on a whirlwind. Soon after, according to legend, the Sun and the Moon, two other gods, mated to create the first human boy. He, too, was carried down to Earth on a whirlwind. The Pawnee believed that when humans died, their spirits followed the Milky Way to heaven where they lived with Tirawa forever.

*A captured maiden is about to be sacrificed to the Morning Star to insure fertility. The ceremony was performed in spring or summer when Mars was the Morning Star. This is the Skidi (Wolf) tribe.*

# Ceremonies

To thank Tirawa and other gods, and to assure good harvests and hunting, the Pawnee held a variety of religious ceremonies. There were two basic kinds of ceremonies: those that honored the bundles, the gifts from the gods, and those that honored seasonal events such as the harvest and the buffalo hunt.

To pay respect to the sacred bundles in the village, the priests gathered in the appropriate lodge to perform a ritual and to make offerings to the gods. The offering could be food, plants, or animals, depending on the nature of the god. The offering to Evening Star, for example, was tobacco and the heart and the tongue of a buffalo. The offering to Morning Star, however, was, for many years, a human sacrifice. Until the mid-19th century, the Pawnee often sacrificed a young maiden captured from an enemy tribe as a tribute to the Morning Star.

The Pawnee also performed ceremonial dances to honor their gods. These dances usually lasted four days. One of the most famous was the Buffalo Dance, performed to please the Buffalo Spirit so that this Spirit would provide many buffalo for the hunt.

In the Buffalo Dance, a buffalo-head mask was put over the head of each dancer. Generally a long piece of buffalo hide was attached to the back of the head mask. It hung down the back of the dancer and trailed along the floor as the dancer moved. The dancers yelped and chanted as they danced to a constantly beating drum. The drum not only provided the music for the dancers, it also represented the beating heart of the Pawnee people.

The dancers' moves tried to imitate the motions of the great buffalo. When a dancer got tired, he bent forward, sink-ing his body toward the ground. Another dancer drew a bow and hit him with a blunt arrow. The tired dancer then fell like a dead buffalo, and was dragged by his heels out of the dance space. Brandishing knives, the nondancers went through the motions of skinning and cutting up the "buffalo." Then they let him go and his place was taken by a new dancer.

*Medal struck in honor of Petalesharo, found on Indian Hill, Nance Co., NE, 1884.*

# A Great Pawnee Chief

Petalesharo was a famous Pawnee chief who was respected as a warrior and as a humanitarian. He put an end to the annual ceremonial practice of sacrificing a maiden from an enemy tribe to honor the Morning Star.

In 1817, as priests were preparing to burn alive a Comanche girl prisoner, Petalesharo defied the age-old religious custom of his people and stopped the sacrifice. It is said that he rode through 400 warriors to reach the stake where the young girl was tied. He cut her rawhide bonds, pulled her up on his horse, and rode back through his stunned warriors. Then he gave her food and a horse so that she could return to her people.

Normally, any Pawnee who committed such a sacrilege would have been killed, but no one dared touch Petalesharo. In later years, priests secretly tried to continue the custom of making human sacrifices, but Petalesharo always found out and freed the victims. Because of his persistence, the Pawnee finally gave up the practice of making human sacrifices.

*Petalesharo in full regalia, 1868.*

20

# Sign Language

There were many different languages spoken among the various tribes of Plains Indians. As a result, no two tribes could understand one another. Though intertribal encounters were not common, occasionally disputes needed to be settled, alliances confirmed, and trade agreements negotiated. Gradually, a universal language was created by using hand symbols.

These hand symbols or signs were easily learned, and the language spread quickly among the different tribes. Signs were as readily understood by the Pawnee in Nebraska as by the Blackfeet, who lived more than 1,000 miles to the northwest. Traders and soldiers also learned the sign language, to better their communication with the Native Americans.

*(Photo courtesy of Nebraska State Historical Society)*

*A buffalo hide made into a robe is painted with scenes of horses.*

*A ceremonial drum decorated with feathers and a painting of a buffalo.*

*Brave Chief, a Skidi (Wolf) Pawnee as painted by George Catlin in 1882.*

# Art

The Pawnee loved to decorate their clothing, tents, equipment, and household items with colorful feathers, beads, and paint. They were especially talented in painting, beadwork, and porcupine quill art.

Before the white settlers came with their colored glass beads, the Pawnee used porcupine quills for decorating purposes. They dyed the quills different colors; then the women sewed or wove the quills into designs on clothing, hunting shields, and other items. Because porcupines were not often found on the Plains, the tribes of the region had to obtain the quills through barter with the Native Americans who lived in the woods to the north. Later, glass beads, which were smaller and came in a great variety of colors, let the Pawnee create far more elaborate designs. The fanciest beaded garments were worn only on ceremonial occasions.

The Pawnee painted on many different objects, from buffalo hide canvases, to their own bodies. Some paintings were a kind of biography, or a pictorial story, of a special event or a significant battle.

The design on a shirt, for example, could identify the man who wore it, but the art could also convey information such as his age, his marital status, and any special feats he had performed on a hunt or in battle. Face and body paint protected individuals from the sun or from windburn, and also symbolized spirits or gods whose protection a warrior hoped to have in battle.

Animals, the land itself, and the sky and stars were all included in Pawnee paintings. Realistic or pictorial art was usually done by the men, and geometric patterns were often painted by women. Even Pawnee abstract patterns had specific meanings and represented particular animals or objects.

Colors were created from many different sources. Blue, for example, was made from dried duck manure mixed with water; yellow from bullberries or buffalo gallstones; black from burnt wood; green from plants; and white from certain clays. These materials were crushed into powder and mixed with water and gummy substances to help the paint stick. Paint brushes were made from buffalo hair, porous buffalo bone, or sticks whose tips the Pawnee chewed into soft bristles.

23

*An unidentified warrior prepares for battle.*

# Warfare

The Pawnee did not fight white settlers as much as they fought other tribes. They counted the Cheyenne, and especially the Sioux, their natural enemies. These tribes would often make surprise attacks on the Pawnee. When the Pawnee were away on buffalo hunts, usually only a few old or sick people and some small children stayed behind in the earth lodge villages. This left the villages almost defenseless, so the enemy tribes

24

would swoop in on a raid, killing people, destroying lodges, burning crops, and stealing whatever horses had been left behind. Even in such dire circumstances, the elders and children fought back valiantly.

The Pawnee have a story about an old warrior named Crooked Hand who once saved a village. When he learned that a war party of 600 Sioux was about to attack his village, he left his own sickbed to organize a small force of feeble elders and young children with their tiny bows and arrows. At first the Sioux laughed when they saw such a pathetic looking army, but the villagers fought so fiercely to protect their homes that the Sioux soon were forced to flee.

The Pawnee, not just victims of hostile attacks, themselves raided enemy villages, killing residents and even taking scalps as trophies. They did not initiate the attacks, however, just to do battle and kill hated foes. Their raids were mostly driven by their need to acquire more horses, which were crucial to their survival.

# The Pawnee Lose Their Lands

From the time that the Pawnee first encountered white people—the Spanish exploration party of Vasquez de Coronado, in 1541—they had little trouble with white settlers—until the mid-1800s. The first evidence of the white people came in the form of diseases—plagues for which the Native Americans had no natural resistance. In 1831, a small pox epidemic killed more than half of the Pawnee, and in 1849, cholera wiped out many more.

It wasn't only disease that took a toll on the Pawnee. It was also the white settlers' greed. Beginning in 1818, the tribe was pushed into making several treaties with the United States government, relinquishing much of their land. Still, it was not enough for the white settlers. They virtually flooded the Plains in the great American westward expansion, wanting more and more of the

Pawnee land, and the government forced the Pawnee to sell it to them.

By 1859, the government had ordered all Pawnee to move to a small reservation on the treaty land granted to them beside the Loup River in Nebraska. For the next 14 years, the once proud and powerful tribe suffered one disaster after another. They were raided by the Sioux, whom the U.S. government had not yet succeeded in controlling. Furthermore, drought and grasshoppers destroyed Pawnee crops, and the buffalo herds were diminishing. There had been an estimated 60 million buffalo on the Plains in 1800. Seventy years later, there were only 13 million. By 1900, fewer than 1,000 buffalo remained.

Even so, the Pawnee continued to work for peaceful coexistence with the white settlers. In 1864, the U.S. Army launched a campaign to subdue the hostile Sioux, and Pawnee warriors volunteered to help. Major Frank North formed a company of Pawnee Scouts who fought courageously alongside the army regulars. The scouts soon became famous and, in 1867, were asked to continue to help by guarding the Union Pacific workers who were building the first transcontinental railroad. Ironically, the railroad that the Pawnee helped build also sped up their demise, for the railroad brought more and more settlers to the West.

Even more tragically, the railroad also brought buffalo hunting parties. During the 1860s and 1870s, the railroad ran special trains for this new sport. The trains would literally stop in the middle of the plains, where hunters on board fired repeatedly at the unsuspecting buffalo. Sometimes these hunters would take only the hide or maybe the horns and the tongue of the buffalo as trophies. They would leave the rest of the buffalo carcass to rot.

Even more destructive were the professional buffalo hunters who did a brisk and profitable business in buffalo hides. They killed millions of buffalo in the late 1800s. Like the sports hunters, these professionals stripped the animals of their valuable hides, and left thousands of carcasses strewn over the plains after each foray. No one considered what the buffalo meant to the life of Native Americans.

In 1876, even the reservation land in Nebraska, which had been given by treaty to the Pawnee, was taken back by the U.S. government. The tribe was forced to move again—this time to Oklahoma. The government pushed the Pawnee out of Nebraska so abruptly that the tribe could not even harvest its crops. By the time they got to the new Indian Territory, it was too late to plant again, so there was little food that

winter. Even more hopelessly, the Pawnee came to be afflicted with a new disease that people called Indian Territory Fever. By 1890, fewer than 1,000 Pawnee had survived.

With the white people's continued push westward, it was inevitable that the settlers would eventually want the Pawnee lands in Oklahoma, too. In 1887, President Benjamin Harrison signed the Dawes Act. It forced the Pawnee to accept individual 160-acre farms. All the rest of the Indian Territory in what became the state of Oklahoma was opened to new settlers. As they poured in, the Pawnee were pushed yet farther into a small area of the territory that later became Pawnee, Oklahoma, as it is known today.

In 1898, Congress passed the Curtis Act. This legislation abolished the rights of all tribal governments and began what the whites referred to as the assimilation or Americanization process for all Native Americans.

*President Benjamin Harrison.*

# The Pawnee Today

In the early part of the 20th century, the Pawnee seemed all but to disappear. Finally, the U.S. government began to realize the tragic position of Native Americans. In 1934, Congress passed the Wheeler-Howard Act, which allowed Native Americans to reinstitute self-government. The Pawnee, though still without land, took actions to reorganize their tribe. Twenty-three years later, in 1957, the Pawnee were allowed to use the reservation lands that had not been distributed to the white people. Then, in 1968, the U.S. government finally re-turned ownership of the Pawnee reserve to the tribe—land that had originally been given to the Pawnee in exchange for their lands in Nebraska.

Today, most of the more than 3,000 existing Pawnee live in Pawnee, Oklahoma, where their tribal government is located. They live and dress like other Americans, and they work in many of the same kinds of jobs. Each summer, the Pawnee have a Homecoming celebration. They dress in their ancient costumes, perform ritual ceremonies and dances, and pass age-old stories on to new generations. Perhaps most of all, they celebrate their survival as a people and a culture.

*George Catlin's portrait of Big Elk,*
*chief of the Skidi (Wolf) Pawnee, 1832.*

# Important Dates in Pawnee History

| | |
|---|---|
| 1300s | An estimated 15,000 Pawnee begin to migrate north from parts of Texas and Kansas into Nebraska. |
| 1541 | The Pawnee meet the Spanish explorer, Coronado, in a friendly encounter. The Spanish introduce the Pawnee to the horse. |
| 1500-1700s | Pawnee civilization flourishes on the Great Plains. The Pawnee coexist peacefully with white settlers. |
| 1600s | The Pawnee secure horses from French and Spanish traders, and begin to breed their own. |
| 1817 | Chief Petalesharo rescues a captive maiden from becoming a human sacrifice in a Pawnee religious ceremony. After many more years, Chief Petalesharo will finally succeed in eliminating the practice of human sacrifice among the Pawnee. |
| 1818 | The Pawnee begin to agree to a long series of treaties with the U.S. government that will eventually convey all Pawnee lands to white settlers. |
| 1831 | Smallpox, a disease for which the Pawnee have no natural resistance, is carried into Pawnee territory by white traders, and results in the death of more than half of the Pawnee. |
| 1849 | Cholera, another white man's disease, reaches epidemic proportions among the Pawnee, causing many more deaths. |
| 1859 | The U.S. government orders all Pawnee to move to Nebraska to a small reservation on land that is granted by treaty to the tribe. |
| 1864 | Major Frank North organizes the Pawnee Scouts, a small group of Pawnee warriors who volunteer to help the U.S. Army fight the hostile Sioux. |
| 1876 | The Pawnee cede their Nebraska reservation to the U.S. government, and the tribe is forced to move to Oklahoma. |
| 1887 | U.S. Congress passes The Dawes Act, which divides the Oklahoma reservation lands into small parcels and requires the Pawnee to accept individual tracts of 160 acres each. |
| 1889 | The U.S. government opens the Territory of Oklahoma to white settlers for homesteading. |
| 1898 | Congress passes the Curtis Act, abolishing the rights of all tribal governments, and beginning the assimilation or Americanization process for all Native Americans. |
| 1934 | Congress passes the Wheeler-Howard Act, allowing Native Americans to reinstitute their tribal governments. |
| 1957 | The U.S. government allows the Pawnee to use those reservation lands that had not been distributed to white settlers in Oklahoma. |
| 1968 | The U.S. government finally returns ownership of the Oklahoma Pawnee Reservation to the tribe. These are the same lands that had originally been given to the Pawnee in exchange for their lands in Nebraska. |

# INDEX